THE
MILITANT
SUFFRAGETTES

THE
MILITANT
SUFFRAGETTES

Antonia Raeburn

INTRODUCTION BY
J. B. PRIESTLEY

VICTORIAN (& MODERN HISTORY)
BOOK CLUB
Newton Abbot 1974

First published by Michael Joseph

This edition was produced in 1974 for sale to its members
only by the proprietors, Readers Union Limited, PO Box 6
Newton Abbot, Devon, TQ12 2DW. Full details of
membership will gladly be sent on request

Printed in Great Britain by
Redwood Burn Limited
Trowbridge & Esher for Readers Union

For Alexandra Raeburn

Contents

Illustrations

FRONT ENDPAPER

Mrs Anne Cobden Sanderson	Mrs Joan Dacre Fox	Lilian Lenton	Harriet Kerr	Mrs Mildred Mansel	Ada Flatman	Mrs Hilda Brackenbury	Grace Roe
Emily Wilding Davison	George Lansbury	Mrs Lilian Dove Wilcox	James Keir Hardie	Kitty Marion	Mrs E. M. Blathwayt	Mrs Flora Drummond	Mrs Leonora Cohen
Mrs Elizabeth Garrett Anderson	Theresa Garnett	Charlotte Marsh	Rachel Barrett	May Billinghurst	Marie Brackenbury	Gladys Roberts	Elsie Howey
Muriel Matters	Hon. Mrs Evelina Haverfield	Dorothy Pethick	Una Dugdale	Laurence Housman	Dr Ethel Smyth	Beatrice Harraden	Jessie Kenney
Victor Duval	Mary Allen	Mrs Edith Garrud	Joan Wickham	Teresa Billington	Adela Pankhurst	Helen Craggs	Mrs Mary Clarke
Mrs Charlotte Despard	Frederick Pethick Lawrence	Sylvia Pankhurst	Marian Lawson	Dr Louisa Garrett Anderson	Clara Codd	Mary Gawthorpe	Vida Goldstein

BACK ENDPAPER

Edith New	Helen Ogston	Isabel Seymour	Cecily Hale	Mary Richardson	Cecily Hamilton	Mary Leigh	Gertrude Elliott (Mrs Forbes-Robertson)
Mrs Emily Katharine Marshall	Mrs Hertha Ayrton	Mrs Minnie Baldock	Mrs O. H. P. Belmont.	Esther Knowles	Arthur Marshall	Vera Holme	Mrs Frances Bartlett
Laura Ainsworth	Mrs Nellie Alma Martel	Maud Joachim	Gertrude Harding	Nellie Hall	H. W. Nevinson	Johnston Forbes-Robertson	Geraldine Lennox
Mary Phillips	Winifred Jones	Lord Lytton	Harry Pankhurst	Dora Marsden	Evelyn Sharp	Marion Wallace Dunlop	Mrs Beatrice Sanders
Georgina Brackenbury	Gladice Keevil	Mrs Edith Ruth Mansell-Moullin	Alice Paul	Mrs Mabel Tuke	Hugh Franklin	Margaret West	Mrs Dora Montefiore
Mary Blathwayt	Ada Wright	Mrs Saul Soloman	Mrs Emmeline Pethick Lawrence	Olive Bartels	Edith Craig	Henry Harben	Mrs Jennie Baines

The photographs of Mrs Anne Cobden Sanderson, Lilian Lenton, Beatrice Harraden, Mrs E. K. Marshall, Dora Marsden, Evelyn Sharp, Ada Wright and Jennie Baines appear by courtesy of the London Museum, that of Henry Nevinson by courtesy of the Mansell Collection, that of Lord Lytton by courtesy of the Lady Cobbold and that of Harry Pankhurst by courtesy of Mr W. Baylis.

Acknowledgements

It is a long time since I started tentatively working on this book in 1964 after the discovery of a collection of Suffragette portraits taken by Colonel Linley Blathwayt of Eagle House, Batheaston, between 1909 and 1911. I abandoned the work at several stages but always had to return to it because of the enthusiasm, encouragement and friendly help of all those whose contributions make up this story.

There are so many to thank—many now no longer here—and the comparatively few surviving Suffragettes I was able to meet must represent the hundreds of others who were equally enterprising. One could tell the same story with the help of an entirely different group, but those who have come forward to take part in this version will, I think, give the reader a sympathetic understanding of their unique struggle.

The text is drawn mainly from three sources—from recorded interviews with the Suffragettes, from the contemporary Press and from personal reminiscences, letters and cuttings in the Suffragette Fellowship archive at the London Museum. The Fellowship collection is a wonderfully documented record, both from the literary and the pictorial point of view.

My thanks are due to all the staff at the London Museum who have so patiently allowed me to spend hours in the basement store and the library. In particular I should like to mention Miss Susan Davis, formerly Assistant Curator, and Mrs Alice Prochaska who is now in charge of the Suffragette collection. From personal papers in the London Museum I have quoted Mrs Ashworth Hallett, Mrs Baldock, Mrs Bartlett, Miss Marie Brackenbury, Miss Ada Flatman, Miss Mary Gawthorpe, Miss Marion Milner and Mrs Marshall.

In the very early days of the project, Miss Vera Douie, librarian of the Fawcett Society, most generously allowed me to borrow the Suffragette classics, and it was she who introduced me to my first two Suffragette acquaintances and later good friends, Miss Theresa Garnett and Miss Mary Phillips. From this beginning I met many Suffragettes and others who invited me to their homes and allowed me to tape-record their reminiscences. The visits were most enjoyable and I should like to thank all the people who have talked with me and those who have written to me about their experiences in the movement. I should especially like to mention Miss Olive Bartels O.B.E., Miss Elsie Bowerman M.A., Barrister at Law, Alderman Dorothy Bowker, Mrs Phoebe Bendit (née Payne), Sir Lewis Casson, Miss Clara Codd, Mrs Leonora Cohen

O.B.E., J.P., Miss Katharine Douglas Smith, Mrs Edith Garrud, Mrs Aileen Graham-Jones (née Preston), Miss Gertrude Harding, Mrs Eleanor Higginson J.P., Miss Vera Holme, Mrs Phyllis Murray (née Keller), Mrs Isabel Kemp (née Tippett), Miss Jessie Kenney, Miss Esther Knowles, Miss Marian Lawson, Freeman of the City of London, Miss Lilian Lenton, Miss Kathleen Pepper, Miss Dorothy Pethick, Mr Charles Price, Mrs Millicent Price (née Browne), Miss Gladys Roberts, Miss Grace Roe, Alderman Isabel Seymour and Dame Sybil Thorndike.

Here I must also mention Miss Cecily Hale, former head of the W.S.P.U. Information Department, who lent me her marvellous collection of cuttings and photographs which have been an invaluable source of reference. Miss Vera Holme, Miss Mary Phillips and Miss Gladys Roberts provided similar material and I am delighted to be able to include excerpts from Miss Roberts's prison diary translated by her from the original shorthand.

A valuable source of insight into the movement and the people involved was the record kept by Miss Mary Blathwayt and her mother in their diaries. Miss Sheila Blathwayt most kindly allowed me to read these and to make use of the unique descriptions they give of Suffragette activities in the west country. Mrs Kate Harvey provided another interesting sideline—the dairy farm run by Suffragettes at Checkendon in Berkshire. She was the dairymaid. Dr Watney Roe, the brother of Grace Roe, has allowed me to use part of a very moving letter he wrote to his fiancée after being present at his sister's trial. To all these people, my thanks.

For permission to use quotations from Bernard Shaw, Laurence Housman and Mrs E. R. Mansell-Moullin, I am grateful to the Society of Authors on behalf of the Bernard Shaw Estate, Jonathan Cape Limited on behalf of the Executors of the Laurence Housman Estate and Mr Peter Mansell-Moullin. For permission to quote the letter by H. D. Harben I must thank Mrs Harben. I have been unable to trace Bayard Simmons, but hope that I may be able to acknowledge his poem in due course.

I am most grateful to the Hon. Mrs Michael Joseph for her enthusiasm and encouragement, and to Miss Jane Sykes for all her editorial assistance.

Finally I must thank the five people who initially made this work possible. Rosemary Ellis of the Bath Academy of Art had already sent me on a search for early photographs when I made the discovery at Batheaston. She then persuaded me—no feminist—to find out more about the Suffragettes whose portraits I had discovered.

I have had the amazing good fortune of being helped and guided throughout the writing of the book by the two people more closely connected with the W.S.P.U. leaders than anyone else living—Grace Roe, Mrs Pankhurst's chief organiser during the final stages of the movement, and Esther Knowles who has been closely connected with the Pethick Lawrences since she was a small child. Mrs Pethick Lawrence selected her at four years old to perform with Mary Neal's child folk dancers, she started work in the W.S.P.U. offices at the age of fourteen, and she later became Lord Pethick Lawrence's personal secretary. Both Miss Roe and Miss Knowles have worked with me tirelessly on the script and Miss Knowles gave hours of her time to typing all the preliminary drafts of the book. From my friendship with them I have learnt a great deal—not about the Suffragette movement alone.

The last two people to mention are members of my family, my aunt, Joan Williams, who typed the final script with such interest and understanding, and my father, Walter Raeburn Q.C. He wholeheartedly encouraged the venture at every stage and participated in the work, from reading reference books and visiting Suffragettes to numbering the pages of my final typescript just before his death. We had recently heard confirmation of the book's publication and he was delighted with this outcome of our eight-year attachment to the militant Suffragette Movement.

Antonia Raeburn
London 1972

Introduction

Do we need a new book on the Suffragette Movement? I think we do, especially when it has been written by somebody born long after the movement vanished, and not by a student of history and politics (Antonia Raeburn is an art teacher) nor by a professional hack, wanting to put another book together. Miss Raeburn was gradually drawn into a study of the Suffragettes because chance had brought her a bunch of their old photographs. She is therefore able to offer us a fresh account of these brave, devoted, often fanatical women, who had first to suffer stupid and vulgar abuse and then, if they turned sharply militant, had to take dreadful risks, including torture (by forcible feeding), grave illnesses, even death.

The decision of the militants, which split the movement, to take 'direct action' by attacks on property, by setting letter boxes and even houses on fire, by threatening visiting politicians with horsewhips, by planting bombs, brings us close to our own time. For my part I think it was a mistake then, just as I think similar courses of action are a mistake now. To add to the horrible sum total of violence in this world will never improve it. (All violent revolutions everywhere have had to pay heavy prices for them.) Alive myself at the time, and with many older friends who were active supporters of the movement, I believe that constant and earnest persuasion did more for it than the sensational publicity the militants received. The opposition to the Women's Vote by a man like Asquith (the devoted friend of so many women) was political. He felt—and he was quite right—that female suffrage at that time would give the Tories a huge bonus. Though in general sympathy with the movement, I am certain it was really the First War itself that made further opposition to the Women's Vote clearly ridiculous. When girls and women had been making munitions and driving heavy lorries, it was no use telling them any longer that God and Nature intended them only to make ginger puddings and darn socks.

But what kind of women were these Suffragettes—man-hating, shrieking viragos or attractive, intelligent, sensitive members of their sex? What brought them together and then held them, through many dangers? Was it the immediate cause or some lack of direction in their own lives? Did they in fact need a common purpose, afterwards offered to them by the war? Was there in many of the militant Suffragettes a naïve and even childlike quality, which might encourage irrationality and deliberate misbehaviour? Did the influence of the movement enable thousands of women, when their help was needed by the nation, to work in close co-operation with one another and not to shrink from unfamiliar responsibilities? I am merely asking the questions. It is Miss Raeburn, taking a fresh contemporary view of this old battlefield and its combatants, who has to supply the answers. Nor is anything here really out of date. The militant section of Women's Lib. is now threatening to take direct action against 'male chauvinism', even though male chauvinism could be even worse if augmented by female-male chauvinism. So I am really introducing a timely work.

J. B. Priestley

Chapter One: The First Suffragettes 1905-06

THE PANKHURSTS—THE FOUNDATION OF THE W.S.P.U.—A
UNIQUE DEMONSTRATION IN MANCHESTER—ANNIE KENNEY
COMES TO LONDON—WORKING WOMEN DEMONSTRATE—MR
ASQUITH'S PRISONERS—KEEP THE LIBERAL OUT!

Mrs Pankhurst once remarked to an American audience, 'England is the most conservative country on earth. Nothing has ever been got out of the British Parliament without something very nearly approaching a revolution!'

Arson and bloodshed brought about the Electoral Reform Bill of 1832 and the franchise was extended to a new section of the population. Previously men and women had shared equal political rights, but this was a reform for men only, and furthermore, by the wording of the Reform Bill which referred exclusively to 'male persons', women were completely disqualified from voting.

Perhaps in fear of the freedom that an industrial age might bring, women were to be restricted. An attitude prevailed in the early nineteenth century that 'the woman, the cat and the chimney should never leave the house'. A woman and all her belongings were the property of her male relatives and uneducated, and without prospect of a career, she remained an isolated unit within the household.

In spite of the rigid ties of an increasingly conventional way of life, the benefits of Victorian prosperity and industry overruled many domestic restrictions, and by 1850 education for women was accepted and a woman could go out and earn in a factory where she was one of an organised group. A Parliamentary Bill to include women where the word 'man' appeared in any Act of Parliament, signalled a change in female status and the advent of 'Bloomerism' in 1851 was taken very seriously. Although only a new fashion from America—the wearing of pantaloons—a popular broadsheet of the day, *I'll be a Bloomer*, proclaimed a severe warning to men:

> Their husbands they will wop
> And squander all their riches
> Make them nurse the kids
> And wash their shirts and breeches.

In 1865 the first women's suffrage society was formed in Manchester and the movement spread slowly to Edinburgh, London, Birmingham and Bristol. The pioneers were exceptional people—women who had managed in spite of all prejudice to bring about reforms in medical practice, education and in social conditions. Among the early campaigners were Florence Nightingale, Dorothea Beale and Josephine Butler.

In 1866 a new Electoral Reform Bill came before Parliament and the case for women's suffrage was put forward by John Stuart Mill who together with Richard Marsden Pankhurst had drafted an amendment to re-enfranchise women on the same terms as men. One of the largest collections of signatures ever made was sent to Parliament in support of the proposal, but the amendment was killed in debate. Nevertheless the newly formed suffrage societies commanded powerful support and within two years members were enthusiastically hopeful that the country had been converted. The 'sixties and 'seventies were decades of tremendous activity. Millicent Fawcett in London, Flora Stevenson in Edinburgh and Lydia Becker in Manchester were dynamic propagandists and organisers.

Dr Pankhurst was one of the founders of the pioneer Manchester Committee for Woman Suffrage. He was a brilliant intellectual and a lawyer, but although he stood three times for Parliament he was too great an idealist to succeed as a professional politician. 'His ideas are his ideas, not those of any section of the Liberal Party,' said the *Spectator*. He did, however, draft two Parliamentary Bills which became law and which were landmarks in the struggle for emancipation. He was largely responsible for the municipal vote being restored to women in 1869, and in 1882, his triumph, the Married Women's Property Act, at last allowed a wife to retain for herself her inheritance and earnings.

He had resolved to remain a bachelor and to devote his life to public work, but at the age of forty he fell in love with Emmeline Goulden, the eldest girl of a large family of Lancastrian and Manx liberationist descent. Her father was a Manchester textile manufacturer—a political supporter of Dr Pankhurst—and it was while the two men were campaigning together in 1878 that the doctor began to notice Emmeline, newly returned from completing her education in Paris. She was then twenty, slender and beautiful, with violet-blue eyes, a clear olive skin and jet-black hair. Her education in France and her background of radical politics had inspired her with revolutionary ideals, and the date of her birth, July 14, the anniversary of the Storming of the Bastille, gave her a sense of destiny. She admired and adored Dr Pankhurst, and after a brief and romantic engagement they were married in 1879.

Among the many other pioneers, the Pankhursts campaigned together for women's suffrage while the question was debated again and again in Parliament. Three times Bills passed a second reading and Members pledged their support, but the Cabinet was primarily interested in questions concerning the male electorate and the Bills were shelved.

The upbringing of her four children occupied much of Mrs Pankhurst's early married life, but as soon as they were old enough, she left them in charge of a competent nursemaid and resumed public work. She played a considerable part in assisting the doctor in his Parliamentary activities, and together they joined various political groups in the hope of forwarding the women's franchise question. In 1893 Mrs Pankhurst was elected to the Board of Guardians, a governing body concerned with the running of the workhouse, and in this position she had a direct opportunity to remedy some of the social ills that had been overlooked by an all-male administration.

The Pankhurst children were brought up to share their parents' interests and as their home had always been a political meeting ground, the two elder girls, Christabel and Sylvia, attended drawing-room gatherings at an early age. In their own illustrated paper, *Home News*, they wrote admiring reports:

> Mrs Pankhurst held an At Home at her beautiful house on May 28. There was a great number of people there. Dr Pankhurst said in his speech that if the suffrage were not given to women the result would be terrible. If a body was half of it bound, how was it to be expected that it would grow and develop properly ... Mrs Pankhurst wore a black sort of grenadine with a train from the shoulders and looked very handsome indeed.

There was a close companionship between the parents and children and the girls were given every encouragement in intellectual and artistic pursuits. The Pankhursts' only sorrow was the death of their first son, Frank, at four years old. Although another boy was born within a year the loss was never forgotten.

In the summer of 1898 Mrs Pankhurst and Christabel, then aged seventeen, were on their way to Geneva where it had been arranged that Christabel should complete her studies. While they were with friends in France an urgent telegram arrived: 'Father ill. Come.' Christabel was left behind: 'Mother was off by the first train ... to Paris, London, into the Manchester train. There she read in the evening paper: "Dr Pankhurst dead!" It was the collapse of our happy life.'

Mrs Pankhurst now had to support her children—Sylvia, fifteen, and Adela and Harry, twelve and eight. She opened a fancy goods shop, but her colleagues on the Board of Guardians soon nominated her for the vacant position of Registrar of Births and Deaths—a salaried appointment in keeping with her abilities. She now had to give up her guardianship but at the same time, her new post kept her closely in touch with social problems, and her election to the School Board in 1901, gave her yet a further opportunity to make much needed improvements in public welfare.

On her return from Switzerland, Christabel began to work in the business her mother had started, but she was unsuited to selling and unhappy with nothing to satisfy her intellect. Mrs Pankhurst suggested that she should take some classes at the university and soon she was not only attending lectures, but she had also become involved in work for the newly formed Labour Party. By 1901 Christabel had been appointed to the Committee of the North of England Society for Woman Suffrage, and inspired by its two dynamic leaders, Esther Roper and Eva Gore-Booth—agitators on behalf of the working woman—she addressed meetings all over the district, pioneering the women's suffrage cause amongst the poorer classes.

The north of England society was unique, for by the turn of the century the Suffrage Movement was almost dead. 'The women had lost heart. You could not get a suffrage meeting that was attended by members of the general public. We used to have about twenty-four adherents in the front row. We carried our resolutions and heard no more about them.' Highbrow gatherings of elderly suffragists held little to attract the new woman—a product of universal education, freed from the tight restriction of home life, yet useless in a rigidly narrow society. The intelligent working girl faced sweated labour and poverty, while marriage was the only safe career for the educated middle-class girl.

'We were burning up, we knew there was something we had to do.' After hearing the great American suffrage pioneer, Susan B. Anthony, speaking in Manchester in 1902, Christabel was profoundly moved: 'It is unendurable to think of another generation of women wasting their lives for the vote. We must not lose any more time. We must act.'

Mrs Pankhurst and Christabel at last reached the conclusion that women could only gain recognition by fighting for themselves, and in 1903 they founded the Women's Social and Political Union. Their policy was to admit women only and to be independent of any political party. At first there was necessarily some compromise as the Pankhursts were very closely associated with the Independent Labour Party and its leader, James Keir Hardie. The fact that almost every potential W.S.P.U. recruit was an I.L.P. member made the absolute maintenance of W.S.P.U. policy impossible at this early stage.

It was extremely difficult to establish any new methods when in 1903 Mrs Pankhurst joined the annual suffrage deputation to the House of

Commons. It was the custom to interview Members pledged in favour of women's suffrage, but these visits had become a mere formality and subsequent action was never taken by either side. On this occasion the women were received by Sir Charles McLaren and several of his Liberal colleagues. They gave the usual assurances and the ceremony was closing when suddenly Mrs Pankhurst broke in: 'Will Sir Charles McLaren tell us if any Member is preparing to introduce a Bill for women's suffrage? Will he tell us what he and other Members will pledge themselves to *do* for the reform they so warmly endorse?' Sir Charles was silent, and in great embarrassment the deputation departed, feeling, as the conventional always did at the start of a new Pankhurst enterprise, that the clock had been set back.

The W.S.P.U. was now in need of influential help and in 1904 Keir Hardie prevailed on his party to put before Parliament the original franchise amendment of 1866. After eight days of persistent lobbying Mrs Pankhurst secured a place for the Bill, and on May 12, the date appointed for the debate, crowds of suffragists of every class filled the Lobby and adjoining passages in the House of Commons. Four hundred working women, confident and excited, had come under the leadership of the Australian suffragist, Mrs Nellie Alma Martel, already a voter in her own country.

In spite of Mrs Pankhurst's objections, a Roadway Lighting Bill was to be heard first, and while the women waited anxiously, the discussion on the lighting of carts went on continuously all afternoon until only half an hour of debating time remained. The Suffrage Bill had been successfully 'talked out' and its farcical introduction was received in the Chamber with hoots and cheers.

The women in the Lobby were indignant and dismayed and Mrs Pankhurst felt that the moment had come to depart from old-fashioned suffragist methods. She called on the women to follow her outside. They swarmed out into the open and Mrs Wolstonholme Elmy, one of the oldest suffrage workers, began to speak. Instantly the police pushed into the crowd of women, pushing them about and ordering them to disperse. The women moved away to the statue of Richard Cœur de Lion, Mrs Pankhurst helped Mrs Elmy, a little Victorian figure with grey ringlets, on to the plinth of the statue and the old lady began her speech again. Once more the police intervened, but at that moment Keir Hardie arrived and after he had spoken with the inspector the women were told that they might gather at the gates of Westminster Abbey. Mrs Pankhurst, quick to take advantage of circumstances, called on Mrs Martel, as a voter, to lead the women on to the meeting place. There they made speeches and adopted a resolution condemning the Government.

This was the first militant act of the W.S.P.U. It caused comment and even some alarm, but the police contented themselves with taking names.

In 1904 Christabel decided to read law as a career and as her father had been a member of Lincoln's Inn, she applied to be admitted as a student. However, the Inn did not accept women and Christabel finally took up studies at Owen's College, Manchester. She was a keen student —in 1905 she won the prize for International Law—but she still found time to continue her political work and she spoke at many local Trades' Council meetings addressing the workers on the need for women's suffrage. She was often accompanied by Teresa Billington, an outstanding young headmistress, the first woman I.L.P. National Organiser and one of the earliest W.S.P.U. recruits.

While they were speaking at Oldham in the spring of 1905 they met Annie Kenney, a cotton mill worker. She had come to the Trades' Council meeting at the invitation of a friend. 'I had never heard about votes for women and politics did not interest me in the least.' But now Annie was fascinated:

Miss Pankhurst was more hesitating, more nervous than Miss Billington. She impressed me though. When the meeting was over, those in the audience whose minds responded more to cold logic drifted towards Teresa Billington; those who responded towards the human side drifted towards Miss Pankhurst. It was like a table where two courses were being served, one hot, the other cold. I found myself plate in hand where the hot course was being served. Before I knew what I had done I had promised to work up a meeting for Miss Pankhurst among the factory women of Oldham and Leeds. I walked to the station with her and before we separated she asked me to spend the following Saturday afternoon with them at their home in Nelson Street.

On the Saturday, after work, Annie arrived at the Pankhursts' house in Manchester: 'I was shown into a drawing-room very artistically furnished and Christabel introduced me to her mother. Mrs Pankhurst had the gift of putting you at your ease immediately.'

Filled with enthusiasm, Annie now spent every Saturday with the Pankhursts at Nelson Street. It was her idea that they should speak on Sundays at the Wakes—the country fairs. She persuaded her sisters Nellie and Jennie to join the venture and week by week throughout the summer, the Pankhursts and Kenneys toured the little Lancashire towns and villages speaking in the fairgrounds beside the travelling showmen, the Salvation Army, and the sellers of quack medicine.

In the autumn of 1905 the country was preparing for a general election and political meetings provided an opportunity to put the suffrage question before Members of Parliament in the presence of the public.

The Liberal revival which was sweeping over the country was nowhere stronger and more triumphant than in Manchester. On Friday, October 13, at an important rally in the Free Trade Hall two professed supporters of women's suffrage, Sir Edward Grey and Winston Churchill, the candidate for North-West Manchester, were to speak.

By tradition women were silent at political meetings but Christabel was now determined to question the ministers on the Liberal attitude towards women's suffrage. She asked Annie to go with her to the rally and the working women of the W.S.P.U. raised ten shillings to pay for their seats. In case their question should be ignored, Christabel decided that they should display a banner: WILL THE LIBERAL PARTY GIVE VOTES FOR WOMEN? The message was printed in black letters on a long piece of white calico but at the last minute they felt that the banner was too unwieldy. Hurriedly a smaller piece of material was printed with the three-word slogan: VOTES FOR WOMEN and with the banner tightly rolled the girls set out for the meeting.

Christabel and Annie listened attentively to Sir Edward Grey's speech. Twice he was interrupted by men whose questions he answered, but the women waited quietly until he had finished. Then Annie Kenney stood up: 'Will the Liberal Government give the vote to women?' There was no reply and the chairman called for other questions. 'I rose again and was pulled down by two enthusiastic Liberals behind me. We then unfolded the flag and that was enough.' Roars of laughter and catcalls filled the hall, and Annie was surrounded by Liberal stewards who forced her to sit down. 'Why doesn't he answer my question?'

The Chief Constable of Manchester came down from the platform and advised her to present it in writing and accordingly Annie sent a slip of paper up to the platform: 'Will the Liberal Government give votes to working women? Signed, on behalf of the W.S.P.U., Annie Kenney (member of the Oldham Committee of the Card and Blowing-room Operatives).' She added that for the sake of the ninety-six thousand organised women cotton workers, of whom she was one, she wished her question to be answered. Her note was passed round, read with amusement and set aside.

Once again she rose to speak and, as the stewards seized her, Christabel leapt up to defend her. Elbowing away the plain-clothes police who had arrived, Christabel jumped on to a seat and called out the question again before she was pulled down. The two women were dragged into the

7

gangway and swept out of the hall past the platform. 'You're a coward,' Annie called to Sir Edward Grey. 'If I leave this hall I shall hold a meeting of protest outside.' Struggling to resist her escort, Christabel halted directly below the speakers, and looking straight up at Sir Edward she asked the question once again. 'I remember thinking that suitably wreathed and attired he would have looked exactly like a Roman emperor. Pale, expressionless and immovable he returned me look for look.'

Christabel felt that for the protest to be effective they must be imprisoned. Outside the auditorium, held down by police and unable to move, lectures on the law flashed into her mind. How could she commit a technical offence? All she could do was to spit. 'It was not a real spit but only, shall we call it, a pout, a perfectly dry purse of the mouth.'

Christabel and Annie were thrown out into the street and many of the audience followed to join them at the street corner for a protest meeting. Here the girls were arrested, taken off to the police station, and charged with obstruction. Next morning the court was crowded. Manchester was excited, the name of Pankhurst being well known in the City. Not only was Manchester roused but the whole country read about the episode in the morning papers.

Annie was sentenced to three days' imprisonment and Christabel was given one week after being found guilty on the additional charge of assault—spitting at a policeman. Both refused the option of paying fines, causing considerable embarrassment in political circles. Sir Edward Grey excused himself from involvement in the episode by explaining that he had not pursued the women's suffrage question as it seemed unlikely to be a party issue. Churchill, on the other hand, was rumoured to have offered privately to pay Christabel's fine, realising how much publicity the imprisonments would attract. The Press carried long articles on the incident and the public was curious to know what lay behind the protest. Suddenly votes for women became a vital topic.

On the evening of Saturday, October 14, after the court hearing, a great meeting was held in Stevenson Square, Manchester, to protest against the imprisonments. In pouring rain, Mrs Pankhurst, Teresa Billington and other men and women of the town addressed crowds from a 'lurry', and they proposed to work up a rally in the Free Trade Hall itself to welcome the prisoners on their release.

Among the crowd was Flora Drummond, a stocky little Scotswoman. She had been sent by her husband to join the protest because of her strong views on women's rights. She began her career in the Isle of Aran as a girl telegraphist, and after passing all the examinations for qualification as a postmistress, she was unable to take up the position, being one inch shorter than the newly prescribed height. After her marriage she had come to Manchester and she now worked as manager of the Oliver Typewriter Company.

On the morning of Christabel's release a crowd was waiting outside the prison. As Christabel came out, everyone rushed forward, 'but one outstripped the rest. She was a complete stranger to me, but she gave me the first greeting. It was Flora Drummond. We were friends at sight.'

All seats were taken for the welcome reception at the Free Trade Hall that evening and many Manchester people who had come out of curiosity had to be turned away. In their speeches Christabel and Annie made no mention of their prison experiences, for their one object was now to promote the future of the cause.

Because Owen's College had threatened to expel Christabel if she became involved in any further incident, Sylvia now took on much of the responsibility of keeping the movement in the public eye. She had taken up Art as a career, and in 1905 she was one of the outstanding students at the Royal College. She had a studio in London, and was in close touch with many of her parents' political associates.

At the beginning of December 1905 the Conservative Government resigned. Sir Henry Campbell-Bannerman, the Liberal leader, was appointed temporary Prime Minister and electioneering began in earnest. One of the first London rallies of the Liberal campaign was to be held in the Albert Hall on December 21 and it was decided that Annie Kenney and Teresa Billington should attend. It was not easy for Sylvia to get tickets, but through Keir Hardie several seats were eventually obtained for 'friends from the country'. Annie was to sit in a Liberal minister's box, and in order to look suitably impressive, she went disguised as 'a lady', with an East End woman from the Un-employed Movement in attendance as her maid.

Annie had written to the Prime Minister asking him to declare his policy on votes for women, and she informed him that she would be at the meeting to hear what he had to say. Sir Henry spoke. Annie waited patiently. But there was no reference to woman's suffrage. Annie could wait no longer, and standing up, holding a banner over the side of the box, she called out her question. At the same time, Teresa Billington unfurled a nine-foot banner from a balcony near the platform. It appeared upside down, adding to the consternation, and while the audience shouted and the organ blared to drown the noise, the women were hurried outside.

During the Christmas holidays, the Pankhursts prepared for a W.S.P.U. election campaign and Sylvia, home from London, organised the painting of yet more banners. The W.S.P.U. drew up an election manifesto which ended: 'INHABITANTS OF MANCHESTER, if you believe that women ought to have political freedom, better wages and fairer treatment all round, VOTE and WORK AGAINST WINSTON CHURCHILL AS A MEMBER OF THE LIBERAL GOVERNMENT.'

Churchill's supporters had covered all the hoardings with enormous red and white posters, 'the largest that had been seen since Barnum and Bailey went away'. One night Harry Pankhurst, then aged fifteen, went round the city with some friends and pasted strips reading, VOTES FOR WOMEN across all Churchill's bills.

Harry and Sylvia were both at Churchill's first election meeting at Cheetham Hill School. Churchill opened his speech by condemning the unsatisfactory behaviour of the late Government: 'The will of the people has been ignored. But now you have got your chance!' 'Yes we have got our chance and mean to use it,' called Sylvia standing up and displaying a banner. Her question was drowned in the uproar and she sat down until quiet was restored.

Hardly had Churchill started speaking again when Sylvia broke in once more, and this time the hall was thrown into pandemonium. The stewards threatened to remove her but hesitated, because the Pankhursts were much esteemed in Manchester and a group of I.L.P. men sitting with Harry at the back of the hall were obviously supporting the interruptions. The chairman tried in vain to persuade Churchill to answer Sylvia and he then suggested that Sylvia should come up on to the platform and address the meeting herself for five minutes. She approached the foot of the platform: 'Don't you understand what it is I want?' Churchill hid his face with a quick impatient movement of his arm: 'Get away, I won't have anything to do with you.'

Reluctantly Sylvia tried to make a speech while the Liberals in the front seats yelled continuously. When she turned to leave, Churchill grabbed her by the arm and forced her to sit down on a chair at the back of the platform: 'You must wait here till you have heard what I have got to say.' He then told the audience that having witnessed the methods the women were using for the destruction of great public meetings, nothing would induce him to vote for women's suffrage, and he went on to protest that he would not be henpecked into a question of such grave importance.

The Manchester voters were sympathetic and the women could not be prevented from appearing with their banners at all Churchill's meetings. Mrs Drummond would present herself at every hall where he was speaking, and either question him in a resounding voice, or herself hold a meeting outside. Churchill won the election, but his majority was remarkably small, and the result attracted national interest. Undoubtedly the suffragists were to some extent responsible, and the *Daily Mail* invented a name for them—*The Suffragettes*.

Mrs Pankhurst was in Wales during the election campaign canvassing for Keir Hardie as candidate for Merthyr Tydfil. She knew that it was vital for the future of the W.S.P.U. that he should win the seat, and she sent for Annie Kenney to join her in addressing the miners at pit-brows and at trade union gatherings. For weeks they worked to further the cause of Socialism while Keir Hardie was characteristically involved in some other project. He only arrived in the constituency for the last two days of the contest and, after winning the seat, he attributed the result largely to Mrs Pankhurst's work.

The general election proved a triumph for the Liberals and the Pankhursts believed that suffragists should make an impression on the new Government as soon as possible. Annie Kenney was sent to 'rouse London':

> I packed my little wicker basket, and with two pounds I started out. When I had paid my fare I had one pound and a few shillings change. Where the next money would come from and what I would live on were questions that never came into my mind. My ignorance or innocence of political life in London were my best protection. Though I was twenty-six, I knew very little of life. A city had no terrors for me. Opposition in London meant no more than opposition in a little Lancashire town. I had no idea how I should begin my work, having come without instructions.

Annie lodged at 45 Park Walk, Chelsea, where Sylvia had her studio. 'It became a matter of course to write Annie's letters and convey her hither and thither.' Sylvia's acquaintances in the Labour and Unemployed Movements helped Annie to start her campaign; W. T. Stead the journalist wrote about her in his *Review of Reviews* and the Socialist pioneers, George Lansbury, Will Crooks and Dora Montefiore, put Annie in touch with groups likely to support the Suffragettes.

Mrs Montefiore introduced Annie to the working women of the East End. 'I don't know how I had the audacity to talk votes for women to those thin, sallow, pinched, poverty-lined faces. I enjoyed their quick tongues, their prying little gossips and their love of company. To give no offence I would drink a cup of tea with every woman I called to see.'

Annie intended to hold a meeting in Trafalgar Square to coincide with the opening of the new Parliament, but on making enquiries she discovered that outdoor meetings were illegal while Parliament was sitting. She went to Keir Hardie for advice, and with his help the Caxton Hall was hired for the demonstration. It was an ambitious scheme and Mrs Pankhurst and Teresa Billington came to London to assist with the canvassing. Handbills were printed, calls were made on influential people and announcements of the meeting were chalked on pavements.

Sylvia found it almost impossible to stir the great city: 'Its busy millions appeared to have no time to think of anything but their own affairs. The thoughtless apathy of those we met with money and leisure at their disposal . . .' At this point Mrs Drummond came to the rescue. She arrived from Manchester, and immediately took over the necessary secretarial work after borrowing a typewriter from the Oliver Company's London branch. Her inexhaustible fund of good humour brought with her a spirit of renewed hope and energy, and after rattling off the correspondence she was always ready to join in delivering handbills and house-to-house canvassing.

Parliament opened on Monday, February 19, 1906 and at three o'clock that afternoon five hundred of Annie's East End supporters emerged from St James's Park Underground Station. Because Annie was doubtful how many would be able to come, she had arranged for their fares to be paid and they were to be served with tea and buns before the meeting. As they marched towards the Caxton Hall, the police ordered them to roll up their red Labour flags and onlookers stared at the curious procession: 'What about the washing?' 'Go home and darn the old man's socks!'

It was a unique gathering at the hall. 'Working women with babies rubbed shoulders with their sisters in a very different social position.' 'We are mostly Socialists,' said Mrs Montefiore, but several aristocratic patrons of old-established suffrage societies were seen sitting discreetly in the audience, among them the Countess of Carlisle and Lady Frances Balfour.

While the women awaited the arrival of their champion, Keir Hardie, they sang unaccompanied to the tune of 'Auld Lang Syne', their own song about the cause:

> They say we are so ignorant
> We don't know right from wrong
> But we can tell them what we want
> And what we'll have ere long.

Soon the audience was told that Keir Hardie had sent a letter of apology and regret—he would not be coming to the meeting.

The King's Speech was at that moment being read in Parliament and everyone knew that the outcome of the Caxton Hall demonstration would depend on whether women's suffrage was to be included in the new Government programme. The audience was excited, and when Annie began to speak she was frequently interrupted by bursts of warm and enthusiastic applause. Before she had finished, however, a message was brought in to say that there had been no mention of votes for women in the King's Speech. What steps would Mrs Pankhurst take? As soon as she began to speak she strongly condemned the Government's omission and resolved that the meeting should form itself into a lobbying committee and go to the House of Commons. The resolution was carried with one dissentient—a man. The *Daily Mail* reported that hundreds of eyes glared at him, and as he left the hall a way was made for him. Women with one accord cried 'Shame' and hissed, but the hardened man actually smiled cheerfully at a lady who, with scornful look, ostentatiously gathered in her skirts as he passed by.

In small groups the women left the hall and made their way through the rain to the House of Commons. This mass deputation was a departure from all convention. It was usual for a chosen few ladies to make an appointment with the Member they wished to see and they would arrive by cab at the House of Commons to be received with due ceremony. Now, as the women approached on foot, police stood at the Strangers' Entrance with orders to admit no one.

Hundreds of women waited outside in the cold and rain, and at last two relays of twenty were admitted. Members came to meet them in the Lobby, but without exception pledged supporters now refused to commit themselves on the suffrage question. The women were disappointed and angry and their only consolation was to learn that they had managed to hold a public meeting within a mile of St Stephen's— an illegal act on the opening day of Parliament.

Mrs Pankhurst, on the contrary, saw the episode as a triumphant turning point: 'Those women had followed me to the House of Commons. They had defied the police. They were awake at last . . . Women had always fought for men and for their children. Now they were ready to fight for their own human rights. Our militant movement was established.'

The Caxton Hall meeting brought many new recruits to the W.S.P.U., and the growing union was in need of an experienced organiser. At Keir Hardie's recommendation, Emmeline Pethick Lawrence came into the movement. 'She was a woman of intense vitality, poetic magnetism and ungrudging power of work.'

Emmeline Pethick, born on October 21, 1867, was one of a large well-to-do family of Cornish descent living in Weston-super-Mare. Her happy home life and her Quaker upbringing had given her a love of beauty and a sense of calling, and at the age of twenty-three she left home to work for the West London Mission as 'Sister Emmeline' among the women in the London slums. Through the mission she met Mary Neal, a pioneer in the Folk Dance Movement, and together in 1895 they decided to branch out in a personal venture to enliven the lot of working girls. They established the Esperance Girls' Club, and their later enterprises included the Maison Esperance, a co-operative workshop, and the Green Lady Hostel, a holiday home in Littlehampton which gave working women a rare opportunity of spending some time in the country.

In 1899 while Frederick Lawrence was working in an East End Settlement, the Esperance Girls' Club came to give a folk dancing display. 'It so happened that Mr Lawrence and Miss Pethick were on the stage, one drawing aside the curtain on one side and one on the other.' This was the first time they met, and in 1901 they were married. Frederick Lawrence was four years younger than Emmeline, but like her, an idealist. Educated at Eton and a highly successful Cambridge graduate, he was brilliant and wealthy. After his marriage, although a qualified barrister, he worked as the editor of various Socialist publications, and in 1906 he was editing the monthly, *Labour Record and Review.*

Marriage did not prevent the Pethick Lawrences continuing to share their personal life with others. Having no family, they built a cottage, the Sundial, near their own Surrey home and invited London children for holidays. Emmeline's concern was to introduce them to the joys of the country and gracious living. 'But I realised that we were only making in a great wilderness a tiny garden enclosed by the wall of human fellowship.'

Mrs Pethick Lawrence met Mrs Pankhurst but did not immediately decide to join the W.S.P.U. It was Annie who eventually persuaded her: 'Mr Keir Hardie told me to ask you to be our national treasurer.' 'Your treasurer! What funds have you?' 'That is just the trouble, I have spent all the money already and have got into debt. I do not understand money, it worries me; that is why I have come to you for your help . . . You need not decide at once.' Mrs Lawrence was beginning to show a lack of enthusiasm. She was very doubtful when she reached home, but on considering Annie's heartfelt appeal she decided, in spite of

everything, to accept the challenge and she was immediately appoi
Hon. Treasurer of the union's empty treasury.

A new committee was formed with Sylvia as Hon. Secretary and Mary
Neal, Mrs Martel and Irene Fenwick Miller, members. Irene Miller
was a young journalist and a childhood friend of the Pankhursts through
her suffragist parents. Gradually the centre of activity began to move
from Sylvia's studio to the Pethick Lawrences' flat above the *Labour
Record* offices at 4 Clement's Inn. The Lawrences had many influential
friends and the union now began to get useful help and support.
Manifestos and leaflets were typed for distribution by voluntary workers
and the Lawrences' car, 'La Suffragette', placarded with VOTES FOR
WOMEN, was put into service to further the propaganda campaign.

It was less than a month since the Caxton Hall meeting and a great
advance had been made, but Mrs Pankhurst and Mrs Drummond had
soon to return to Manchester and they felt that it was a matter of urgency
to interview the Prime Minister. On March 3, after they had received an
unsatisfactory reply to a written request for an audience, Mrs
Drummond and Annie Kenney set out with a small group for 10
Downing Street. Sir Henry Campbell-Bannerman had been ill, they
were not admitted and they were told that, in any case, they must apply
in writing to see the Premier. A further letter was duly sent asking the
Prime Minister to receive a deputation. This time the reply stated that
all form of communication must be made in writing.

To prevent further delay, the W.S.P.U. waited until Sir Henry had
recovered and then a deputation was organised to call on him uninvited.
Annie wrote personally to some of her supporters:

> We have decided to go on a deputation to the Prime Minister on
> Friday morning. He is doing his best to get out of it but we are
> going to be there . . . The women will not get in any trouble so they
> have no occasion to be nervous. We are meeting at Westminster
> Bridge Station on Friday morning at 10.15. It is very early but it is
> for the cause we are going to win, so come and bring as many as
> possible.

Annie's confidence inspired her followers and on March 9 about
thirty women met her as arranged and made their way in small groups
to Downing Street. The Press had been notified, and reporters and
photographers were waiting near Number Ten to witness the scene.
Irene Miller, Mrs Drummond and Annie were among the first to arrive.
An elderly retainer answered the door and while he went off to deliver
their message they were left waiting on the doorstep. Three-quarters of
an hour later, two officials came to tell the women that there was no

1905-06

...essage and when they began to protest the door was

...English women!' called Irene Miller, banging on the ...mped on to the step of the Premier's car which stood in ...house and began to address the crowd. While police ...h Irene Miller on the doorstep, Mrs Drummond pulled at the litt... ...ss knob in the centre of the door and to her amazement the door flew open. She rushed inside, but was hastily shown out again. Soon all three ringleaders were arrested and taken off to Cannon Row Police Station.

They were detained for an hour, and then word came from the Prime Minister that they were to be released. At the same time he stated that he would in the near future receive a deputation from the W.S.P.U. and any other suffrage societies.

After the Downing Street incident George Bernard Shaw, interviewed by a *Tribune* reporter, said:

If I were a woman I'd simply refuse to speak to any man or do anything for men until I'd got the vote. I'd make my husband's life a burden and everybody miserable generally. Women should have a revolution. They should shoot, kill, maim, destroy until they are given the vote.

Asked what he would consider the proper qualifications, Shaw replied:

There's none necessary, the qualification of being human is enough; I would make the conditions exactly the same as for men; it's no use women claiming more than men though probably in the end they'll get more as they invariably do whenever women agitate for equality with men in any respect.

What sort of Bill would I introduce, did you say? Simply a short Act to have the word 'men' in all relevant statutes construed as human beings—as mankind—though as you hear people talking of womankind, I suppose even that would not be understood. It's one of the many drawbacks to our ridiculous language we have no word which includes men and women. It just shows how little we realise men and women belong to the same species. No one denies that a stallion and a mare are both horses—they wear just the same kind of harness—but a woman is looked upon as an entirely different animal to a man. So everything, costume, coiffure, customs, political rights, everything is arranged as far as possible to accentuate the supposed differences between two human beings practically identical. Of course it's a great advantage to women to be regarded as a race apart, an advantage which, as usual, they abuse unscrupulously.

While the Suffragettes were preparing for the deputation to the Prime Minister, Keir Hardie had secured a reading in Parliament for a women's franchise resolution. April 25 was the date appointed, and on that evening a strange assembly crowded the Ladies' Gallery behind the grille in the House of Commons. The wives of Members who supported the suffrage resolution were present wearing full evening dress, while the suffragettes—Mrs Pankhurst, Sylvia and their new supporters—were still in day clothes.

At ten o'clock Keir Hardie introduced the motion that sex should be no bar to Parliamentary franchise and an aimless debate began. The women listened quietly for an hour until M.P.s started to ridicule the motion. 'Hear! Hear!' called a voice from the Ladies' Gallery. Whispers and murmurs followed and the Speaker sent orders to have the women removed if they made further disturbance. Mrs Pankhurst signalled them to refrain, but it was too late, time was running out and M.P.s were laughing at them. Someone looked round and saw that the police were already in the gallery. 'Divide!—vide!—vide!'

'Justice for women!' Teresa Billington pushed a white banner through the bars of the grille and waved it over Members' heads. Laughter and shouts drowned the speaking and the debate ended in pandemonium as M.P.s rushed in from all parts of the House to see what was happening.

An order was given to clear the gallery, and the Serjeant-at-arms with a force of police broke into the crowd of women, who refused to leave. As they were dragged out, hats and coats were pulled off in the struggle, and later a crushed pile of belongings was dumped into Palace Yard.

'Amazing Scenes in the House'. 'Scandalised Commons'. Next morning the Press told the story under prominent headlines and the Suffragettes were universally condemned for their disgraceful behaviour. The Conservative women suffragists and members of the National Union of Women's Suffrage Societies were particularly upset by the incident. Some had actually been present in the Ladies' Gallery, and they were now so loth to be further associated with the Suffragettes that they tried to discourage the W.S.P.U. from joining the deputation to Sir Henry Campbell-Bannerman.

Early on the morning of May 19 one thousand demonstrators assembled on the Embankment. The Prime Minister had kept his promise to the

W.S.P.U. and representatives of suffrage societies were to be received at the Foreign Office. Members of trades' organisations and suffrage groups from all over the country had arrived to march in procession with their delegates. Women weavers, winders, reelers, shirtmakers, chairmakers, iron-workers, cigar-makers, bookbinders, college graduates and pit-brow women all stood waiting in ranks. A group of mill girls were conspicuous in their clogs and shawls and a contingent of mothers carrying children had come from London's East End. Even international suffragists were represented by two women carrying a banner inscribed, DROIT VOTER. The W.S.P.U. leaders were in high spirits—Annie in mill girl costume and Teresa Billington, as Chief Marshal, in blue with a large red sash lettered VOTES FOR WOMEN.

The main part of the procession with its bands waited on the Embankment by Cleopatra's Needle while the chosen deputation marched to the Foreign Office. The traffic had not been officially stopped for the occasion and amused cabmen and omnibus men had to pull up to make way for the suffragists. The women carried their banners past Big Ben and across Whitehall until, at Downing Street, the police had them rolled up.

On the doorstep of the Foreign Office the leaders halted and, a few minutes later, the deputation was admitted and conducted to the Deputation Chamber. The assembly was remarkable. Several M.P.s had come to represent the women's suffrage signatories in Parliament, twenty-five different trades' organisations had sent delegates and some of the pioneer suffragists were present. Emily Davies, LL.D., then seventy-six years old, was among the ten women to address the Prime Minister. It was she who had handed the first women's suffrage petition to John Stuart Mill in 1866.

After hearing all the speakers, Sir Henry told the meeting that he was personally in favour of women's suffrage. 'But there is opposition in the Cabinet. It would never do for me to make any statement or pledge under these circumstances. All I can do is to advise a policy of patience.'

Feeble cheers and hisses accompanied Keir Hardie's vote of thanks. 'Patience like many other virtues can be carried to excess,' he said. As the meeting prepared to close Annie Kenney jumped up: 'Sir, we are not satisfied!' The meeting came out looking very crestfallen. Annie stamped her clog foot on the courtyard: 'We are not going to stop for this, we are going on with our agitation.'

In the afternoon the demonstrators marched from the Embankment to a mass meeting in Trafalgar Square. The crowds were deeply impressed by the speakers—Mrs Pankhurst, calm and persuasive, Keir Hardie in rough tweeds, 'the only prophet in Parliament', and Annie in simple costume with a brilliant red rosette pinned to her breast. Mrs

Wolstonholme Elmy stepped forward to the front of the plinth and listened while her speech was read to the crowd. She had been a school teacher in Congleton, Cheshire, and had helped to found the first Manchester Women's Suffrage Committee. As she heard her words delivered, the old lady burst into tears:

When you have enthusiasm for a real cause, you know you have discovered eternal youth. I have been fighting for this cause all my life and yet I am as enthusiastic as when I started. Of course I feel disappointed today for the Prime Minister's words showed that he had little real sympathy with our movement. I sometimes wonder whether we are not as far off as we were forty years ago. Yet, I shall go on fighting still. Even an old woman can do something when she is in earnest!

In protest against the result of the deputation, Mrs Montefiore refused to pay her taxes. 'Taxation without representation is tyranny.' Twice before she had been sold up, but now on May 24, she locked her gates against the bailiffs and placed herself in a state of siege. Her house in Hammersmith stood back from the road and a tall spiked wall shut off the garden. Nailed high on a summer-house in full view of passers-by was a huge banner: WOMEN SHOULD VOTE FOR THE LAWS THEY OBEY AND THE TAXES THEY PAY.

Reporters were already waiting outside 'Fort Montefiore', when Annie, Teresa Billington and Mrs Martel arrived with placards and flags to hang on the railings. As crowds gathered, Annie handed a pot of marmalade and two half quarterns of bread over the wall. These were received by a servant and taken into the house.

A few moments later Mrs Montefiore appeared at an upper window with a favourite dog and her maid. 'Speech! Speech!' 'Certainly,' she replied. 'Now we have been told that there are ministers in the Cabinet who are against us. There is Asquith—Assassin Asquith—who is against the women because they are for peace and he is on the side of the capitalists. If I were free, I should break Asquith's windows!'

An exchange of protestations followed and Annie called up from the road: 'We are going on with the movement and we will raise earth itself if we do not get the vote.' The crowd cheered and the Irish terrier yelped as Mrs Montefiore leaned further out of the window, 'Yes,' she said purposefully. 'Twenty Cavendish Square has windows!' She then sent a message down to reporters:

If, as Sir Walter McLaren said at the Exeter Hall, Asquith, Bryce and Lord Crewe are the most active and determined opponents of women's suffrage in the Cabinet, then we active 'forwards' mean to work up and down the country to prove our hostility to those who are hostile to our claims.

Some years previously, Asquith, then Home Secretary, had acquired the name 'Assassin' after a mining dispute at Featherstone. The military were sent to quell the uprising; soldiers had opened fire on the men and seven strikers were killed. Asquith, now Chancellor of the Exchequer, was the most noted of all members of the Cabinet in opposition to women's suffrage.

The Suffragettes decided that the only possible way of getting an immediate hearing in Parliament was to put pressure on Cabinet Ministers opposed to their cause. Lloyd George had said in Liverpool on May 24: 'Why do not the women go for their worst enemy?' Accordingly the W.S.P.U. wrote to Asquith asking for an interview, but their requests were unsuccessful. Asquith refused to meet the women.

Finally a deputation went unannounced to call on him at his home, 20 Cavendish Square. He was out. When the deputation called a second time, the butler gave long explanations, and meanwhile Asquith escaped by a back door and drove off in a closed car.

On June 21 Annie Kenney and Teresa Billington led a third attempt and arrived at Cavendish Square with a procession of forty women. Police were waiting, the procession was halted and officers snatched the women's banners.

We were walking peaceably within our rights [says Mrs Baldock, an East End Poor Law Guardian]. Miss Billington tried to force her way on. A policeman struck her in the face and she retaliated by one slap on his face with her open hand. Another policeman caught her by the throat until her face became purple. A fat woman in the crowd interfered and had her wrists torn by the policeman's nails. Miss Billington was taken off, then I saw a number of women with a banner come up to the front of Mr Asquith's house.

Annie was leading the group and making for Asquith's front door. A policeman prevented her from ringing the bell. Alice Toyne, another member of the deputation, was watching:

The policeman said Miss Kenney knew jolly well Mr Asquith would not see a person like her. So Miss Kenney said she would walk about there and find out; and she *walked about*. Then the policeman began to hustle her and tell her to move off, but she said she had a right to walk about, she liked to walk about there and she would walk about. Thereupon they arrested her.

Mrs Knight, a little lame woman, hobbled with an umbrella to defend Annie and she, too, was arrested. Then Mrs Sparboro, an elderly seamstress, noticed that two ladies at an upper window of Asquith's house were beginning to laugh and clap. 'Don't do that—oh don't do that! That is how the soldiers were sent to Featherstone.' As she stood in the middle of the road wagging her finger up at the women, the police seized her.

The four arrested Suffragettes were taken to the police station, and later that day they came up for trial. When charged with assault, Teresa Billington refused to be tried by a Court composed entirely of men: she would call no witnesses and give no evidence. Promptly, the magistrate gave sentence—two months' imprisonment with the option of a ten-pound fine. It was a shock. The sentence was excessive, and the W.S.P.U. immediately asked to have the cases of the other three women adjourned so that they could take legal advice.

Keir Hardie brought up Teresa Billington's case in Parliament, and through his intervention the term of imprisonment was halved. In fact she never served her sentence because her fine was paid, against all W.S.P.U. principles, by an anonymous reader of the *Daily Mirror*.

Mrs Pethick Lawrence sent a telegram to her husband in the country asking him to come immediately to London to help secure a defence.

> I went up at once [he says] and joined my wife in a police court. It was a dingy and dirty place, and as we waited for the three Suffragettes to be brought in, I noticed the dock was not clean. I stepped forward and rubbed it with my pocket handkerchief. It was a great demand on my courage, but it testified that in this matter of the women's revolt, I had taken sides with the dock against the bench.
>
> The three prisoners presented a sorry spectacle. All were working women and poorly dressed. Apart from her flaming eyes, Annie Kenney looked an ordinary north-country mill girl. Mrs Sparboro was the wife of an Italian workman resident in East London and Mrs Knight was lame and insignificant.

The women were charged with disorderly conduct and the magistrate asked Mrs Sparboro why, at the age of sixty-four, she allowed herself to be influenced by younger irresponsible people. She drew herself up: 'You would be astonished if you knew the poverty and goodness of them. They are braver and better than I am, and many of them have done without their breakfast.'

The three offenders were each given six weeks in Holloway. Mrs

Baldock visited Mrs Sparboro in prison and recorded what the old lady told her:

> I feel so well. I eat, drink and sleep well. I think to myself, perhaps it is because my conscience is clear that I feel so happy. I have a dear little cell all to myself. It has been newly decorated and it is so clean and nice. I always wanted a place of retreat somewhere, where I could be quiet. Be still and serve—that is what I am doing. We can't all serve the same. I have a book—I read, I knit, I go to chapel, and I must say that the parsons here are better than those outside. We see each other but we are not allowed to speak. But [she added in a whisper] we throw kisses at each other and Miss Kenney holds up her fingers one less each week. Tell my husband I am all right. I was thinking about him. He is so worried with flies this weather. One thing, we have no fleas and no flies in prison. He will be glad to know I am not worried with them flies.

Although there was a Suffragette outcry over the imprisonments, the public was unsympathetic, Keir Hardie made vain protests and the Press ridiculed the situation. The women were released on August 14, and next day small handbills were seen all over London inviting people to Hyde Park to welcome 'Asquith's Prisoners'. That afternoon Annie, Mrs Sparboro and Mrs Knight were received by rowdy crowds who had come out of curiosity and to make fun of them.

Provincial crowds were kinder as Christabel discovered when she embarked on a new line of policy in the late summer of 1906. She had completed her Law studies in June and the results of the Bar Exams showed her name bracketed with one other at the head of the honours list. She had been the only woman candidate and as a woman, she was now unable to practise. She was therefore free to devote all her time to the W.S.P.U.

The Suffragettes had proved a remarkable influence on voters during the general election and Christabel's plan was now to put pressure on the Government through the electors: 'Obviously the best way of forcing the Government to act is to bring about the defeat of its candidates at by-elections. As soon as a Parliamentary vacancy is announced, a party of speakers will go to the constituency and begin an active campaign against the Government.'

Christabel arrived alone to launch a by-election campaign at Cockermouth. The *Cockermouth Free Press* reported:

On Monday night, Miss Pankhurst, one of the notorious band of lady suffragists, held a meeting at the Clock. She was certainly an object of interest, and had to encounter a considerable amount of interruption, but was equal to the occasion. A large crowd escorted her to the station after the meeting, but in order that she might take no harm, several young men gallantly lent her their arm!

Christabel's persuasive enthusiasm stirred up fierce competition between the parties, and at the poll the Government candidate was defeated in a constituency which had long been a Liberal stronghold.

In the history of Cumberland politics there has never been such a flood of oratory from M.P.s, ex M.P.s, would-be M.P.s, Tory, Liberal and Labour. The redoubtable Suffragettes active with hand and voice spared us the sight of their flag-wagging, for which most of us are extremely thankful.

From a man's point of view, women had played a useful part in electioneering in recent years. Now, Christabel in carrying out the W.S.P.U. policy of independence had created a new role for women in the political field. M.P.s were beginning to see the danger of losing valuable supporters and those women suffragists who were affiliated to a party were in an uncomfortable position. They did not wish to be classed with the 'hooligan Suffragettes', and yet they recognised the expediency of the W.S.P.U. policy.

The policy had stabilised itself to such an extent that Mrs Pankhurst and Christabel now openly denounced affiliation with the Labour Movement. However, Sylvia and Adela still adhered firmly to the party. Without the support of Keir Hardie, the W.S.P.U. could never have flourished as it did. Keir Hardie himself recognised Christabel's policy as the only effective one, and at this juncture he even considered abandoning his own party to champion the women's cause. But he realised that this idealistic move would be detrimental to both sides. He continued all the same to put the women's point of view before Parliament on every occasion.

Chapter Two: Headquarters at
4 Clement's Inn 1906-08

Sylvia resigned as Hon. Secretary of the W.S.P.U. four months before
Christabel had completed her studies. Her studio had been overrun by
W.S.P.U. workers, a large stock of banners was stored there, and Sylvia
had no time for her own work. Mrs Pankhurst had hoped that Sylvia
would hold her position, maintaining a Pankhurst stronghold in the
W.S.P.U. until Christabel was free to come to London, but now Mrs
Edith How Martyn, a science graduate of London University, and Mrs
Despard were appointed jointly to replace Sylvia on the committee.

Charlotte Despard, Irish by descent, was the sister of General
French. When she joined the W.S.P.U. she was over sixty and a most
remarkable woman for her time. She believed passionately in the
progression of humanity, and saw the women's movement as a significant
gathering together to reach a new stage in the evolution of the race. She
advocated absolute freedom of the individual and her life's work had
been amongst the poorer classes. Phoebe Payne, the prominent theoso-
phist, met her at the Dublin home of George Russell: 'She had a
flamelike quality, finely chiselled features and blue eyes, oh so blue! She
always appeared to look the same—long frock to her ankles—black
mantilla flowing away from her pure white hair—and a sense of authority
emanated from her.'

Pethick Lawrence watched the growth of the movement closely:

> I did not at first deem it my business to take any active part in the
> struggle. This was a campaign organised by women and executed by
> women who were out to show the stuff they were made of. There
> was no lack of initiative, drive, courage and enthusiasm, but there
> was a danger that by the very exuberance of its growth, the move-
> ment would outrun its own co-ordination. There was a need for
> 'planning', on the business side. The first step was to take an office.

Some of the lower floors in 4 Clement's Inn were opened as London headquarters in September 1906, and the Pethick Lawrences were not sorry to recover undisputed possession of their own flat which was just above.

At Pethick Lawrence's suggestion, Miss Kerr, a friend of E. V. Lucas, gave up her own secretarial business and became general office manager. Mrs Sparboro on her release from prison became the office 'tea lady'.

Isabel Seymour, a young friend of the Pethick Lawrences, came to work in the office when it first opened:

It was very happy-go-lucky—envelope addressing, and the almost daily tea party. Mrs Pankhurst used to descend but she wasn't permanently there. I remember the sort of feeling that she was still a bit of an outsider. But of course Christabel was always at Clement's Inn. The Pethick Lawrences had put the spare room of their flat at her disposal. They really were like overshadowing guardian angels.

Mrs Pethick Lawrence had a genius for raising money. She gave generously herself and her personal appeals attracted many wealthy subscribers. The funds increased quickly, a financial secretary, Mrs Sanders, was engaged and affairs were conducted in a strictly official way which particularly impressed Annie:

If we were out in our petty cash book, it had to come out of our own pockets. I always admired the careful and methodical way in which the money was spent. If a chair would be suitable as a platform, why pay a few shillings for a trolley? If the weather was fine, why have a hall? If the pavements were dry, why not chalk the advertisements of the meetings instead of paying printers' bills? If a tram would take us, why have a taxi?

Throughout the summer of 1906 W.S.P.U. speakers held street-corner meetings in various parts of London. Mrs Martel wrote to Mrs Baldock enthusiastically proposing that they should organise six meetings every night in London's East End. 'These and an occasional "smash up", are the methods we must maintain to give publicity to our cause.'

It was a real fight to go through with some of their meetings. Mrs Bartlett, a working woman and one of Christabel's earliest recruits, was helping her on a campaign in Battersea. At the sound of her muffin bell people would come flocking to hear Christabel speaking from a box. Undeterred by rude remarks and rowdiness, she could hold an audience by charm and lively argument and before the autumn, Mrs Bartlett had obtained permission for her to hold meetings indoors and on Clapham Common. Already Mrs Despard and Richard Cobden's daughter, Mrs Anne Cobden Sanderson, were holding weekly meetings in Hyde Park near the Reformers' Tree.

Later that summer the W.S.P.U. began a campaign of widespread propaganda in the provinces. Mrs Pethick Lawrence toured Yorkshire and Mrs Pankhurst worked in Wales with Mary Gawthorpe, a brilliant young teacher from Leeds. Mary was petite and attractive and with her quick Yorkshire repartee she rivalled Christabel in popularity as a speaker.

Annie was received as a heroine when she returned home to Lancashire and from there she went on to join Teresa Billington in Asquith's own constituency, East Fife. Eventually the Suffragettes prevailed on the local Women's Liberal Association to seek an interview with Asquith. The interview was granted, but the Chancellor firmly announced that he would meet only members of his constituency. 'Women must work out their own salvation,' he told the deputation when they met.

The extensive propaganda drew new recruits to the movement. Women from every walk of life would turn up daily at Clement's Inn to offer their voluntary services and by the autumn of 1906, the W.S.P.U. membership had increased beyond all expectation. The leaders had allowed this to happen spontaneously, without giving any thought to organisation, and on October 22—the eve of the re-opening of Parliament —they called an emergency meeting. A strategy had been planned for the following day; arrests were expected and in the event of legal proceedings being taken, a constitution was hastily drawn up to afford some protection for W.S.P.U. members.

Next morning, as M.P.s were returning to the House of Commons, a gathering of Suffragettes waited outside the Strangers' Entrance. They asked to be allowed to enter the Lobby and each named a particular Member she wished to see. Officials said that only twenty women would be admitted and they then proceeded to select the privileged few according to their dress. No working women were among the small groups to go into St Stephen's Hall.

At the request of Mrs Pankhurst and Mrs Pethick Lawrence the Liberal Chief Whip arrived and they asked him to discover whether the Prime Minister intended to consider the women's suffrage question during the forthcoming session. The Chief Whip soon returned with an unfavourable answer. 'Does the Prime Minister hold out any hope for the women for any session during this Parliament or for any future session? The Prime Minister, you will remember, called himself a suffragist.' 'No, Mrs Pankhurst,' the Liberal Chief Whip replied, 'he does not.'

When the leaders again joined their group in the Lobby, no M.P. had yet appeared although many of the women had asked to see the most sober and sedate type of country squire Member. After a short consultation they decided to protest, and Mary Gawthorpe jumped on to a settee behind the statue of Lord Iddesleigh and began to make a speech. The women closed in round her.

Chief Inspector Scantlebury pushed his way through the jostling crowds, hastily removed Mary, and put her outside. Mrs Despard stood up to take her place. She, too, was pulled down and frog-marched away. Mrs Cobden Sanderson followed, then Mrs Martel, Mrs Montefiore and others. Policemen arrived in force and Inspector Scantlebury gave an order to clear the Lobby. The police were faced with a unique situation. They were quite unused to handling women of class and the outburst provoked an atmosphere of intense excitement. A *Daily Mirror* reporter wrote:

> The martyrs clutched the bench. A stalwart officer placed his arms gently but firmly round the waist of a Suffragette who in her desperate protests threw her arms around the constable's neck to the great embarrassment of the officer and the immense amusement of the crowd. 'This is how the women of England are treated,' she shrieked over the constable's shoulder, shaking a small white fist at the lookers-on. 'This is how you men . . .' The rest of the sentence was lost as the great glass doors of St Stephen's Hall swung back again and the shrill voice died away in the distance.

In the mêlée Mrs Pankhurst was thrown to the floor and painfully hurt. 'The women thinking me seriously injured, crowded around me and refused to move until I was able to regain myself. This angered the police who were still more incensed when they found that the demonstration was continued outside.'

Annie was waiting in the street as a spectator. She had been given orders not to take part in this demonstration, but when she saw Mrs Pethick Lawrence struggling in the brawl, she rushed forward to try and reach her. At once the police seized Annie. 'You shall not take the girl,' cried Mrs Pethick Lawrence, 'she has done nothing.' Immediately Mrs Pethick Lawrence was herself arrested. Mrs Despard was disappointed to be exempted from similar treatment. 'When I saw little Annie Kenney being taken away, I told the police, "You won't arrest me because I am well known, but because she happens to be a factory girl you take her." '

Ten women were held at Rochester Row Police Station that evening and they were eventually released on bail for the night. Next morning the prisoners' friends and relations arrived early at Rochester Row to make certain of getting a place in court. Mrs Cobden Sanderson's two sisters, Mrs Cobden Unwin and Mrs Cobden Sickert, were among the first to take seats, but before the trial came on they were asked to leave the court to make room for people who had come to hear another case. Once removed, they were not readmitted, and no other women sympathisers were allowed into the hearing of the Suffragettes' case.

Pethick Lawrence brought his wife to the court by car. Her arrest had been a great shock to him: 'Things which happen to other people assume an entirely different aspect when they come right home to one's family circle.' Pethick Lawrence was present at the trial: 'The police evidence was confined to the element of public disorder, the magistrate cut short Mrs Cobden Sanderson's attempt at a political defence, and the women were all sentenced as common criminals to two months' imprisonment in the second division.'

After the trial Sylvia went to the door of the court and asked to be admitted. 'It is all over. There is nothing to interest you now.' But Sylvia walked past the doorkeepers, straight into the court and standing before the magistrate, she complained that women had been unjustly excluded from the hearing. 'There is no truth in any of your statements,' said Mr Horace Smith and without giving Sylvia time to answer, he ordered two policemen to remove her. She was dragged out and thrown into the street where she did her best to hold a protest meeting. Very soon she was arrested. Back in court again, now in the dock, she was sentenced to two weeks' imprisonment in the third division and she was then taken to join the other prisoners in the cells.

Isabel Seymour came to Rochester Row to bring lunch for the prisoners:

They were all up a long staircase in a range of cells at the top, Adela, the How Martyns, the Pethick Lawrences and Teresa Billington. The How Martyns were very newly married and the Pethick Lawrences reasonably newly married—(My dear!). The How Martyns were locked in an embrace for a whole hour more or less, quite unable to eat and in tears. The Pethick Lawrences were equally segregated in another cell, but as the cells were open to the front, I could circulate from one to the other nourishing the birds like a mother.

At last they heard the black Maria rumble into the courtyard but Mrs Lawrence was not prepared for the new horror:

> I had imagined that it would be a sort of bus with hard benches on each side. When I saw that it consisted of low, narrow compartments, hardly enough for a full-grown person to sit in, and realised that in one of these narrow compartments I was going to be locked up, my heart died within me. The only aperture admitting air or light was a small barred grating opening into a narrow passage between the two rows of these cages.

On the same afternoon that the prisoners went to Holloway, Pethick Lawrence took over his wife's role as treasurer. At a W.S.P.U. meeting he made an appeal for funds and promised to contribute ten pounds for every day that his wife spent in prison. 'I intended it as a public gesture, but it was as a jest that the story went all round the world!' At a Covent Garden fancy dress ball the prize-winning costume was placarded:

> Ten Pounds a day
> He said he'd pay
> To keep this face
> In Holloway.

The shock of the arrest, the experience of the black Maria and the harshness of prison treatment, were too much for Mrs Pethick Lawrence. Almost immediately she became ill and overwrought and her husband had to fetch her away from prison on the verge of a breakdown. Some days later he took her to Italy and left her there to recover, while he returned to London to carry on the work at Clement's Inn.

The Suffragettes were condemned and ridiculed for several days after the Lobby incident, but soon the Press began to consider the question more seriously. The *Daily Mail* now headed its editorial, 'Cruel Treatment of English Ladies'. The *Daily News* commented:

> The plain man is content to dismiss the whole affair as if these people were a set of criminal lunatics. The observer who looks beneath the surface is unable to accept such a pleasant and plausible explanation. Such social reformers as Cobden's daughter and Mrs Despard cannot be condemned as oppressed with a desire for silly self-advertisement.

The report then goes on to tell of Mrs Cobden Sanderson's work with the Independent Labour Party, of Mrs Despard's remarkable achievements in the slums of Battersea, and of Mrs Pethick Lawrence's social work in London's West End.

These women were being treated not as political offenders but as common criminals. As second-class prisoners they were stripped, forced to wear prison clothes, scrub stone floors and live in solitary confinement. Soon Mrs Montefiore was released with a breakdown and it was known that several women had been removed to the prison hospital. Questions were asked in Parliament by Keir Hardie and Lord Robert Cecil and within a week, the Home Secretary, Herbert Gladstone, ordered the prisoners' transfer to the first division.

Mary Gawthorpe and Annie Kenney were better conditioned to the prison life than the other women.

We knitted and footed socks for men prisoners—socks with the regulation stripes of red alternating with grey. Annie Kenney and I were the only ones who received full marks, hence payment amounting to thirteen shillings and fourpence for our work when at the end of four weeks we were all thrown out of prison.

There had been such a public outcry at the length of the imprisonments that the women were released on November 24 after serving only one month of their sentences. In appreciation of the prisoners, Mrs Fawcett—soon to become President of the National Union of Women's Suffrage Societies—arranged a welcome dinner at the Savoy Hotel. The released Suffragettes were given a tremendous reception, and when it was all over, an elated Annie and Mary Gawthorpe set off by train for Huddersfield.

A by-election was in progress there, and Christabel was already waging a most successful campaign. She had been exploiting the imprisonments as anti-Government propaganda, and now she was delighted to be able to produce the prisoners themselves. The Press reported:

As the train came in a great cheer went up. The two martyrs alighted, and were met by Christabel Pankhurst who kissed them warmly as the crowd cheered again. Then the three, arm in arm, guarded by stalwart policemen and followed by hundreds of cheering Yorkshire men, made their way slowly into the station square where a meeting was in progress.

Here the noise became deafening. Women waved handkerchiefs from windows and the townspeople yelled and clapped as Annie and Mary mounted the speakers' lorry. Annie was the heroine of the day. Traffic was dislocated and tram-cars had to stop while cheering crowds followed the Suffragettes up the main street after they had spoken.

'We are all hoarse and tired,' Christabel told reporters, 'but we are happy. Never have we had such a reception as we have had here. Men as well as women listened to us earnestly, and there was an absence of those silly interruptions and heckling we experienced in Hyde Park.'

When the election results were announced on November 30, the Liberals still held the seat, but with a greatly reduced majority. It was generally believed that this was due to the Suffragette intervention and the *Daily Mirror* commented:

When the Suffragettes began their campaign they were mistaken for notoriety hunters, featherheads, flibbertigibbets. Their proceedings were not taken seriously. Now they have proved that they are in dead earnest, they have frightened the Government, they have broken through the law, they have made votes for women practical politics.

During the last few weeks of 1906 the subject was constantly brought up in Parliament, always to be opposed by some members of the Cabinet. Three times small groups of Suffragettes demonstrated at Westminster in defiance of the Government attitude, and twenty-one more women were imprisoned as a result. Mrs Drummond led one of the protests, and while her companions were in the Lobby trying to speak, she resourcefully managed to enter the House by the underground passage reserved for Members. She was caught as she headed for the Debating Chamber, and consequently she was among those to spend Christmas in Holloway.

There was now a genuine public interest in the movement, and many women of rank, intellectuals and university women joined the constitutional suffragists as members of the National Union of Women's Suffrage Societies. Before Parliament reassembled on February 12, 1907, the N.U.W.S.S. planned that they would hold a demonstration.

The 'Mud March' on Saturday February 9 was the first great assembly of the 'constitutionals' and many of the suffrage pioneers took part with their now grown-up daughters. In pouring rain a sober crowd assembled at Hyde Park Corner and the women, dressed mostly in black, then proceeded to the Strand for a meeting in the Exeter Hall. The militant brigade was conspicuously absent, and the *Daily Graphic* said of the half-mile-long procession: 'Indeed, although feminine, it was anything but effeminate. It bore with dignified contempt the ribaldrous remarks which now and again some wag would throw at it. On the whole, however, the attitude of the crowd was distinctly respectful.'

A notable group of politicians and intellectuals addressed the suffragists at the Exeter Hall. Many of the women were unexpectedly surprised by the attitude of some of the speakers; both Israel Zangwill

31

and Mrs Fawcett gave credit to the militants for revitalising the movement. The Liberal women on the platform were very disapproving that any credit should go to the Suffragettes and they actively showed their displeasure by interrupting the speakers and hissing when Keir Hardie rose to wind up the debate.

'I have come to this meeting to show that I still support your cause, but if it is advanced today, you have to thank the militant tactics of the fighting brigade. It is due to no effort I have made.' Keir Hardie then went on to stress the necessity for a policy of independence: 'Women must put the suffrage question before all party considerations.'

The Suffragettes decided to hold a 'Women's Parliament' on the day following the opening of the new session at Westminster. 'Deeds not words' was the W.S.P.U. motto and the 'Parliament' was an assembly gathered with the specific intention of taking immediate action.

Votes for women was not mentioned at the opening of Parliament, and on February 13 at three o'clock both the Caxton Hall and the Exeter Hall were filled with Suffragettes eagerly awaiting a demonstration. 'Rise up!' came the watchword from the Caxton Hall platform. 'Now!' responded hundreds of women and amidst deafening cheers they rose from their seats and prepared to take a resolution to the House. Mrs Despard came forward to lead the deputation, and as soon as the volunteers were organised into ranks, they set out with an escort of police on either side. Each woman carried a rolled-up copy of the resolution and as they marched towards the House of Commons, they sang to the tune of 'John Brown's Body':

> Rise up women! for the fight is hard and long;
> Rise in thousands, singing loud a battle song.
> Right is might, and in its strength we'll be strong
> And the cause goes marching on;
> Glory, glory, hallelujah . . . etc.

A cordon of police confronted the women at the Abbey Green. They tried to break up the procession, but the Suffragettes tightened their ranks and refused to be turned away. Suddenly the mounted police appeared. They took the place of Cossacks and rode down the women moving peaceably in procession. Scattered into small groups, the Suffragettes now tried to get through the police cordons and reach the doors of St Stephen's Hall.

Mrs Lilias Ashworth Hallett was a noted suffrage pioneer from Bath. Dignified and white-haired, she had come to London for the Women's Parliament and this was her first connection with the W.S.P.U.:

My astonishment was great when I found myself suddenly encompassed by police on foot and on horseback, and my courage rose in proportion to the indignation which I felt.

Police blocked the footway. They laughed and jeered. When I endeavoured to get on the road I found myself in serious danger from the mounted men whose horses moved restlessly on and off the pavement. Twice I eluded these men charging down upon us. I was twice arrested, and when I found the hands of the police upon me, I pointed to the Houses of Parliament and said: 'If you don't take your hands off me there are men in the House who will want to know the reason why.' They then dropped me; they were not sure who I might be.

Evidently the police had been given orders to drive away the women but to arrest as few as possible. The constable who took Marion Milner in charge proved unexpectedly helpful. After escorting her down the steps from the entrance to St Stephen's Hall, he released her to her great surprise. 'Haven't you arrested me?' 'No.' Then as she looked rather nonplussed, he added encouragingly: 'Go on, missie—try again. You do it often enough and I'll have to arrest you.' After about the sixth attempt to enter the hall, he said: 'That's enough—you done your part noble— now we'll go.' And go they did—amicably—hand in hand to Cannon Row Police Station, and it was there she was charged with resisting the police.

Christabel, Sylvia and Mrs Despard were among the women arrested that afternoon. Mrs Despard was triumphant that she had at last obtained her objective—imprisonment for the cause. Over fifty women were taken into custody, and while they were released overnight, Pethick Lawrence stood bail for them all. Police and prisoners were on extraordinarily friendly terms as they waited for the trials next morning, and several constables begged souvenirs—*Votes for Women* badges—from the Suffragettes they had captured.

Christabel's case was the first to be heard. She blamed the Government for what had happened on the previous day. Some of the women had suffered from rough handling by the police. 'If lives are lost,' Christabel said, 'the Liberals will be responsible. One thing is certain, there can be no going back for us and more will happen if we do not get justice.' Here the magistrate intervened and denounced Suffragette tactics as a means of getting votes: 'These disorderly scenes in the streets must be stopped.' 'They can be,' Christabel broke in, 'but only in one way.' 'Twenty shillings or fourteen days,' said Mr Curtis Bennett sternly.

Christabel and some fifty-three other women chose to go to prison. 'Holloway is full up,' the *Daily Mirror* reported. 'Yesterday some seventy or eighty convicts were moved to Aylesbury. The authorities, fearing another raid, are at their wits' end to know how to accommodate further political prisoners.' A description of Holloway by Christabel appeared in the *Penny Magazine* shortly after her release:

In the old part of the prison the cells are gloomy in the extreme. A perpetual twilight reigns there—but in the new wing the cells are perfectly light and clean. Until the last visit to Holloway the Suffragettes were placed in the old cells; latterly they have occupied the new ones.

The arrival of more than fifty Suffragettes means that some of them do not reach their cells on the first night until midnight or after. Hastily, therefore, each prisoner lays on the floor the plank bed which she finds reared up against the wall. On this is placed a mattress stuffed with cocoa-nut fibre. Coarse sheets, two blankets and a rug complete the bedding.

The next morning the cell door is thrown open and the prisoner is asked if she wishes to make application to see the governor, the matron or the doctor. In case of illness, unless she applied then, she cannot see the doctor until the following day.

Before breakfast, cells are cleaned and beds are made. That meal consists for those in the first and second divisions of a brown loaf and a pint of tea. The bread is fairly good, the tea very much the reverse. At half-past eight comes the summons to chapel. Here a suffragist prisoner sees not only her colleagues but all the other inmates. In chapel, before the chaplain enters, smiles are exchanged and attempts at conversation are made.

These are noticed and forbidden. What are known as the criminal prisoners are a source of interest to the suffragists, who realise that many of them are more sinned against than sinning. Almost all are poor, and the majority would not be there at all if they could afford the fines imposed by the magistrates. There are very few really wicked and depraved looking women. Suffragists believe that a great and priceless opportunity of regenerating these women is being neglected. The discipline is of a kind to harden the prisoners and tends to make them deceitful. There is much religion (chapel every day and twice on Sundays), but it all seems to the women unreal and mechanical.

For twenty-three hours out of twenty-four they are alone. During the twenty-fourth hour, though not alone, they are forbidden to speak, and none speaks to them. Prison undoubtedly punishes but it does not reform.

After chapel all return to their cells. Later in the morning the prisoners enter the yard for exercise. Round and round they march in single file, a considerable space between each for the sake of preventing conversation. To do that is a matter of some difficulty but prisoners manage to exchange a word now and then. Soon after the return from exercise, dinner is brought to the cells. Brown bread and potatoes form part of every midday meal, but the third factor varies. On Monday it is boiled beans with a small piece of bacon. On Tuesday and Friday it is plain unsweetened suet pudding. On Wednesday and Saturday it is soup, on Thursday it is boiled beef and on Sunday tinned meat, having a pronounced odour and evidently hailing from Chicago.

The afternoon is unbroken save by visits of inspectors, by the matron, on some days by the governor and occasionally by the visiting magistrate. At four o'clock comes supper, consisting of brown bread and cocoa which is even more undrinkable than the tea. At eight o'clock the lights are turned out and all prisoners go to bed.

Some of the more objectionable features of prison life are the provision of a very unwholesome wooden spoon which is handed down from prisoner to prisoner, the scanty supply of water for washing, the use of cold water only for cleaning purposes, the use of tins more or less unclean for serving soup and other food; the supply of food of very inferior quality. In the first division, prisoners may wear their own clothing if they please, and many suffragist prisoners do so, but in the second division this privilege is not allowed. No nightdresses are provided and the clothing might be better adapted than it is to secure the health and comfort of the wearers.

When the prisoners were released two weeks later, the W.S.P.U. arranged a welcome breakfast. Christabel spoke, and referred to the first Women's Parliament as the twentieth-century Peterloo. It certainly looked as though the demonstration had produced some results, for events in Parliament had moved towards the introduction of a Women's Suffrage Bill.

Mrs Fawcett and four of her colleagues had asked to be allowed the privilege of pleading their cause at the Bar of the House. Their request was refused, but it seemed to impress several private Members with the seriousness of the women's demand and they agreed to introduce a Suffrage Bill if they won a place in the ballot. One of these supporters, W. H. Dickinson, the Liberal M.P. for North St Pancras, won first place; he decided to put forward a Women's Enfranchisement Bill and the debate was arranged for March 19.

Christabel was hopeful but never over confident: 'If they kill this Bill policies will change. If we do not get the vote, it will mean revolution amongst women.' In fact Mrs Pankhurst's professional future rested on the outcome of the Bill. Her position as registrar was threatened unless she gave up Suffragette work. She had carefully avoided imprisonment while still employed, and the registrarship was never neglected. Mrs Clarke, her sister, was a staunch deputy but the authorities had sent Mrs Pankhurst a severe warning. Always optimistic, she held hopes of being able to keep the post.

The Ladies' Gallery was closed to visitors during the reading of Dickinson's Bill, and in order to get up-to-the-minute news on the debate, Mrs Pankhurst and Christabel went to the *Daily Mirror* offices and read the details as they came over the tape. After five hours the question was still under discussion and the Speaker refused to call a division. Time ran out. Waiting anxiously in the newspaper office, the Pankhursts realised that yet another Bill was lost. Mrs Pankhurst regretfully resigned from the registrarship and now devoted her entire time to campaigning for the vote.

Suffragette meetings followed one another in quick succession. They felt it was imperative to make an effort to save the Bill, and a week later, a second Women's Parliament assembled in the Caxton Hall. The Suffragettes hoped to get into the House by means of a carefully planned coup. A contingent of 'Lancashire lassies' had travelled down from the industrial north, and dressed in their clogs and shawls, they arrived outside the Houses of Parliament and alighted from a bus as though on a sightseeing tour. The police were out in force expecting a march from the Caxton Hall, and for a few moments they did not realise what was happening. It was only as the women began to make for the door of St Stephen's Hall that they were recognised as Suffragettes and seized before they could go further.

Christabel was presiding at the Caxton Hall, and now contingents of women were sent out from there. As they returned dishevelled and breathless from the tussle, Christabel urged them to go back to the field, break through the police ranks and get into the House: 'Seize the mace and you will be the Cromwells of the twentieth century!' Again and again the women tried to get past the cordons until finally over seventy arrests had been made.

The Government remained indifferent to the pleas of suffragists and anti-suffragists alike. A strong group of 'antis' had come forward when it looked as though votes for women might become a reality through Dickinson's Bill. Within four weeks over thirty-seven thousand signatures were collected from people against women's suffrage. The speed of the operation amazed some of the suffragists who had long been preparing a women's suffrage declaration, and they demanded an enquiry. On examination, the 'anti' petitions were condemned as 'informal'. Many of the names were written in the same hand, and batches of signatures had been collected on separate sheets not headed by an official demand so that there was no evidence to show that a signatory knew to what cause he was adding his name.

The Suffragettes realised that it was to be a longer struggle than they had at first visualised. There were no more demonstrations in 1907 and the women now embarked on a widespread campaign of winning popular support by peaceful means. An unusual number of Parliamentary by-elections that summer provided ideal conditions for propaganda work. By this time the W.S.P.U. had gathered a number of very competent organisers and where, in the early days, one or two Suffragettes would manage an election campaign with any local help they could get, several organisers would now go to a constituency and work with some thirty or forty of their own volunteers in addition to local helpers.

The Suffragettes were used to jeering crowds and a certain amount of rowdiness, but during the Rutland by-election they experienced violent opposition for the first time. In the small towns of Oakham and Uppingham gangs of youths howled them down; their speeches were drowned by horns and rattles and they were bombarded with bad eggs and rotten fruit and vegetables. It was alleged that a wealthy Liberal at Oakham was paying a gang to terrorise supporters and to create havoc at Suffragette meetings. Extra police reinforcements had to be brought in from Leicestershire and local sympathisers dared not openly help the Suffragettes. Although the women eventually managed to hire a 'lurry' as a platform, they had to venture out by night to fetch it themselves from the barn where it was being stored, and it was painted with the name of a farmer who lived miles outside the constituency.

One evening when Mary Gawthorpe was addressing an outdoor meeting at Uppingham, some men in the crowd began to pelt her with peppermint bull's-eyes. 'Sweets to the sweet,' she remarked and went on speaking. Suddenly a china 'pot egg' flew through the air and hit her on the head. She fell down, stunned, and was carried away unconscious to an hotel. When she appeared again on the Suffragette platform next morning the local inhabitants were amazed and full of admiration. In fact, the Suffragettes were popular with the majority of the electors and most of the hostility they experienced was stirred up by the lower-paid labourers who were themselves still unqualified to vote.

Propaganda work was not confined to by-elections. Branches of the W.S.P.U. had been started in many of the larger towns in the Midlands and north of England and chosen organisers were now sent to help increase membership. Edith Rigby, the Secretary of the Preston branch, writes enthusiastically about the daily routine during Annie Kenney's visit to the town.

In the morning Annie would visit 'people worth winning to a more generous and intelligent understanding of the women's claims'. Apparently many of these better-class people were sympathetic and promised help and financial support.

The active members of the Preston branch were all working women and each afternoon at three o'clock one of them would organise a parlour meeting to which she invited her neighbours. Crowded into a little room, they listened appreciatively while Annie gave them a short talk.

Shortly after three-thirty, the textile workers began to pour out of the largest mills in the town and at a busy street corner, Annie stood on a 'lurry' and addressed the men and women on their way home. 'Hundreds pressed round,' says Mrs Rigby, 'jeering until sobered by remarks that touched tender places.' These meetings lasted for nearly an hour, and many people came to hear Annie speak again in the evening in the covered market.

When the Suffragettes journeyed out to hamlets and villages, they always met with friendliness and respect. Many of the agricultural workers remembered the bad days before the 1884 Reform Act when they had no vote. At that time, a labourer's widow and children were frequently turned out of their farm if he died. The country women were now quite satisfied with their own lot, but they did feel that women workers in industrial cities had a need of the vote in order to improve conditions.

Although they were poor, the country people would buy badges and pamphlets and they eagerly accepted the free propaganda leaflets that were offered. As the Suffragettes travelled from village to village, drivers of passing carts and workers in the fields would hail them. Sometimes the labourers would call out, ask the women to stop, and come hurrying up to the roadside to collect Suffragette literature.

The Literature Department of the W.S.P.U. had developed considerably under the direction of Pethick Lawrence. When his wife was imprisoned, he took on the title of Hon. Secretary and made himself almost entirely responsible for the running of the office at Clement's Inn. He re-organised the accounting system and formed a separate literature sales department—the Woman's Press. Alice Knight, a shopkeeper, was engaged to take over the new enterprise which offered penny pamphlets, badges, postcard photographs of the leaders and books on the Suffrage Movement. Between the March and August of 1907 the Woman's Press made four hundred and fifty pounds.

As soon as Mrs Pethick Lawrence was fit to return to work as treasurer, she inaugurated a votes for women campaign fund aiming at twenty thousand pounds. Circulars were sent to known suffrage supporters in every part of the country, explaining the difficulties involved in con-tacting new subscribers and asking their help to bring in new recruits. The appeal brought a generous response from members of all suffrage societies and W.S.P.U. membership steadily increased.

As the W.S.P.U. was essentially a fast-moving political organisation all speakers and organisers were advised to keep strictly up to date with current events. In the autumn of 1906 weekly Monday 'At Homes' were started to help to clarify the immediate political situation and to explain W.S.P.U. strategy. These began as informal gatherings at Clement's Inn, but as numbers increased the Portman Rooms were taken. The leaders presided on the platform, and in addition to explaining policy, they would announce the forthcoming programme and there would be a collection and enrolments. Later the meetings were often held in the larger Queen's Hall.

All organisers were encouraged to attend the 'At Homes', and Mrs Pethick Lawrence advocated that they should read at least two news-papers with differing political views each day. Christabel was an avid reader and when she spent week-ends with the Pethick Lawrences in Surrey, she was always the first to look at the morning papers. As she finished a page, it was thrown to the floor, and someone had carefully to collect up and reassemble the scattered papers before the master of the house appeared.

By the autumn of 1907 there were already seventy branches of the W.S.P.U. The movement had become so popular that many members of old-established politically affiliated suffrage societies joined the militants while still involving themselves in party activities. This allowed for the infiltration of policy alien to W.S.P.U. tactics, and in spite of every effort on the part of the leaders to maintain unity, destructive criticism of their methods led to disruption within the branches. The Pankhursts and the Pethick Lawrences acted on their own decisions without consulting delegates or anyone else, and although these means were vital for the growth of the movement, they met with disapproval from many members who saw them as undemocratic.

For this reason, and because all branches subscribed to the W.S.P.U. funds, the members were most anxious that their representatives should be heard at the annual conference which had been agreed to when the constitution was drafted in the previous year. It had become increasingly clear to the leaders that it would be impossible to run the movement on a representational basis as it was originally conceived, and a month before the conference was due Mrs Pankhurst dramatically tore up the constitution and announced that she had decided to reorganise the union. A new committee was to be selected, and the annual conference abandoned.

The national W.S.P.U. under the control of Mrs Pankhurst was now to be responsible for the entire organisation and the union branches would become local W.S.P.U.s subject to direction from headquarters. There would now be no membership fee—all affiliation fees already received would be returned and the only condition of enrolment was the signing of a membership pledge: 'I endorse the objects and methods of the Women's Social and Political Union and I hereby undertake not to support the candidate of any political party at Parliamentary elections until women have obtained the Parliamentary vote.'

Mrs Despard, Mrs How Martyn and Teresa Billington (now Mrs Billington Greig), broke away from the W.S.P.U. at this stage. They had long been in disagreement with much of the W.S.P.U. policy; Mrs Despard felt that she could not condone methods so alien to her beliefs in the freedom of the individual, and Teresa Billington, herself an extreme individualist, was hurt that her opinions no longer held sway within the union. The three seceders now formed their own democratically controlled organisation, the Women's Freedom League.

From W.S.P.U. headquarters, a long letter dated September 19, 1907 was sent to all organisers and enquirers. The situation was described very frankly and reasons for the W.S.P.U. policy were clearly explained:

. . . We are not playing experiments with representative Government. We are not a school for teaching women how to use the vote. We are a militant movement and we have to get the vote next session. The leaders of this movement are practical politicians; they have set out to do an almost impossible task—that of creating an independent political party of women. They are fighting the strongest Government of modern times and the strongest prejudice in human nature. They cannot afford to dally with the issue. It is after all a voluntary militant movement; those who cannot follow the general must drop out of the ranks . . .

Every political movement has this crisis to face and at such times strong leadership is essential. Apart from those whose past associations and life have been bound up with political causes that are dear to them and which they can hardly be expected at an advanced age to leave, we have against us others whose motives are less pure. There are disappointed place-seekers and those who have thought that they were more capable of filling certain posts than those who have been selected . . .

In a personal letter to an organiser who wondered what she should tell enquirers, Mrs Pankhurst wrote:

> . . . All that is good for the general world outside is the assurance that our policy is unchanged and that our political independence is stronger than ever . . . I am resolutely refusing to reply to any personal statements made by the seceders. The sooner the incident is closed, the better it will be for the women's cause.

Pethick Lawrence had given invaluable advice on manoeuvring the difficult situation and the executive running of the reformed organisation now fell entirely to him and his wife and Christabel. Mrs Pankhurst herself took no active part in the day-to-day business at headquarters although she was kept informed on every move and consulted over major developments. She had complete confidence in Christabel's judgement and left her to make decisions on policy. Pethick Lawrence says that Mrs Pankhurst was a consummate evangelist, and preferred to expound the gospel of militancy in an endless succession of great meetings up and down the country.

Almost immediately after the 'split', Pethick Lawrence brought out the first number of the new W.S.P.U. paper *Votes for Women*. A striking cover picture, 'The Haunted House' by David Wilson, represented a seated woman brooding over the Houses of Parliament. The paper began as a monthly at threepence a copy and at the same time, in order to keep workers and organisers in constant touch with the movement, a halfpenny weekly bulletin was published, giving the Suffragette news and a programme of forthcoming events. Each number of *Votes for Women* contained news items and leading articles by the Pethick Lawrences who were joint editors. Christabel wrote on policy, Sylvia on the history of the Suffrage Movement, and there were also extracts from the Press, and reports from local W.S.P.U.s telling of their latest activities. In addition, the paper usually included an article by some well-known writer such as Laurence Housman or Elizabeth Robins.

One early number had an allegorical story, 'The Sleeping Beauty in the Wood Retold', by a certain Trotty Tadpole. In this version the Princess awakes before the Prince comes to claim her and she is told to go out and seek him. After passing through a mass of tribulations, each representing a political barrier, she at length overcomes all with the help of inspiring visions and reaches the Prince, having proved herself his equal. The story ends: 'She went her way through the world by the Prince's side, everywhere setting free the captives and bringing hope to the despairing.'

There was a growing national awareness of the changing status of women. 'The Mere Man', writing in the *Sphere*, observes:

> The homes must be comparatively few in which three or four maiden daughters live on with their parents. The last quarter of a century has seen the gradual uprising of the latchkey girl, who is determined to make her own living and make her own way in life. There has grown up a race of bachelor girls in flats who live on caramels and sausages. We have most decidedly changed for the better; the majority of unmarried girls now have their own employment and as long as they are not absolutely dependent on it for their bread they do very well.
>
> A father never thinks of keeping his sons at home; he sets them up for life or gives them an allowance which enables them to live in their own rooms. If he can afford it he might do the same for the girls. It would obviate the necessity for the huge houses of the Victorian family and so would not really be much more expensive than the old-fashioned establishment.

The first members of suffrage societies had joined on account of their intellectual or benevolent convictions. They were people with security, whereas many of the new young W.S.P.U. recruits were middle-class women—already victims of changing conditions. Some came from large families, others had lost their parents or had married at an early age, and they were all having to face life without the shelter and support that would have been assured them in the Victorian era. The Suffragette Movement provided these women with a certain security, fulfilment for their intellectual abilities, and above all with a comradeship they had never previously known. As most of them had no important occupation, they were able to devote their entire time to W.S.P.U. activities, and it was from this group that many of the W.S.P.U. national speakers and organisers were drawn.

Working-class women, teachers, nurses and social workers also joined the movement. They knew from experience to what conditions the women of the poorer classes and women in industry were subjected.

A biography of Mrs Baldock was given in *Votes for Women*:

> As a working woman she knows the difficulties and sorrows of their lives and she has now given up all political life to fight for the political power of women. She brings to her work the experience gained as a Poor Law Guardian and by work in the I.L.P. and on distress committees.

After hearing Mrs Baldock speak in Victoria Park, one of the boys of whom she was a guardian wrote:

> Dear Mother,
> I saw and heard you at Victoria Park last Sunday. When I first saw you I thought I would wait until afterwards and speak to you. Then I saw you had some lady friends with you so I went home. I felt somewhat proud of the fact that the lady who was speaking so beautifully was known by me.

Christabel had an eye for selecting workers and a magnetic personality which drew people into the movement.

Ada Flatman was indifferent to the Suffragettes until she travelled abroad and was constantly asked about her views on the question. When she returned she was curious to find out more about it and she was taken by friends to several meetings held by the constitutional suffragists:

> I was not impressed but got the idea of the suffrage and wanted to hear the militants. I went to a meeting in the Horticultural Hall, Westminster, where Christabel Pankhurst was to be the speaker. There I saw a young girl in her early twenties giving out handbills at the door and speaking to people as they came in. She later went on to the platform and made a fighting speech which thrilled me through and through and I knew that I must be one of that valiant band.

Frances Bartlett was one of Christabel's first recruits. She had left school at the age of nine to work in a dairy; later she came to London as a children's nurse, and by the time she was twenty-one she was married with three children. Mrs Bartlett decided to take up political work and as a keen Liberal supporter she attended a debate on militant tactics at the National Liberal Club. Christabel, newly arrived in London, was also at the meeting, and when she stood up at question time, she was roughly pulled down and prevented from speaking. Mrs Bartlett then jumped up in a fury:

> I said that if that was the way Liberals treated women, I for one refused to give them any more of my time. Miss Pankhurst who was sitting in the front row turned round and shook my hand and when the meeting was over she asked me to call and see her at Clement's Inn the following morning.
>
> I was a voluntary worker for a few years and my work consisted of chalking pavements for meetings, working up processions, attending to banners, selling the paper, working at all by-elections and going to protest at meetings; I would travel up and down the country following Cabinet Ministers about and making myself a nuisance to them wherever they went. We never knew what was in store for us but we braved the fury and sometimes extreme violence.

Marie Brackenbury, an artist, and one of the nine children of General Charles Brackenbury, says: 'Gentle cultured women handing notices of meetings became quite used to such expressions as "you ought to be beaten and then dragged round Trafalgar Square by the hair of your head." '

Paper selling was one of the chief activities of voluntary workers, and by law the women had to stand off the pavement so as not to obstruct pedestrians. *Votes for Women* soon came out in a weekly edition and a new verse was chanted in the streets:

> Votes for Women
> Price one penny
> Articles by Annie Kenney
> Mrs Lawrence—Christabel
> Other Suffragettes as well.

'The truth for a penny! The truth for a penny!' Marie Brackenbury would cry as she stood with her papers. 'No, thank you!' said a haughty dame, and gathering up her voluminous skirts she was about to pass on in disgust. 'What! Don't you like the truth?' 'Certainly not!' replied the lady with a disdainful toss of her head.

'Sometimes people would spit in our faces,' says Marie Brackenbury, 'but nothing mattered except faithfulness to our cause. We were roused to throw aside all conventions and cost what it might to break down the barriers of false prejudice and false conceptions of the ideal woman.'

Mrs Pankhurst brought the militant campaign to the west country for the first time during the Newton Abbot by-election in January 1908. The local people were interested to hear the Suffragettes' point of view and they gave them enthusiastic support, never imagining that women might affect the political issue.

The Mid-Devon Constituency had always been a Liberal stronghold, and the local Liberals were so sure of success that they had printed a mock mourning card in anticipation of the election results:

IN MEMORY OF THE SUFFRAGETTES AND
TARIFF REFORMERS WHO FELL ASLEEP
AT MID-DEVON ON JANUARY 7, 1908

By tradition, the Liberals would break up the meetings of any opposing party. At Bovey Tracey a Conservative candidate was once nearly shut in a cage, and now, gangs of rowdy Liberals would wreck every Conservative and Unionist meeting, pelting the speakers with rotten vegetables and muddy snowballs.

The Suffragettes had been continuously urging the electors to vote against the Government, but no one realised until the count of the poll that their words had made an impression. When it was announced that the Unionist candidate had won the election by twelve hundred and eighty votes, the Liberals were astounded. They massed together in angry groups, and the police, foreseeing a riot, hurriedly escorted the newly elected candidate from the town hall and motored him out of the town.

Mrs Pankhurst and Mrs Martel started walking calmly back to their lodgings. Friends warned Mrs Pankhurst to be careful and she laughingly assured them that she was not afraid to trust herself in a crowd. As they walked on, they met a group of young clay cutters wearing red Liberal rosettes. The men were angry and agitated; their pride had been wounded and they were ready to make a scene. Suddenly one of them recognised the Suffragettes: 'They did it! Those women did it!' he roared, and immediately the crowd rushed forward and began to pelt the women with clay and rotten eggs.

Mrs Pankhurst and Mrs Martel ran for a near-by grocer's shop. Mrs Banbury, the grocer's wife, hastily let them in and bolted the door, but the men outside battered on the shop front so violently that the grocer was terrified that they would wreck his shop. As Mrs Pankhurst did not wish to be the cause of damage, she asked if they could leave by the back way and Mrs Banbury led them out into a small yard which opened into a side lane. Unknown to the Suffragettes, the angry mob had come round to the gate and as soon as it was unlatched the men rushed in. With shouts and oaths, they seized Mrs Martel and beat her over the head with their fists. Mrs Pankhurst and Mrs Banbury eventually managed to tear her away and the grocer's wife dragged Mrs Martel back into the house.

Mrs Pankhurst had just reached the threshold when a staggering blow fell on the back of her head.

> Rough hands grasped the collar of my coat and I was flung violently to the ground. Stunned, I must have lost consciousness for a moment, for my next sensation was of cold wet mud seeping through my clothing. Sight returning to me, I perceived the men, silent now, but with a dreadful, lowering silence, closing in a ring around me. In the centre of the ring was an empty barrel, and the horrid thought occurred to me that they might intend putting me in it. A long time seemed to pass, while the ring of men drew closer. I looked at them, in their drab clothes smeared with yellow pit-clay. 'Poor souls,' I thought, and then I said suddenly, 'Are none of you *men*?' Then one of the youths darted toward me, and I knew that whatever was going to happen to me was about to begin.

> At that very moment came shouts and a rush of police who had fought their way through hostile crowds to rescue us. Of course the mob turned tail and fled, and I was carried gently into the shop, which the police guarded for two hours, before it was deemed safe for us to leave in a closed motor-car. It was many months before either Mrs Martel or I recovered from our injuries.

Before Parliament reassembled for the 1908 session, renewed efforts were made to persuade Cabinet Ministers to act on the votes for women issue. Because the Suffragettes would now ask questions at every Liberal meeting, the Liberal organisers began to make it difficult for women to get tickets. In spite of this, the Suffragettes managed to secure seats through their men supporters and they were present at every important political gathering strategically placed and ready to interrupt when an opportunity occurred.

When Asquith spoke on franchise issues at a rally in Aberdeen, the entire seating in the hall was reserved for specially selected ticket holders. It was clear that Asquith did not intend to mention the women's suffrage question and a resolution was passed without reference to it. All was peaceful until the Rev. Webster, a known supporter of women's suffrage, rose on the platform to propose an amendment to the resolution. Three men seized him, a brawl ensued, and when Mrs Pankhurst stood up to protest she was promptly removed. A Liberal woman who tried to object was taken out soon afterwards. The *Aberdeen Press* reported:

> The scene absorbed all thoughts and many a Liberal left the meeting with the uneasy feeling that the suffragists had had the

LEFT: Christabel Pankhurst in academic dress soon after she had qualified as an LL.B. RIGHT: Annie Kenney in mill girl costume.

Mr Asquith's Prisoners: Annie Kenney, Mrs Knight and Mrs Sparboro.

An early meeting of the W.S.P.U. at the Pethick Lawrences' flat in 4 Clement's Inn. *From left to right:* Mrs Drummond, Christabel Pankhurst, Jessie Kenney, Mrs Martel, Mrs Pankhurst, Mrs Despard.

The first arrest of Mrs Pankhurst. February 13, 1908.

Suffragette prisoners released from Holloway. July 31, 1908.

W.S.P.U. members prepare for the Hyde Park meeting on June 21, 1908. These young women do not match the popular image of the aggressive Suffragette.

THIS IS "THE HOUSE" THAT MAN BUILT,

AND these are a few of the women of note Who say that they want, and they will have the vote; And think that they ought, To have Man's support: Even although HE should have to go short, The sly Suffragette Who is all on the get And wants all, in THE HOUSE that man built.

A picture postcard representing Suffragettes as a group of grasping harridans. (London Museum.)

Vera Wentworth
advertising the Hyde Park
meeting of June 21, 1908.

Annie Kenney and Mary Gawthorpe leaving Hyde Park after the
meeting. June 21, 1908.

From a window overlooking Holloway Gaol Christabel waves to the hunger strikers. July 1909.

The hunger strikers wave scarves and regalia from their broken windows. July 1909.

A Suffragette cartoon of 1909 illustrates the horrors of forcible feeding—
a tame representation according to those who have undergone the process.

LEFT: Lady Constance Lytton.
RIGHT: Lady Constance disguised
as Jane Warton. January 14, 1910.

Black Friday. November 18, 1910. Volunteers for the deputation to Parliament fill the platform at the Caxton Hall.

The battle in Parliament Square on Black Friday. Pictures showing attacks on the Suffragettes were suppressed and those showing the women as aggressors were published.

Mrs Fawcett plants a holly tree in Colonel Blathwayt's Suffragette arboretum. 1910.

A Suffragette dairy and farming school in Checkendon, Berkshire, was run by two Cambridge graduates (right), Kate Lelacheur and Fanny Parker.

Suffragette window smashing raid in Regent Street. March 1, 1912. (British Museum).

After a window smashing raid police guard a shop, while placards proclaim the latest number of Suffragette arrests.

Mrs Pankhurst rearrested under the Cat and Mouse Act. May 26, 1913. After defying detectives who intend to take her back to Holloway, Mrs Pankhurst falls fainting into the arms of Dr Ethel Smyth. Nurse Pine and Dr Flora Murray attend.

Derby Day. June 4, 1913. Emily Wilding Davison stops the King's horse and is hurled across the turf.

The Emily Wilding Davison funeral procession. June 14, 1913. Women in white carrying madonna lilies solemnly march through the streets of London.

ABOVE: Reginald McKenna who introduced the Cat and Mouse Act of 1913.

RIGHT: Suffragette anti Cat and Mouse cartoon.

THE CAT AND MOUSE ACT

PASSED BY THE LIBERAL GOVERNMENT

THE LIBERAL CAT
ELECTORS VOTE AGAINST HIM!
KEEP THE LIBERAL OUT!

Suffragette prisoners parched by hunger and thirst strike. 1913.

Suffragette arson. April 15, 1913. Levetleigh the seaside house of
Arthur du Cros, M.P. for St Leonards, is gutted by fire.

Mrs Pankhurst sails from France to the United States. October 11, 1913.

Mrs Pankhurst is detained at Ellis Island as an undesirable alien. October 18, 1913.

'Arrested at the gates of the Palace. Tell the King!' May 21, 1914.

Women battle with police at the gates of Constitution Hill. May 21, 1914.

best of it. They had entered their protest constitutionally and respectfully and yet they had been refused a hearing. There was head-shaking last night amongst the Liberals and there will be more today.

On January 17 the Cabinet Council was to meet at 10 Downing Street to draw up the outline of the future Parliamentary programme. The Suffragettes saw this as an opportunity to make an impression on the Government, and a few minutes before the council meeting was due to start, a taxi drew up in Downing Street and a small group of women stepped out. Another group followed and the police and news reporters watched closely as the women paced up and down in front of the Prime Minister's house obviously waiting for someone. Asquith had still not yet arrived.

Soon a two-horse brougham, followed by two taxis, turned into Downing Street and pulled up a few yards away from Number Ten on the opposite side of the road. As police approached the carriage door from the pavement, out stepped Mrs Drummond on the road side together with three supporters, one of them Mary MacArthur, a pioneer in the Women's Trade Union Movement. Several more women emerged from the taxis.

Hardly had they alighted when Asquith drew up in his carriage. As he stepped down, the Suffragettes made a combined rush for the door of Number Ten, but the police were too quick for them. A clear space was made for the Chancellor to pass through and the police managed to hold the women back until he was safely inside the house.

Now they had to handle another disturbance. Two of the Suffragettes, Edith New and Nurse Olivia Smith, had come wearing belts of heavy steel chain. Each woman held a padlock, but the keys had been given to an old gentleman—a bookseller—in the crowd. While the police were engaged at the entrance of Number Ten, the two women had run to the iron railings, and slipping another chain through the waist chain and round the bars, each had fastened herself with her padlock. 'Votes for women! Votes for women!' they cried out: 'We want votes for women in the King's Speech.' 'Votes for women!' chorused the other Suffragettes in the street.

As the police went hurriedly from the entrance of Number Ten to deal with the chained women and their supporters, Mrs Drummond seized her chance. Two years before she had discovered the secret of the brass knob in the centre of the door. Now she ran up the steps, pulled at the knob, and the door opened. Followed by Mary MacArthur, Mrs Drummond rushed into the hall and ran on until she reached the swing doors opening into the council chamber passage. Here both women were caught by a police inspector, and within seconds, more policemen and house officials had come running to his assistance.

Meanwhile, the women outside were ordered to leave the street, but the chained Suffragettes refused to undo their padlocks and eventually the police had to break the chains with their hands. Even then, the women would not go away and at last Superintendent Wells gave orders to his men to arrest all those who continued to resist. The four principal offenders were taken to the police station and charged with disorderly conduct. All were later sentenced to three weeks in Holloway; this time in the second division.

In *Votes for Women* of March 1908, Mrs Pethick Lawrence comments on the episode and in answer to the remark, 'How silly of women to chain themselves to the railings of Downing Street,' she replies: 'Doing something silly is the women's alternative for doing something cruel. The effect is the same. We use no violence because we can win freedom for women without it; because we have discovered an alternative.'

It seemed very unlikely that the suffrage question would be included in the business of the new Parliamentary session, but now, more than ever before, the suffrage societies felt a sense of urgency. Four members of the Women's Freedom League actually attempted to waylay the royal coach and present a petition to the King as he was on his way to open Parliament on January 29.

There was no mention of votes for women in the King's Speech, but shortly after the session opened, a place was given for the reading of a Women's Suffrage Bill put forward by H. Y. Stanger, the Liberal M.P. for Kensington. A debate on the Bill was arranged for February 28 and the three most active suffrage societies felt that they must put all possible pressure on the Government before that date.

On January 30, members of the Women's Freedom League tried to call, without appointment, on six prominent Cabinet Ministers. They were not welcome and the 'naughty' Suffragettes, as the *Daily Mirror* called them, were arrested. On the same day, a deputation of 'the good ones', from the National Union, was received by Asquith. He had nothing positive to say on the suffrage question, however, and the deputation left the interview convinced that his attitude would only incite the Suffragettes to further militancy. Next morning the Women's Freedom League decorated the outside of Asquith's house with posters and banners and held a meeting on his doorstep.

The W.S.P.U. had already planned another Women's Parliament; the Caxton Hall had been taken for a three-day session and from this base the women intended to make a series of active attempts to present a petition at Westminster. The Parliament met on February 11, and immediately the first strategy was put into operation. Harry Pankhurst had in fact devised the scheme.

Marie Brackenbury and her sister Georgina were among the twenty women to be hidden in one of two pantechnicons:

> On passing the House of Commons, it was arranged that they should open like the Trojan Horse and let us all fly to the door. Silently, we slipped one at a time into a yard in Theobald's Road. There we found our van and disappeared into it. The doors were shut and the twenty sat quietly in this dark hole. Presently we were aware of a great clattering of horses and a sense of jolting and rumbling which lasted for what seemed to us an age.
>
> Suddenly the van stopped, our hearts beat fast, the doors swung open, we saw the House of Commons before us and out we all flew. We found, standing at the great door, a large body of Westminster police. They told us to go. We, clutching our petitions, stood our ground silently but firmly. Members of Parliament approached. The police made way for them; we made rushes, hoping to pass in behind the Members. The police in the execution of their duty took us by the neck and threw us into the road. We picked ourselves up, and as smilingly as we could, came back to the doors only to be flung down again . . .
>
> We were driven to prison in that terrible vehicle, 'black Maria', each one locked into what seemed like an upright coffin with a small hole for one's face to look through.
>
> Two days after our disappearance into Holloway Gaol the following lines appeared in the *Daily Mail* written by one of the prisoners who had managed to smuggle in a pencil, in spite of the stripping and searching ordeal which we all went through:

> Sing a song of Christabel's clever little plan
> Four and twenty Suffragettes packed in a van
> When the van was opened they to the Commons ran
> Wasn't that a dainty dish for Campbell-Bannerman?
> Asquith was in the treasury, counting out the money
> Lloyd George among the Liberal women speaking
>   words of honey
> And then there came a bright idea to all those
>   little men
> 'Let's give the women votes,' they cried, 'and all
>   be friends again.'

While the pantechnicon group was being turned away from the entrance to the House of Commons, Mrs Pethick Lawrence with the support of Annie and Christabel, was organising a more ordinary deputation from the Caxton Hall. Annie urged the audience not to leave all the fighting to the working women on this occasion. 'We want rich women and middle-class women to go out and help.' Of the dozens of volunteers who eventually came forward many wore sables and furs and the Press reported that they presented all the evidence of social standing.

'Suffragette Smart Set to the Fore' headed a description of the ensuing battle. As the women tried bravely to reach the House of Commons, forcing their way through the crowd and the police barriers, their leaders urged them on from the safety of wheeled vehicles. The *Daily Mirror* reported:

Miss Annie Kenney, a striking figure in electric blue and without a hat, surveyed the troops from a hansom cab. Miss Christabel Pankhurst sought to direct operations from another. Her cab was nearly overturned at one point of the proceedings when their passage was barred. Mrs Baldock drove round with a megaphone and shouted 'Votes for women' as far up the stairs of St Stephen's entrance as the megaphone could send the words. Other women with megaphones drove past in cabs shouting their battle cry.

These are new W.S.P.U. tactics. Among the methods which the Suffrage Movement has so far introduced into political warfare are: Bell ringing—door knocking—police court protests—voluntary imprisonment—chain and padlock tableaux—systematic minister baiting—the pantechnicon—megaphone and taxi appeal.

Some fifty Suffragettes were arrested as a result of the day's attempts. After all the excitement they now waited quietly at Cannon Row Police Station looking pale and agitated. Many were married women with families and commitments and they were unable to leave the station until late that night after they had all been bailed out by Pethick Lawrence.

When they appeared for trial at the Westminster Police Court the following morning, Mr Muskett prosecuting for the Crown threatened that if disturbances continued, the authorities would reintroduce the Tumultuous Petitions Act—a statute dating from the time of Charles II. The Act prohibited processions of more than thirteen people to the House of Commons and the prescribed penalty was either a fine of one hundred pounds or three months' imprisonment. The latter would necessitate a trial by jury and although the Home Secretary was anxious to mete out heavy punishment, he did not favour the idea of giving the public a say in the prosecution of the Suffragettes. Government policy still assumed that harsh treatment would be a deterrent, and on this occasion the women were sentenced to six weeks in the second division.

The Women's Parliament assembled for a second day of business after the trials had taken place. No active demonstration was planned and the meeting was one of indignation and protest. Mary Blathwayt, a Bath supporter, writes in her diary: 'Annie Kenney said that she was ready to go to prison for three months. For a few minutes after this, Mrs Pethick Lawrence who is generally all smiles, nearly broke down. She had to lean forward and cover her eyes with her handkerchief.'

A great wave of enthusiasm and excitement came over the Parliament on the third day of the session. Mrs Pankhurst had returned that morning from South Leeds where she had just completed an astonishingly successful by-election campaign. She appeared on the Caxton Hall platform, elated: 'I have come back to London, feeling as I have never felt before that we are near the end of the struggle.' After telling of her marvellous reception in Yorkshire, Mrs Pankhurst then proposed to form a deputation in accordance with the Charles II Act and herself carry a resolution to the House of Commons. Twelve chosen women including Annie came forward to accompany her and as they left the hall, the audience crowded out of their seats to watch them go.

Mrs Pankhurst was still very lame from her Newton Abbot experience and walked with difficulty. Seeing this, Mrs Drummond with characteristic blunt kindness, called to a man with a dog-cart and asked him if he would drive Mrs Pankhurst to the House of Commons. He agreed and Mrs Pankhurst mounted the cart, but as soon as they reached Victoria Street the police ordered her to get down.

Of course I obeyed and walked, or rather limped along with my companions. They would have supported me, but the police insisted that we should walk single-file. Presently I grew so faint from the pain of the ankle that I called to two of the women, who took hold of my arms and helped me on my way. This was our one act of disobedience to police orders. We moved with difficulty for the crowd was of incredible size.

When the small procession arrived at Parliament Square the way was completely barred. Suddenly two policemen seized Mrs Pankhurst by the wrists, told her that she was under arrest and led her away. Still holding a rolled petition in one hand, and a small bunch of lilies of the valley in the other, she reached Cannon Row Police Station some minutes later, supported by officials and exhausted.

The Women's Parliament ended with a dramatic evening session. Mrs Pethick Lawrence presided, a great show of support was given in the form of contributions to the funds and Mrs Despard appeared on the platform to offer her sympathy as leader of the Freedom League. There were comments on the fact that Parliament had adjourned early that afternoon. 'At any rate the Members are safe for one night more,' said Mrs Lawrence jokingly, 'and we have learned this. "Never put off till the evening what you can possibly do in the afternoon." '

Suddenly Mrs Pankhurst entered. She had just been released on bail with the other members of her deputation. Cries of 'Bravo', the singing of 'Rule, Britannia', and wild applause greeted her appearance.

Next morning the Westminster Police Court was so crowded that many of the prisoners' relatives and personal friends could not get in for the trial. Even Harry Pankhurst had to wait outside in the hall while friendly W.S.P.U. members plied him with buns and chocolate. It was expected that Mrs Pankhurst would be prosecuted under the Charles II Act, but finally the threatened measure was not taken, and Mrs Pankhurst and her companions received the same sentence as the women of the previous deputations.

Beatrice Harraden the writer describes the *Alice in Wonderland* court proceedings:

No statements except those of the constables were deemed of any importance, and writ in large invisible but flaming letters on the magistrate's forehead were: 'Six weeks in the second division by order of the Government.' Well—Mrs Pankhurst will not mind whether she is legally or illegally imprisoned. She and her brave followers are in Holloway for a principle. But it would be cowardly for us who believe in the same principle not to rally round her and ask the simple question, 'Why is Mrs Pankhurst in prison?'

Mrs Pankhurst describes how when they arrived, they groped their way through dim corridors into the reception ward where they were lined up against the wall for a superficial examination. Prison was degrading. 'Only when a prisoner is coming out do the officials begin to speak humanly,' said Mrs Pankhurst. 'The prison officials have a special voice—a voice of iron. You get a special voice too and you become cowed and humbled.'

A week of self denial had been arranged to start on February 15, as soon as the Women's Parliament ended. 'The time has come,' Mrs Pethick Lawrence said, 'to pour as much money as women can get together into

this movement; we must neither stint nor spare in a crisis like this.'
Immediately generous sums of money were sent in by wealthy supporters, but Mrs Lawrence stressed that everyone, however pressed by
home cares and business, could help.

Special collecting cards were sent to all members to hang on the wall
at home so that family and visitors could drop pennies in. Numerous
drawing-room meetings, tea-parties, concerts and work parties were
held to raise funds. Some families gave up sugar and sweets; others
adopted a 'prison diet', and gave all the money saved to the W.S.P.U.
It was even suggested that a member might invite herself out to every
meal during self-denial week, taking her collecting card with her, and
then give the proceeds of a week's housekeeping and a week's begging to
the fund.

At a meeting in the Portman Rooms, members offered jewellery for
sale. Prominent authors gave autographed copies of their books and John
Galsworthy wrote on the opening page of his donation, *The Island of the
Pharisees*: 'The institutions of this country, like the institutions of all
other countries, are but half truths.'

The self-denial week was an unqualified success, and Mrs Pethick
Lawrence decided to keep the campaign going for a further month until
the first W.S.P.U. mass meeting in the Albert Hall. Meanwhile she
wrote endless personal letters to secure promises of money and the total
collection finally reached the sum of seven thousand pounds.

On March 19 the Albert Hall was packed for the great meeting. No
one sat in the chair of state on the platform, but dramatically placed on
the seat was a large placard reading, 'Mrs Pankhurst's Chair'. Everyone
believed that she was still in prison, and when, at the last possible
moment, Christabel announced that the Government had released her
mother that afternoon, the audience was astounded. Some rose to their
feet, some waved handkerchiefs, everyone clapped and cheered, and at
the height of the applause Mrs Pankhurst walked slowly up the steps
leading to the platform.

Offers of money were made impulsively. Hundreds of promise cards
were sent up to the platform as the excitement rose, and while the
amounts were read out, a great scoring board marked the rapidly
increasing funds.

Triumphant, twelve brakeloads of Suffragettes drove through Peckham
on the following day—nomination day for the forthcoming by-election.
Inspired by recent successes, the Suffragettes ran this election campaign
with fanatical enthusiasm.

Other political groups with a grievance to air decided to join the contest and during the campaign every principal square and open space in Peckham was occupied by speakers. At the poll the Liberal candidate suffered a major defeat, and public opinion held that the result was largely due to Suffragette propaganda. Churchill angrily described Peckham as a 'capricious little London slum'.

Churchill was standing for re-election in his own constituency of North-West Manchester. Thirteen parties were campaigning in the election on various political issues. One of the most important was the Licensing Bill which suggested prohibiting the employment of women as barmaids.

The *Daily Mirror* reported that there were so many associations of politically minded ladies at work that it was necessary to distinguish them by short titles. The 'Anti Barmaids' believed that the Licensing Bill should go through and they supported Churchill's re-election. The 'Barmaids', on the other hand, were advocates of employment for women—supporters of the Unemployed Movement and members of the Women's Freedom League. The National Union of Women's Suffrage Societies had also decided to take part in this particular election and they were nicknamed the 'Nusses', while W.S.P.U. members became 'Wasps' or 'Spankers'. There were other strong forces on both sides, including, for Churchill, his mother, Mrs Cornwallis West.

Detailed newspaper accounts reported the daily events:

Miss Pankhurst is suffering slightly from hoarseness but never misses a meeting. Miss Millar, the titled Suffragette incognito, has spent most of her day chalking announcements of 'Wasp' meetings on the pavement. Miss Millar's chief occupations are assisting in the control of canvassers at one of the committee rooms, ringing the big bell that summons audiences at open air-meetings, selling Suffragette picture postcards and contradicting absurd rumours about the exalted rank of her father.

'As you know,' she said, 'he does not approve of women taking an active part in politics, but he has allowed me to come here and he let me go to help in the Peckham election though neither he nor my mother would let me join in any of the raids on the House of Commons. He gives me my dress allowance and I am here in the care of Mrs Drummond. I have two brothers and five sisters and there is really nothing for me to do at home.'

The most spectacular piece of propaganda was the Manchester to Sheffield pleasure coach—the Atlanta—decked out with yellow ribbons and driven by Eva Gore-Booth and her elder sister, Countess Markieviez, on behalf of the 'Barmaids'. The coachman in a white beaver hat sat behind them blowing the yard-long coach-horn, as the passengers showered literature from the roof at every corner.

Whenever they stopped, the Countess and her sister announced to the crowd that they were not themselves barmaids, but would rather, far rather, be barmaids than 'sew, sew, sew, twelve hours a day for five shillings a week.' They said that ninety-seven thousand licensed premises in the country each employed one or more barmaids. The Conservative candidate, Joynson Hicks, must be returned or at least one hundred thousand barmaids might be turned out 'to starve or sew, sew, sew, an industry for which they were most of them quite unfitted.'

There was heavy snow on polling day, April 25, but that did not hinder the polling, and when the votes were counted it was announced that Joynson Hicks had won the election. Churchill was extremely pale as he seconded Hicks's vote of thanks to the returning officer, and his lips trembled as he concluded:

> I think there is something in the election on which we should dwell, I mean the general feeling of good will and good humour and restraint that has characterised all parties and all classes in what has been one of the fiercest and one of the most strenuously contested elections which our country has known.

Several weeks later, in early May, Churchill stood for re-election at Dundee where he was almost certain of a Liberal majority. Although the W.S.P.U. adhered to their usual policy of addressing meetings, the Women's Freedom League, inspired by the North-West Manchester success, adopted new tactics. Miss Molony, one of their members, followed Churchill to each of his meetings and rang a muffin bell continuously while he was speaking. Finally, in the middle of an address to a group of factory men, he gave up struggling against the noise. 'If she thinks it is a reasonable argument, she may use it. I don't care and I bid you good afternoon.'

The unfortunate bell-ringing alienated the sympathy of a number of people who had started to believe in militancy and members of the Women's Liberal Federation immediately withdrew all support for the Suffragettes. Churchill won the election, and he commented later: 'Mistakes by my opponents undoubtedly assisted the Liberal cause; the ridiculous antics of the professional suffragists and their frenzied behaviour had the effect of rallying an enormous mass of Liberal women, and to their work a fair share of the results of the election must be attributed.'

Even Bernard Shaw wrote to the Suffragettes:

You've got to win over the average male elector. I am an average male elector. Here I am and you've got to reckon with me. I have always been in favour of votes for women. I still am. But if your present methods are to continue, if the introduction of women into politics is going to mean the argument of the muffin bell, interference with the right of public meeting, saturating politics generally with still further doses of unreasonableness—then I should vote against any candidate Liberal or Conservative who put votes for women in his election address.

This was a critical moment to have lost public support, for the Government was in a weak position owing to the recent illness and death of Sir Henry Campbell-Bannerman. Asquith had been appointed the new Prime Minister of a rather ineffectual Government in its third year of office.

On May 20, replying to Members on the question of women's suffrage, Asquith refused to consider the next stage of Stanger's Women's Enfranchisement Bill which had duly passed its second reading on February 28 with a majority of one hundred and seventy-nine votes. Asquith pledged not to oppose any amendment on behalf of women that might be made to a general Electoral Reform Bill, but he said that no change of this kind could be carried into effect unless it had behind it the support of the women of the country.

Chapter Three: Masses of Women 1908

THE GREAT HYDE PARK MEETING—A THEATRICAL DEPUTATION
—THE WEST OF ENGLAND CAMPAIGN—THE SUFFRAGETTES
'RUSH' THE HOUSE OF COMMONS.

'Women's Sunday' in Hyde Park was to be the greatest franchise demonstration ever known. Pethick Lawrence had devised the scheme to prove that the women's movement held overwhelming public support. No cost was spared and detailed plans were made for accommodating the vast crowds expected at the meeting. To prevent a recurrence of the 1886 franchise rioting when the park railings were torn down, Pethick Lawrence arranged with the authorities to have some of the railings temporarily removed.

Four months before the demonstration was to take place, the staff at Clement's Inn began work on a publicity campaign. Mrs Tuke, known as Pansy, was an hon. secretary on the W.S.P.U. committee and her social assets were invaluable in the normal running of the office. Now she was caught up in the general upheaval and she wrote to Isabel Seymour somewhat distractedly: 'You would hardly know the place if you came into it now, a regular hive of busy people jostling and pushing. Two more large rooms have been taken on the ground floor . . .' The Pethick Lawrences engaged extra help and five thousand pounds was set aside for advertising alone.

There were to be eighty women speakers and twenty platforms in the park. Early in the campaign a 'Record Poster' appeared on hoardings throughout the country with life-size portraits of the twenty women chairmen, and handbills were circulated giving details of the seven processions that were to converge on the park from various parts of London. Railway excursions were arranged to bring parties from the provinces, and a quarter of a million mock train tickets were printed to encourage people to make use of the special transport. In London W.S.P.U. canvassers went to factories, shops, hospitals and restaurants, calling on working women to join them. 'Bring your friends and family to Hyde Park, and you must wear the colours.'

Purple, white and green, symbolising justice, purity and hope, had been chosen by Mrs Lawrence to represent the movement. Articles in the colours were soon on sale, and picture hats and baby bonnets could be bought with trimmings stamped *Votes for Women*. The Women's Press stocked striped shantung motor scarves printed with the Suffragette motto, and tricolour ribbon was so popular that it sold out before new supplies could be made. Street vendors carried Suffragette rubber dolls in their trays and offered 'heverlasting sooveeneers of the grite de-mon-steration!'

An enterprising firm presented Mrs Drummond with accessories of military uniform especially designed for her as field marshal of the manoeuvre. She was to wear a peaked cap in the colours, an epaulette and a sash lettered *General*. This well-earned title was to remain with her throughout the movement and soon superseded her nicknames of 'Bluebell' and 'the Precocious Piglet'.

The advertising campaign culminated in a 'crusade fortnight' at the beginning of June. At Mrs Lawrence's suggestion, bands of cyclists went out every evening on illuminated and decorated bicycles to distribute handbills and programmes in the suburbs. In variety theatres, the cinematograph advertisements invited people to the demonstration and featured short scenes from the Suffragette campaign, while every morning the women would be up early to chalk pavements and to distribute the mock tickets at main-line railway stations.

Three days before the demonstration, Mrs Drummond hired a steam launch on the Thames. She drew up to the Terrace of the House of Commons and while a brass band played, she unfurled a banner reading: 'Women's Sunday—June 21—CABINET MINISTERS SPECIALLY INVITED.' M.P.s, officials and amused servants came flocking out to the Terrace to hear Mrs Drummond address them through a megaphone but she was unable to finish her speech, for very soon the river police appeared and her launch was chased back to land.

Mrs Drummond was in complete charge of marshalling the processions. Thousands of women from all over the country were expected to arrive in London and a detailed schedule had been drawn up for their reception at the main-line stations. Stewards were on the platform to place the women in ranks as soon as they alighted from the trains, and once the processions were formed, each group of ten was directly superintended by a leader and a sub-leader.

June 21 was a brilliant summer day, and hundreds of Londoners came out early in the afternoon to watch the long processions making their way to the park with their brass bands and banners. Most of the women were dressed in white with trimmings of ribbon or flower sprays of violet and gardenia. Each marshal could be distinguished by her silken and gilded regalia stamped *Votes for Women*, while the less important officials wore a lettered canvas regalia of purple, white and green. Groups of women from the provinces proudly carried the standards they had embroidered for the occasion and the largest banners, inscribed with long mottoes, were carried by men wearing huge rosettes. At every stage of the procession the women had the friendly co-operation of the police. Two thousand extra men had been recruited for the day, and their presence deterred any rowdy element from the processions.

Twenty waggons serving as platforms were spread out in a great circle over the park, and a pantechnicon stood in the middle of them as an information centre. From its roof, the 'Conning Tower', Pethick Lawrence, reporters, and a changing group of V.I.P.s had an aerial view of the complete operation. Below them stretched a widening sea of summer hats, sombre bowlers, straw boaters, flimsy dresses, dark suits and light suits. As the crowd thickened, Pethick Lawrence shouted instructions down to the police.

Already excited groups were gathering at the platforms and a gang of young men pushed round Number Eight where Christabel was to speak. When she arrived in academic dress, escorted by police, there was a general rush in the direction of her waggon. 'We want Chrissie! We want Chrissie!' yelled the youths and they began to rock the platform. 'All togevva nah!' they shouted and roared out a popular song:

> Put me upon an island where the girls are few,
> Put me amongst the most ferocious lions in the Zoo,
> You can put me upon a treadmill and I'll never never fret,
> But for pity's sake don't put me with a Suffering-gette.

Christabel impulsively decided to start her meeting before the arranged signal and as she spoke, her characteristic gesture—her outstretched arm—brought more people flocking to her platform. She walked round, addressing the crowd on all sides, and soon she threw off her cap and gown and stood simply in a plain holland dress.

For some time she managed to hold the audience with her quick repartee, but the bursts of pushing and fighting became increasingly violent. Children had to be lifted on to the platform for safety, and the mounted police rode through the crowd to loosen the press of people. No one could now hear what Christabel was saying but she continued speaking undeterred.

On the other platforms, the younger Suffragette speakers met little opposition, but rowdies singled out Mrs Pankhurst and Mrs Martel who had so recently been mobbed at Newton Abbot. Mrs Martel's waggon was almost overturned and two sailors, one on the other's shoulders, made constant interruptions at Mrs Pankhurst's platform. When she mentioned married women, one of them bellowed, 'Wives? Why, I've got four—all in different ports!' Then a bell rang and two men in the middle of the crowd started a wrestling match. People were pushed aside and squeezed together as the fighters made a space for themselves.

One of the features of the demonstration was to be a 'Great Shout', called from every platform simultaneously at five o'clock. From the corners of the Conning Tower, four buglers announced the cry, and women with megaphones led the 'Shout'. 'VOTES FOR WOMEN—VOTES FOR WOMEN—VOTES FOR WOMEN—ONE—TWO—THREE . . .' A confused roar came in response from the platforms near the Conning Tower, but further out the 'Great Shout' was drowned in all the other excitement. At Christabel's platform the crowd cheered wildly, and as she drove off with a strong police escort, her enthusiastic audience chased after the van.

Supporters still remained in the park for hours afterwards. A country member wrote: 'It was curious to emerge suddenly from an awful squeeze and a shouting mass of people to come immediately upon a little ring of fathers and mothers and children sitting quietly in the grass.'

The Press was full of glowing accounts next morning. It was estimated that half a million people had come to the park, and these included a number of foreign sympathisers, and such well-known personalities as Thomas Hardy, H. G. Wells, Israel Zangwill, Lillah McCarthy and Bernard Shaw. Shaw's wife marched in the procession with Mrs Pankhurst and he was a very prominent spectator. 'I told my wife,' he said, 'that I'd go in the procession on one condition only—that I should sit in a Bath chair and that she should push it all the way! She didn't accept the offer!' However, Shaw raised his hat to his wife as she passed, and he remarked as he watched the rest of the demonstration: 'Only one baby in the procession and that carried by a man; only one dog in the procession and that carried by a woman!'

After the great display of support at Hyde Park, a letter was sent to Asquith asking him to state the Government's future intentions. The Prime Minister replied that he had nothing further to add to his statement of May 20.

Now Mrs Pankhurst invited the general public to join a militant demonstration. She announced her intention of leading a protest deputation to Parliament and she asked people to assemble in Parliament Square on June 30 in support of the Suffragettes. Although the Commissioner of Police had warned the public against such action, the Suffragettes with their colours and regalia now provided an irresistable spectacle and a vast crowd gathered.

Once again the women assembled in the Caxton Hall and a 'constitutional' deputation was organised. Dressed gaily for the occasion, a group of twelve led by Mrs Pankhurst started out for the House of Commons. Their police escort cleared a way through the cheering crowds and some onlookers tried to run alongside the procession. Others stood up in buses to watch the women's progress. As the Suffragettes marched through the Abbey Close, a group of clergy was held back to make way for them. 'Those women should be whipped,' remarked one of the crowd. At the Strangers' Entrance a barrier of police was drawn up and Inspector Scantlebury stood waiting on the steps. He told Mrs Pankhurst that the Prime Minister refused to see her and he returned the letter that she had sent to Asquith asking him to receive the deputation. Without demonstration the women went back to the Caxton Hall. Mrs Pankhurst then announced an open challenge to the assembly to go to Parliament Square and 'quietly but persistently' protest.

Towards late afternoon small groups of Suffragettes in evening dress began to draw up outside the House of Commons in taxis and hansoms. Others came by bus, and with megaphones, and from the vantage point of the railings of Palace Yard, they asked the help of the people who pressed round. 'But the Parliament Square crowd was skylarking in the street with no more interest than its own amusement,' said a reporter.

Together with other M.P.s, Herbert Gladstone had come out into Palace Yard to enjoy the summer evening and to watch the Suffragette assault. As the women tried to slip through the police cordons, the surrounding crowd encouraged them. They jostled and cheered and became dangerously out of hand whenever the police tried to arrest a Suffragette. Parliament Square was not clear until nightfall and by then nearly thirty arrests had been made.

Later that evening two more women were arrested for breaking the windows of 10 Downing Street. Mary Leigh and Edith New, having done this on their own initiative, were prepared for disapproval from headquarters, but on the contrary, Mrs Pankhurst immediately went to see them at the police station and she assured them that 'the smashing of windows is a time-honoured method of showing displeasure in a political situation.' The Press took a different attitude, and the stone throwing was regarded as an unfortunate incident, while the other events of the day were lightheartedly dismissed.

The Suffragettes had learned that they could achieve popularity through any event which called for a colourful display. When the first prisoners of the June 30 deputation were released, they were met at the gates of Holloway with banners, bands and bouquets. Edith New and Mary Leigh came out of prison on August 22 and the six horses which had drawn their carriage to Holloway were dramatically replaced for the return journey by six Suffragettes in costume. The team had somewhat over-estimated their strength, and only with the help of willing supporters who pushed from behind and augmented their force in front did they eventually arrive in the West End. At the next release a team of fifty uniformed women drew the four prisoners. 'Makes you feel like a bus 'orse, don't it?' remarked the crowd, but the Suffragettes could pull in comparative comfort on this occasion, and each had a special handkerchief in the colours that she was able to wave to supporters along the route.

Mary Phillips, a Scottish Suffragette, was released one day later than all the other prisoners. Scottish thistles and purple heather filled the waggonette that was to carry her to a welcome breakfast, and as she came out, four pipers in full Highland costume struck up 'Macpherson's Farewell to Prison'. Mrs Pethick Lawrence adorned her with a Forbes plaidie and a Glengarry while she was greeted by her parents and a team of Suffragettes in tartan. Mrs Drummond performed the Highland Fling at the gates of the prison yard, and she announced later that they would 'get the Scottish Thistle behind Asquith' when it came to the next big Suffragette demonstration at the re-opening of Parliament.

For most of the W.S.P.U. speakers and organisers the summer of 1908 was one of their happiest times. They had won the friendship and respect of a large section of the public and they now threw themselves into a fearless campaign of converting the country. Following Annie's appointment in the spring, as organiser for the west of England, Suffragettes had become part of west country life. Annie's enthusiasm quickly won support at all levels of society. 'She had a homely way with interrupters,' said Clara Codd who worked with her. 'She never lost her temper or left off good-humouredly smiling. "Now you men!" she would say.'

Speakers were delighted to be sent to the west of England, and Millicent Browne, a school teacher, spent the August holidays working with the W.S.P.U. in Bristol where Annie had taken a furnished house. Adela Pankhurst, now as deeply involved in the cause as her sisters, was there with her dog. Annie Kenney and several others were also in residence, while Mary Blathwayt acted as caterer, cook and housekeeper. They were joined for short intervals by an elderly woman whom they called 'Mother Earth', for she made it her job to see that they took some rest and relaxation. She used to read to them as they lay on the Downs in the sunshine.

The Suffragettes hired a shop in Bristol which was run on the lines of the Woman's Press, and a photo of one of their prettiest speakers—

Gladice Keevil—was displayed in the window. Meetings did not always go smoothly. One day when they were speaking on the quay in Bristol, the women were nearly pushed into the Avon, and on another occasion jealous pierrots on the beach at Weston-super-Mare tried to pitch them into the mud. Men supporters were usually standing by ready to rescue them, but Annie discovered a perfect answer to hooliganism when she bribed two well-known wrestlers to appear at her meetings as a body-guard.

In their leisure time many of the Suffragettes wrote articles and poetry in praise of the movement and their leaders. Flippancy and sincerity were often curiously mixed. The following creed was in fact composed as an exercise in wit:

I believe in Emmeline Pankhurst—Founder of the Women's Social and Political Union.

And in Christabel Pankhurst, her eldest daughter, our Lady, who was inspired by the passion for Liberty—born to be a leader of women. Suffered under the Liberal Government, was arrested, tried and sentenced. She descended into prison; the seventh day she returned again to the world. She was entertained to breakfast, and sat on the right hand of her mother, our glorious Leader, from thence she went forth to judge both the Government and the Antis.

I believe in Votes for Women on the same terms as men, the policy of the Women's Social and Political Union, the equality of the sexes, Representation for Taxation, the necessity for militant tactics, and Freedom Everlasting.

Amen.

'Mrs Pankhurst was not amused,' the writer says, although there was certainly no blasphemous intention behind the creed, and the writer herself held strong religious beliefs. The Suffragettes were not strict church-goers but most of them had a religious faith, and many had become interested in Theosophy. 'Ours is a moral and spiritual movement based on fundamentally religious conceptions,' Mrs Lawrence had said when criticised for holding the Hyde Park demonstration on a Sunday.

The summer was peaceful, and a number of successful mass meetings were held in the provinces. The new session of Parliament was due to open on October 12, and the Suffragettes announced in early September that they would be holding a demonstration on October 13—the anniversary of the first militant protest.

Prior to the demonstration, a letter was sent to Asquith again asking him to consider the further stages of the Women's Enfranchisement Bill. Mrs Pankhurst told Inspector Wells when he called at Clement's Inn to investigate: 'Action of ours will depend on the reply we receive to that letter. If it is a satisfactory reply there will be nothing but great cheering. If the reply is unsatisfactory there will be a great demonstration and we shall try to get into the House of Commons.'

On Friday, October 9, Asquith replied to Mrs Pankhurst's letter that the Government did not intend to carry the women's Bill during the autumn. Accordingly, on Sunday, October 11, the Suffragettes held a mass meeting in Trafalgar Square and invited the public to join their demonstration on the following Tuesday. Mrs Pankhurst, Christabel and Mrs Drummond addressed the crowds from the plinth of Nelson's Column and thousands of handbills were distributed. The wording had been devised by Christabel:

VOTES FOR WOMEN—HELP THE
SUFFRAGETTES TO RUSH THE HOUSE
OF COMMONS ON TUESDAY EVENING
OCTOBER 13 AT 7.30.

Christabel came forward to speak:

I wish you all to be there on the evening of the thirteenth, and I hope that that will be the end of this movement . . . Years ago John Bright told the people that it was only by lining the streets from Charing Cross to Westminster that they could impress the Government. Well, we are only taking a leaf out of his book.

Mrs. Drummond told the public to come 'unarmed', and Mrs Pankhurst deliberately called for self-restraint in order to keep the support and co-operation of the public.

On the following morning each of the leaders received a summons to appear at Bow Street that afternoon. The charge: 'Inciting the public to do a wrongful and illegal act'. The leaders defied the order, and instead of going to the police station, they appeared on the platform for a crowded 'At Home' in the Queen's Hall. 'We are here,' said Mrs Pankhurst, 'and we shall not go to Bow Street until they come and take us.' It was an anxious and dramatic meeting. 'The warrant officers are outside,' announced Mrs Lawrence at one point, but tactful negotiations were made, and the summonses were adjourned until the next day.

On the morning of October 13 there was an atmosphere of suppressed excitement at Clement's Inn. It was like a camp prepared for battle. The women under arrest were not to be found. It was clear that they were there somewhere, but no one knew where. At half past eleven Superintendent Wells and Inspector Jarvis arrived at the office. The Secretary handed them a typewritten note:

Dear Mr Jarvis,
We shall not be at the office 4 Clement's Inn until six o'clock today, but at that hour we shall all three be entirely at your disposal.
(Signed) CHRISTABEL PANKHURST

The police searched all the offices but found no one. The Pankhursts were in fact in the roof garden of the Pethick Lawrences' flat above the W.S.P.U. headquarters, making final arrangements before going to prison.

Inspector Jarvis had always maintained friendly relations with the Suffragettes. He probably knew that the women were in the building, so he waited at W.S.P.U. headquarters with a few of his men, and all day a group of journalists hovered in the office corridors.

Outside, eager and curious crowds had gathered. The gates of the Inn leading to the Strand were temporarily closed and only people on business were admitted. Residents of Clement's Inn watched from their windows as a continuous stream of Suffragettes went in and out. Women from the country—volunteers for prison—arrived one by one to take their orders from Mrs Pethick Lawrence. Spread out in front of her was a huge map of London.

'Now I have a little job for you,' she told Clara Codd who had just arrived from Bath. 'How you will do this I leave to your own initiative and judgement. The police will not let you stand still a moment today. But you must find some means of entering the House of Commons by the Clock Tower door and make a demonstration on the floor of the House.' Mrs Pethick Lawrence described the region of the attack, and Clara was then dismissed to go and work on a plan of campaign.

Lady Constance Lytton had witnessed the dramatic scene at the Queen's Hall and now, against all family principles, she felt drawn to help the Suffragettes. Although she did not sufficiently agree with their policy to offer herself for the deputation, she came to Clement's Inn on the thirteenth prepared if she could to use her influence with the authorities. Her observations on that day made her a complete convert to militancy. She spent most of the afternoon at the House of Commons where she was received with due civility. Her mission was to approach Herbert Gladstone over the question of first-division treatment for Suffragette prisoners, but she was unable to see the Home Secretary personally and her messenger—Arthur Ponsonby, M.P.—finally had to report that Gladstone had angrily refused to make any concessions.

When Lady Constance left the House, late in the afternoon, the crowds in Westminster were dense. Six thousand workmen had assembled in Parliament Square that morning for a demonstration of the unemployed, and crowds had been milling about London ever since. All metropolitan police leave had been cancelled for two days, extra mounted men were brought in from the suburbs, and six thousand police had been put on duty.

The mounted and foot patrols kept people moving all the time, going between the crowds and breaking up any group that massed together. Although the demonstrators booed and hissed they put up no resistance as the police drove them away from Parliament Square. Towards evening, all approaches to the Houses of Parliament were cut off. The traffic was diverted—only mail vans were allowed to pass—and the area was surrounded by cordons of police shoulder to shoulder. M.P.s were shown through to the House. The place was like a besieged city. In the approaches to Westminster, behind the cordons, the crowds were now waiting to see the Suffragettes. They sang popular songs, cheered the mail vans as they passed and from time to time, impatient of standing still, they made dangerous rushes, swaying whole masses of people.

Just before six o'clock Mrs Drummond and her husband arrived at Clement's Inn and entered headquarters, closely followed by Inspector Jarvis. The little group went upstairs to the long outer office which was packed with reporters, photographers, supporters and staff. At six o'clock precisely Mrs Pankhurst and Christabel entered, followed by Sylvia and the Pethick Lawrences. When the leaders were assembled, flash photographs were taken and Jarvis read the arrest warrant. He stumbled over the small print and was evidently glad when it was done. Then, surrounded by members and sympathisers, the leaders made their way downstairs to the two cabs waiting to take them to Bow Street.

When the Women's Parliament opened in the Caxton Hall at seven-thirty, the audience was in a state of excitement. A gang of about a hundred youths had barged in just before the meeting was due to begin. They had seated themselves and seemed to have no intention of leaving, until gently persuaded to do so by Mrs Pethick Lawrence.

The crowd outside could be heard cheering as deputations of women went out to attempt the impossible task of passing the police cordons, and indignant witnesses returned breathless to the hall to describe the struggle and the arrests. Suddenly a woman ran on to the platform waving an evening paper. 'A woman has actually rushed the House of Commons!' she cried. Mrs Pethick Lawrence triumphantly announced the news: 'Now, friends, we have got a woman into the House of Commons—not only into the House of Commons—but into the Debating Chamber itself!'

The woman was Mrs Travers Symons, formerly a secretary to Keir Hardie. She was known at the House, and having gained entrance, she sent her card to Mr Idris, an acquaintance of her father's, and asked if he might show her the Lobbies. Guards watched with suspicion as Mr Idris accompanied Mrs Travers Symons in the direction of the Debating Chamber. When they reached the Inner Lobby, she asked if she might be allowed to look through the 'peephole'—the window beside the main door of the Chamber. For a moment she stood there, watching through the glass, then seeing the main doors unguarded she made a rush. Mr Idris was too startled to stop her, and she was already inside the Chamber and beyond the Bar of the House before the doorkeeper realised what had happened.

Parliament was debating the Children's Bill. 'Leave off discussing the Children's Bill and attend to women first!' called Mrs Travers Symons, with arms outstretched. She was seized, and police hastily carried her out of the Chamber and escorted her from the building.

M.P.s felt that Mr Idris had been made the victim of a gross abuse of privilege and because of the incident the peephole was temporarily closed. Mrs Travers Symons immediately wrote an apologetic letter which was shown by Mr Idris to the Speaker:

Dear Mr Idris,
My action this evening must have surprised you. It surprised me. I had no intention of calling you out. What I did was on the spur of the moment. It would not have occurred to me to call you out, had I not known of your enthusiasm for the women's cause. If I have caused you any annoyance I am sorry. I can only repeat that as far as you are concerned what I did was entirely unpremeditated.

Although her entrance was far less spectacular, Clara Codd also managed to get into the House. After hiding for most of the day in the Westminster Underground Station, she emerged at eight o'clock and miraculously walked straight through the police cordons guarding the entrance at Big Ben. She went into the building but lost her way, and wandering confusedly along a corridor, she was noticed by three house-maids who chivvied her off. As soon as she came outdoors again a policeman approached: 'What are you a doin' of, miss?' 'I wish to see Mr Asquith,' she replied primly. She vaguely remembered a law that no one could be driven away from a certain distance around the People's House. 'I have a right to be here,' she said in a dignified voice, 'and you have no right to drive me away.'

The policeman whistled to another constable and the two men seized Clara.

They gave my arms a peculiar twist which almost forced me to walk on my toes. In this undignified position I was marched to Cannon Row Police Station where I found a number of my compatriots already arrested. They put us all in the billiards-room and there we had to stay until the House rose and Mr Pethick Lawrence came to bail us out.

Mrs Pankhurst, Christabel and Mrs Drummond arrived at Bow Street Police Station after the Court had risen and so no order could be made for their bail. A night in the cells was the only alternative, and as no beds were provided—only wooden benches—Mrs Pankhurst was still anxious to be released so that she could plead properly next morning. Lady Constance Lytton was allowed to visit the cells: 'I saw close to the barred window and in a deep shadow, Mrs Pankhurst's fine face, looking very tired.' This was Lady Con's first meeting with the leader, and after a short discussion she set out to go and find the Bow Street magistrate. She at last ran her quarry to ground somewhere near Olympia. Curtis Bennett listened to her, but said that he could do nothing on behalf of the prisoners. 'As to taking them food and bedding, that is a matter for the police to decide,' he said.

Meanwhile, Mrs Pankhurst had sent telegrams to several M.P.s asking their assistance, and when Lady Constance finally returned to Bow Street with Mrs Pethick Lawrence, bringing blankets, they found that arrangements were already being made for the prisoners' comfort. James Murray, M.P. for East Aberdeen, had arranged with the Savoy Hotel to have dinner sent to the police station. The table was laid with silver and candlesticks and the meal was served by three waiters. Beds were also brought in from the hotel, but Mrs Pankhurst was unable to rest: 'All night I lay awake thinking of the scenes which were going on in the streets.'

At ten o'clock the following morning the leaders appeared in court on a charge of 'circulating a handbill likely to cause a breach of the peace'. After a preliminary hearing, a week's adjournment was granted and during the interval Christabel called on Lloyd George and Herbert Gladstone to appear as witnesses for the defence. Both ministers had been seen outside the House of Commons on the night of the thirteenth and Lloyd George had brought with him his six-year-old daughter, Megan, to watch the scene.

The leaders, on bail during the adjournment, appeared in public at two crowded meetings. Christabel spoke bitterly: 'Parliament is waxing old, if not decrepit, and it is about time it went in for a deathbed repentance ... Women are not allowed to grow in this country. In China, they cripple children's feet. Here they do their best to cripple their minds and souls.'

On October 21, the trial of the leaders re-opened with Lloyd George and Gladstone both present. The Pankhursts conducted their own defence and Max Beerbohm as a reporter was so impressed by Christabel that he wrote an ecstatic article on her for the *Daily Mail Saturday Review*:

> ... Her whole body is alive with her every meaning; and, if you can imagine a very graceful rhythmic dance done by a dancer who moves not her feet, you will have some idea of Miss Pankhurst's method ... I am told that she is great at the mass meetings in Hyde Park, but I doubt whether her effect can be so delightful there. A setting of trees and grass would strike no contrast to her freshness. But put the wood-nymph in the dock of the police court and her effect is quite wonderful ... No, that is a misleading image. The wood-nymph would be shy, uncomfortable, whereas Miss Pankhurst in her barred pen seemed as comfortable and self-possessed as Mr Curtis Bennett on the bench. As she stood there with her head inclined merrily to one side, trilling her questions to the Chancellor of the Exchequer, she was like nothing so much as a little singing bird born in captivity ... Mr Lloyd George did not seem at all as though he had been born in the witness box. His Celtic fire burned very low.

Lloyd George had received a handbill in Trafalgar Square and Christabel asked him what he had taken the bill to mean. 'I really should not like to place an interpretation on the document. I don't think it is quite my function.' 'This word *rush* seems to be at the bottom of it all,' Christabel went on. 'I find that in *Chambers' Dictionary* one of the meanings of the word is *an eager demand*. Now if you were asked to help the Suffragettes to make an eager demand to the House of Commons that they should give votes to women, would you feel we were calling on you to do an illegal act?' 'That is not for me to say.' '*Rush*, we are told in another dictionary means *in a hurry*. There is nothing unlawful in being in a hurry. Did you understand we asked you to go in a hurry to the

House of Commons?' 'I cannot express any opinion as to that,' replied Lloyd George, 'I can only give evidence as to what I saw.' When Christabel asked him whether he had thought that the Trafalgar Square crowd would respond to the handbill, he replied that he had expected nothing formidable, and he had thought it safe to bring his child out into the street on the night of the thirteenth. 'She was very amused,' he added.

Before the Home Secretary was called, Christabel asked leave for another witness to be heard. Already, on the first day of the hearing, Christabel had drawn attention to the fact that in a London drawing-room a magistrate of the Westminster Police Court had admitted that in sentencing Suffragettes his instructions came from the authorities. Now she called on Georgina Brackenbury, who had been sentenced to six weeks by that magistrate, and to whom afterwards he had made the admission. Christabel was allowed to ask one question: 'Did Mr Horace Smith tell you that in sentencing you to six weeks he was doing what he was told?' 'He did,' said Georgina Brackenbury before she could be stopped.

When Gladstone came into the witness box, Christabel tried to discover from him whether he was responsible for the police action and the court proceedings that were taken in the case of Suffragettes. The magistrate constantly interrupted and told the Home Secretary that he need not reply to any questions of State. When Mrs Pankhurst asked Gladstone why the Suffragettes were not treated as political prisoners, the magistrate again intervened.

The examination of the ministers continued all morning, but it only emerged that no unusual violence had taken place on the thirteenth as a result of the handbill. During the entire afternoon and until seven-thirty at night, when the case was adjourned, a succession of witnesses appeared, all supporting Christabel's point that the crowd had been orderly. Fifty more witnesses had still to give evidence at a further hearing.

When the trial re-opened on Saturday October 24, Curtis Bennett announced that the time of the Court was being wasted: 'I may at once state that a simple repetition of the same class of evidence given by the last twenty-four witnesses will not affect my judgement.' He ruled that he would hear only three more witnesses and that the prisoners must then speak in their own defence.

Christabel was put at a disadvantage as she had not expected that the trial would end so soon. She delivered her speech from typewritten notes and acted without her usual self-possession. At one point she burst into tears:

The Government want to keep us in the police court. They know perfectly well that if this case were heard before a jury of our countrymen we should be acquitted. This is a Star Chamber of the twentieth century and it is in order to huddle us into prison without a fair trial that these proceedings have been taken in their present form. I dare say it was not anticipated by the public that this case was ever to be defended. They are accustomed to see us disposed of and sent to Holloway Gaol very much as the animals are dealt with in the Chicago stockyards.

Later, Christabel regained her usual composure: 'Is it, as a matter of fact, an illegal thing to rush the House of Commons? The only woman who has done it has gone scot-free. Mrs Travers Symons rushed the House of Commons. Nobody seems to mind her having done it at all.'

Although Christabel had been caught unawares, her final speech was long and impressive. Each point was backed with apt political or historical precedents and she spoke with passion and fervour.

'When I rose to address the Court,' says Mrs Pankhurst, 'I began by assuming an appearance of calmness which I did not altogether feel.' Whatever their sympathies, everyone in the court was moved by the force of Mrs Pankhurst's personality. She spoke simply: 'We are not women who would come into this court as ordinary law-breakers and we feel that it is a great indignity that for political offences we should come into the ordinary police court.'

Mrs Pankhurst said that she had been brought up to realise that she had a duty towards her country. She told of her share in the public work of her husband, and then she spoke of the experience she had gained when she worked on the Board of Guardians and on the School Board and Education Committee. She had realised then the inadequacy of the laws affecting women—the marriage and divorce laws, the illegitimacy law which was sometimes the cause of infanticide:

Women have persuaded Parliament, they have tried for many years to do something to alter these laws, for they believe as I do, that in the interests of men quite as much as of women, it would be a good thing if laws were made equal between the sexes . . . We have tried to be womanly, we have tried to use feminine influence and we have seen that it is of no use.

My daughter referred to the way in which women are huddled into and out of these police courts without a fair trial. I was in Holloway Gaol and there are women there who have broken no law who are there because they have been able to make no adequate statement . . . we need some legitimate influence to bear upon our law-makers.

In spite of natural diffidence, and the inherited desire to escape publicity, Mrs Pankhurst said that they had been obliged to face misrepresentation and ridicule in order to get popular support for the movement:

> The ignorant mob at the street corner has been incited to offer us violence which we have faced unarmed and unprotected by the safeguards which Cabinet Ministers have. We know that we need the protection of the vote even more than men have needed it.
>
> Although the Government admitted that we are political offenders, we shall be treated as pickpockets and drunkards; we shall be searched. I want you, if you can, as a man, to realise what it means to women like us.
>
> On the night of the thirteenth, after we had been arrested, our followers showed great restraint. They were indignant, but our words have always been 'be patient—show our so-called superiors that the criterion of women being hysterical is not true.'
>
> We are here not because we are law-breakers; we are here in our efforts to become law-makers.

The burly policemen, the reporters and most of the spectators were in tears as she finished.

Mrs Drummond followed with a short speech and then the magistrate summed up the case.

Curtis Bennett praised the speeches but said that he was not concerned with the political side of the offence. The handbill had been published in spite of warnings. Thousands of police had been put on duty as a result. After the disturbance ten people were taken to hospital, seven policemen put on the sick list and thirty-seven people charged in court. 'Could it be said for one instant that a circular asking the public to rush the House of Commons was not likely to create a breach of the peace?'

The magistrate then sentenced Mrs Pankhurst and Mrs Drummond to three months' and Christabel to ten weeks' imprisonment on their refusing to be bound over.

The women were placed as common criminals in the second division, but as soon as they arrived at Holloway, Mrs Pankhurst refused to submit to the indignity of being searched and having to undress in front of the wardresses. It had been admitted that their offence was political, and Mrs Pankhurst demanded a political prisoner's right to speak with her friends.

The governor, on consideration, allowed the women to undress in private and he placed Mrs Pankhurst and Christabel in adjoining cells, but he would not relax the silence rule. Very soon all communication with Christabel was made temporarily impossible, for Mrs Pankhurst became ill and was moved from the ordinary cells to the hospital.

The Suffragettes took exercise at a different time from the other prisoners and when Mrs Pankhurst recovered she was allowed to join them:

> Single file, we walked at a distance of three or four feet from one another, back and forth under the stony eyes of the wardresses. The rough flags of the pavement hurt our feet shod in heavy shapeless prison boots. The autumn days were cold and cheerless and we shivered violently under our scanty cloaks.

The Suffragettes tramped in parade round two large circles—the small women on the inner ring and the others outside. Because of her height, Clara Codd was very conscious of the ill-fitting prison clothes:

> They were much of a size. The tall women had skirts nearly up to their knees while short Mrs Drummond, even with tucks taken, had to hold up her skirts. She appeared to have what looked like the spur of a cock sticking out from behind each leg. I determined when near her on the other circle to see what it was. The prison stockings were far too large and so the heel stuck out halfway up her leg!

Mrs Drummond was pregnant. On the first morning she found that she could not eat the food and she was removed to the hospital:

> I have never been in hospital in my life. The solitary confinement was enough to drive one out of one's senses. The days were long and dreary—how I longed for some work to break the dreadful monotony. We were allowed to have books from the prison library and I read *The Scottish Chiefs* and *Life and Labour* by Smiles. What I suffered from most was the stuffiness of my cell. The tiny window placed near the ceiling would not open, and the only ventilation came through an iron grating in the wall.

On the Sunday morning of November 1, Mrs Pankhurst and Mrs Drummond were to be taken out to the exercise yard but somehow Mrs Drummond was left behind:

I rang a bell; no one came. Presently I heard a great cheering going on outside. I dragged the bed to the window and climbed up. I saw women running in all directions. I heard no more, and later, when I went out into the corridor, all was quiet. I asked one of the wardresses what had happened but got no answer.

After a week of submitting to silence Mrs Pankhurst had found the situation intolerable and as the Suffragettes paraded monotonously round the yard, she signalled to Christabel to stand still. She then approached her daughter and the two linked arms and spoke. A wardress attempted to stop them while another hastily left the yard to fetch help. Soon she came running back with a small force of wardresses. They seized Mrs Pankhurst and as they took her away the Suffragette prisoners burst into cheers.

All were condemned to solitary confinement and in Mrs Pankhurst's case, as she now refused to submit to the silence rule, a wardress was posted on constant duty outside her cell and communal exercise and chapel were banned.

That evening Mrs Drummond felt ill: 'I must have fainted, for I was found by the wardress lying on the floor.' Two days later she was let out of prison and she returned straight to Clement's Inn to be welcomed by delighted friends. 'The news of my release surprised no one more than myself. What has become of the three long months I thought I was going to spend in the prison cell? I half expect even now to hear the wardress calling: "Come along, H.3." '

While the leaders were in prison, the official side of the union flourished under the expert guidance of the Pethick Lawrences and Sylvia. On October 29 the W.S.P.U. held their second Albert Hall mass meeting. 'Never has a great demonstration been better organised,' said the *Daily Telegraph*. 'All had their instructions and carried them out with ability and promptitude.' A W.S.P.U. member describes how a perfect storm of cheers greeted the Pethick Lawrences as they mounted the platform. She says: 'A thrill of emotion ran through the huge building when Mrs Pethick Lawrence asked the women to rise and give a silent tribute to those in prison.'

Pethick Lawrence took on Christabel's role of addressing the audience on militant policy. He condemned the Government for placing the leaders in the second division. It was obvious, he said, that they were political offenders and it was for that very reason that they were being imprisoned as common criminals to prevent them communicating with the movement outside.

During this period the W.S.P.U. took no militant action, but on October 28 two Women's Freedom League members, Muriel Matters and Helen Fox, chained themselves to the grille of the Ladies' Gallery in the House of Commons. The padlocks could not be undone, officials were unable to break the chains and finally the women were removed still attached to pieces of the wrought-iron grille which officials had wrenched out of the surrounding stonework.

The incident was widely publicised and a public controversy arose over the question of replacing the grille. Laurence Housman wrote in *Votes for Women*:

The one place where the grille of the harem has been obstinately retained is in Parliament itself. There in the people's house the grille stands, a close and fitting symbol of the spirit which still governs the making of our laws. For generations sensible-minded men have tried to get that portion removed, but on each occasion our legislators have gravely decided that to admit women as unobstructed onlookers would cause an emotional disturbance to their systems.

And now, only the other day a portion of that grille had to be removed because women were chained to it, yet in narrating that incident, the bulk of the party Press—alive only to the comedy of the moment, blind to the absurdity which had made it possible—described not the grille but the women as ridiculous! Surely no skeleton has ever tumbled from its cupboard to a more ignominious effect. For there was the barrier which had so long been set up for a protection actually providing the means by which the intruders were able to make their protest known to all the world.

And the joke is not over: having proved its utter ineffectiveness, the grille will go back into its place and there will stand, high behind the Speaker's Chair and behind the Press, a monument of masculine stupidity.

The grille was never in fact replaced; a Select Parliamentary Committee set up to consider the whole question of admission of strangers to the House suggested that in future women accompanied by men should be admitted to the open gallery previously reserved for men only. This suggestion was adopted at the end of the Parliamentary session two months later, and in the meantime the public galleries were closed.

When Mrs Drummond was released on November 3 she had refused to give any undertaking as to her future conduct and immediately she returned to Clement's Inn, a protest march on Holloway was organised:

75

Anyone who has been in 'The Castle' knows that it is a very nice place to be out of! The ground on which I was discharged was that of ill-health. Well, the remedy for that I have always found is hard work and plenty of it. With our leaders in prison we cannot afford to waste a single moment.

Within three days twelve prison dresses of green serge were made. These were identical with the Holloway winter uniform, stamped with the broad arrow in white, and each worn with a check apron, a small linen cap and a large number disc. Perhaps the idea of dressing up had been inspired by the threat of a magistrate who had recently discharged two Suffragettes on the understanding that they would promise not to distribute pamphlets in fantastic costume. In fact, the two women were only dressed in W.S.P.U. colours and they were wearing sandwich boards.

The women in prison garb—all genuine Suffragette ex-prisoners—drove through the West End on Saturday morning to advertise their demonstration, and in the evening at six o'clock the Holloway procession started out from Kingsway. Mrs Drummond rode in a wagonette with Sylvia, next came the Press cart carrying leaflets for distribution along the route, the 'prisoners' followed in a brake, and after them marched ranks of women four abreast. While brass bands played the Women's Marseillaise, 'John Peel', 'Men of Harlech' and 'John Brown's Body', the women joined in, lustily singing their own words to the tunes.

By the time Holloway was reached the procession was about half-a-mile in length and many thousands strong. Two black Marias that passed it on the way were greeted with ironical cheers and everywhere the traffic had to be temporarily diverted. An enormous crowd was gathered around Holloway and a cordon of mounted police had taken up a position in front of the main entrance.

The bands played and the marchers cheered continuously as the procession circled twice round the prison by way of near-by roads. When they passed the quarter of the prison that housed the hospital, a shadow fell across one of the windows and word went round that it was Mrs Pankhurst. 'Three cheers for Mrs Pankhurst!' called the excited crowd. 'Votes for women! Votes for women!' It was a huge gathering and, before they left Holloway, Mrs Drummond said: 'Let us raise our voices in indignation at the treatment of our friends inside these walls.' Then a goodnight cheer was given to the prisoners inside the building and the procession accompanied by the crowd returned to Clement's Inn.

A breakfast was held at the Inns of Court Hotel on the following Friday to welcome the first batch of released prisoners. Mrs Drummond spoke of the Holloway demonstration and said that it had reminded her of the Relief of Lucknow when the besieged asked one another: 'Dinna ye hear it? Dinna ye hear it?' Sounds of the demonstration had only been faintly heard by the prisoners just as they were preparing their plank beds for the night. Mabel Capper says she threw down her plank and got as near to the grating as she could to hear what was going on outside. Mrs Pethick Lawrence, in a typical speech, compared the march to Holloway with its colours, music, shouting and circling of the prison to the observance of a symbolic rite. The released prisoners gave disquieting news of Mrs Pankhurst. Since being in solitary confinement she had begun to suffer from serious depression. Aeta Lamb, who was in the cell next to Mrs Pankhurst in the prison hospital, said that latterly the leader's health had changed for the worse. 'We must do something so desperate and determined as to force the Government to change these conditions,' she said.

M.P.s who supported the suffrage cause asked daily questions in Parliament. Two further Saturday demonstrations crowded the streets round Holloway and the Home Secretary at last made some concessions which he had previously refused; Mrs Pankhurst was allowed to read newspapers and to communicate with Christabel for one hour each day. But the Suffragettes considered that these half-measures were unsatisfactory and they began to feel, as never before, a resentment at the injustice of Cabinet Ministers.

At the Leeds Assizes on November 19 Pethick Lawrence represented the first Suffragette to be tried by jury—Jennie Baines. She was a working woman from a Birmingham family of Salvation Army supporters. Besides helping to keep her husband and three children, Mrs Baines had followed a remarkable career in public work and as a speaker for the Temperance Movement. She joined the W.S.P.U. as a voluntary worker in 1905 after Christabel's first arrest.

On October 10, 1908 Mrs Baines was arrested and charged with inciting a crowd to storm the doors of the Leeds Coliseum while Asquith and Herbert Gladstone were inside holding a meeting. Pethick Lawrence maintained that through the glass doors of the hall, the speakers could have seen clearly what was going on outside, and in his capacity as counsel for the defence, he called on the two ministers to appear as witnesses in the case. The judge agreed to serve subpoenas on Asquith and Gladstone, but both ministers succeeded in getting these set aside and, contrary to all regular procedure, they did not appear in court.

At the trial it was ascertained that no harm had been done as a result of Mrs Baines's speech and she protested that she had no intention of causing a riot. Pethick Lawrence, in justification of her action, spoke at length on the reason for the Suffragette agitation, but the jury were advised that political consideration should not influence their verdict, and Mrs Baines was found guilty and sentenced to six weeks' imprisonment.

Now, when the prison treatment of Suffragettes was such an outstanding Parliamentary issue, Lloyd George offered to give an address on women's suffrage to an Albert Hall meeting of the Women's Liberal Federation. The Liberal women no longer had any sympathy with the militants, and Lloyd George obviously believed that with 'words of honey' he could regain their undivided devotion to the Liberal Party. He promised that he would deliver a 'special message' to the meeting, and this led many suffragists to believe that he intended to make a positive statement on votes for women.

The W.S.P.U. was sceptical, and Mrs Pethick Lawrence described the proposal as a 'political flirtation': 'A member of the Cabinet which is opposed to votes for women is to speak at a meeting for woman suffrage at the Albert Hall. He stands in a false position.' Nevertheless, a large number of W.S.P.U. members proposed to attend the rally and to hear and to disapprove of what the Chancellor had to say to his Liberal supporters. The Liberal organisers of the meeting anticipated that there would be conflict among the audience and they issued a manifesto— 'Official Orders of the Day'—pleading for good behaviour.

Evelyn Sharp, the writer and Suffragette speaker, was at the Albert Hall on December 5:

Everybody knows the look of things outside an ordinary suffrage meeting—the conversational groups of women waiting at the doors, the women stewards sporting their colours as they drive up and hail everybody. The happy hawker selling his toy plaster skeletons to the tune of 'All that's left of the mere man, one penny' . . . The police had turned out in force but they did not show that look of interested sympathy they generally reserve for suffrage meetings. Like many of us who waited almost in silence for the doors to open, they seemed apprehensive.

One felt the same electric atmosphere within the dimly lighted hall. The organist did his best to relieve the tension by playing all the merry, irresponsible tunes he could think of. I noticed that people were not talking quite naturally before the meeting began; they seemed suspicious of their neighbours and were yet nervously eager to meet them halfway if they showed any signs of making advances.

All the front seats nearest the platform were taken by a group of W.S.P.U. members. Before Lloyd George rose to speak, the Suffragettes removed their overcoats, revealing prison costume, and each proceeded to tie on a white cap. 'The ladies in convict dress sat and menaced Lloyd George with unwavering gaze and unbroken silence like any Banquo's ghost at a feast,' says Evelyn Sharp.

Lloyd George rose and began to state his reasons for believing in women's suffrage. 'We've known them for forty years,' called an impatient voice, 'and the whole audience has just passed a resolution to say so.' The interrupter, Helen Ogston, a graduate of St Andrews University, then embarked on a speech of her own. All the gangways in the hall were filled with stewards and now three attempted to approach her in the private box where she was standing. Helen Ogston held them back and *The Times* describes how, flicking at them delicately with a new dog whip, she persisted in addressing the audience. Not a word of her speech was heard in the commotion, and the meeting was brought to a standstill until she had been roughly stewarded out.

When at last the calls of protest and cries of 'Shame!' had died down, Lloyd George began to speak again. 'Deeds not words! Deeds not words!' came a voice from the gallery, and for the next hour and a half each of Lloyd George's statements met an interruption from some part of the hall. The stewards had been advised in their manifesto to do no violence and to treat all with courtesy, but now, regardless of instructions, they set on interrupters, punching them under the chin or gagging them with a hand. 'That's it,' shouted a white-haired man. 'Knock 'em down! Give it to 'em hot! Knock 'em down!' and the stewards dragged the Suffragettes from their seats, bundled them to the exits and flung them downstairs. 'Shame! Shame!' cried the women in the hall.

'We shall get peace and order gradually by this process of elimination,' Lloyd George remarked. 'My words are—' 'Two more years in Holloway Prison,' called a voice from the platform. Other suggestions were shouted out and, as the noise grew, Lloyd George sat down. 'What about the special message?' came a repeated cry, and the organist hearing no speaker, played 'Oh, dear! What can the matter be?' Lady McLaren presiding on behalf of the Liberal women begged Lloyd George to continue, but he refused, insisting that he did not wish to be the cause of violence. Lady McLaren exonerated the Liberals: 'Persons have taken the management of the meeting from the hands of its promoters,' and she persuaded Lloyd George to stand up again.

As soon as he spoke, new interruptions started and several minutes later, a man jumped shouting out of a box and on to the platform. 'Are there no *men* here?' he called out, and as stewards removed him, the manager of the hall appeared to advise Lady McLaren to close the meeting. With the 'special message' still to be delivered, Lloyd George decided to continue his speech, and in anticipation of the promised statement, the audience was comparatively quiet. But Lloyd George still did not come to the point: 'If Queen Elizabeth had been born today, she . . .' 'She would have been in Holloway Gaol,' broke in a Suffragette.

Finally the long-awaited message was given: Lloyd George pronounced his faith in Asquith's proposed Electoral Reform Bill which he said would surely include women. However, few people felt there was anything very 'special' about this, and when Lloyd George sat down, having finished his speech, there were still requests for the message.

Outside the hall photographers had been taking pictures of each ejected woman as she emerged, scratched, dishevelled and with her clothes torn. The general public was disgusted by the whole affair, but the Press dwelt more on the underlying problem, bringing out the real issue for the first time. The *Globe* said in a leading article:

> To give women the vote may bring increased stability to the State or it may on the other hand confuse the whole of our politics by an injection of hysteria. It will surely revolutionise the relations of the sexes. Upon such a question only the most invertebrate of mankind can be without an opinion.

Bayard N. Simmons wrote for *Votes for Women*, a 'Surprised Ode of Remonstrance to a Strong Man Who Sits Still':

> You've splendid muscles; why forswear
>   The privilege of such a frame?
> Listen! that woman over there
>   Is going to urge her monstrous claim:
> Roll up your sleeves, my Hercules
> Have done with empty chivalries.
>
> Have you no outraged feelings, none
>   That such a creature, merely fit
> To be the mother of your son
>   Should want to vote and work for it?
> Should dare to any seriousness
> Beyond the latest thing in dress.

Have you no feelings? Don't you know
  The hearth's the married woman's sphere,
As for the spinsters, they can sew,
  Typewrite and draw the nation's beer.
These are their duties: don't you boil
To hit them when they leave such toil?

I give you up: you're out of date,
  A fossil, not a man at all,
Compared with those, at any rate
  Who triumphed at the Albert Hall . . .

To prevent the recurrence of such a demonstration, the Government hurriedly passed a Bill making the interruption of a public meeting a police court offence.

The first London branch of the Women's National Anti-Suffrage League was inaugurated on November 5, 1908 at the Queen's Gate Hotel, Kensington. The Countess of Ilchester presided and Violet Markham spoke: she regretted the necessity of this struggle being forced on them when so many national problems were calling for attention. The propaganda of the Suffragettes was mischievous and undesirable. There were some rather strong planks on the suffragist platform, but they were built on a structure fundamentally rotten and rickety. It was no business of the State to revolutionise matters because of a minority of exceptional women who were desirous of possessing more political power than now fell to their lot. It was scandalous, if characteristic of the day of cheap notoriety, to read of women being carried struggling from the House of Commons in the arms of policemen.

Charles Mallet, M.P. for Plymouth, said that they must dissociate themselves from the small company whose conduct and violence were lowering the reputation of English women and E. L. Somervell, a prominent anti, wrote: 'If the vote is forced on us, how can we appeal to the protective instinct of the male and demand that matters affecting the welfare of women and children shall be treated as non-party questions?'

The final days of the W.S.P.U. autumn campaign were spent in preparation for the return of Mrs Pankhurst and Christabel. Christabel's prison sentence expired on December 22 and Mrs Pankhurst's on January 9. Mary Leigh was now the only other Suffragette remaining in Holloway and she too was to come out on January 9, after serving an extra long sentence on account of her previous imprisonment for stone throwing.

Mrs Pethick Lawrence had planned a victory procession to escort each leader from Holloway to Clement's Inn on the morning of her release. Ranks of Suffragettes in uniform were to lead the triumphal car while those who 'found it inconvenient to adopt the uniform style of dress' were to follow the carriage carrying tricolours. The uniform was a purple or green skirt—much shorter than usual length—a white jersey golf coat, and a coloured felt hat. The coat could be bought for seven shillings and sixpence and the hat cost two shillings. A regalia worn crosswise over the coat completed the costume.

Charlotte Marsh organised a house-to-house campaign along the route from Kensington to Holloway and a hundred and fifty people promised to hang out flags on December 22. This was to be the first of the many great processions led by Charlotte Marsh as standard bearer.

The order of assembly at Holloway was carefully organised and instructions were given in *Votes for Women*: 'We urge all friends to arrive not a moment later than 7.30 a.m. and to take up their places in the procession at once. It is quite likely that the authorities will release Miss Pankhurst before the appointed hour of 8 a.m. They have done that sort of thing before.' It was even anticipated that the Home Secretary might let out all the Suffragette prisoners together; recently Gladstone had become suspiciously evasive when questioned on 'releasing the Suffragettes for Christmastide'.

Quite unexpectedly, the leaders were released on Saturday, December 19. The Home Office order was given just before six o'clock in the evening when Christabel and Mary Leigh had already gone to bed. The three prisoners were summoned by wardresses, taken from their cells, and told that they could leave immediately. No one was waiting to greet them as they came out of Holloway, and Clement's Inn they knew would be shut for the week-end. So Mrs Pankhurst and Christabel went straight to Waterloo Station to take a train to Dorking, and they arrived at the Pethick Lawrences' house in Holmwood later that evening. Mary Leigh went back to her home in Camden Town.

As soon as Mrs Drummond received the news on Sunday morning, she travelled to Holmwood and with the Pethick Lawrences she re-arranged all the preparations for the following Tuesday's reception. Two long country walks on Sunday helped Christabel to regain her usual liveliness, but Mrs Pankhurst had prepared herself to come out of prison two weeks later, and she found it harder to adjust to the sudden freedom.

The celebrations on December 22 began at a quarter to ten in the morning with a welcome breakfast at the Inns of Court Hotel. There were over five hundred supporters from all parts of the country seated round the tables, and places could not be found for the many more who had hoped to attend. The main hall and side rooms were richly decorated with evergreens and hung with banners and flags in the colours of the union. A report said that 'birdsong trilled forth whenever the cheering was at its height'.

As Mrs Pankhurst rose to speak, the audience broke into the chorus of 'Rule, Britannia'. The situation seemed unreal to Mrs Pankhurst.

It is quite impossible for me to tell you all that I have in my heart and would like to say to you this morning. Had the authorities carried out their original intention, I should have a little while ago have got down from the iron railings at the head of my bed, away from the cell window out of which I had been peering to see the procession depart along the Parkhurst Road with my daughter. I should have been sitting on my hard wooden chair in the cell by the bedside, and taking my unfinished sock in my hand, I should have begun to knit and have tried to imagine myself among you this morning. Well, it seems to me, standing on this chair, that that is, in some strange way, just where I am.

Every woman who has been in prison, I know, can understand how I feel. You know, when we were younger and had time to read romances and ideal writings, we were so fascinated by those stories of people who had a dual personality. Well now, we women who have been to prison have acquired a dual personality which we shall never lose. We are the women out in the open, at the meetings, speaking with fire and enthusiasm, and going to disturb Cabinet Ministers' meetings; and then we are the women who spend so much of our time in that awful solitude.

After breakfast the triumphal procession set out from Kingsway, with Mrs Pankhurst and Christabel standing in the midst of flowers on an open landau drawn by four milk-white horses. Suffragettes in uniform led the team, and four dignified women dressed in riding habits followed on other white horses, while the grooms walked alongside. Mrs Pethick Lawrence with Mrs Drummond and the Kenney sisters led the uniformed ranks at the head of the procession. As they marched through Holborn and along Oxford Street, the bands struck up the Marseillaise and 'See the Conquering Hero Comes'. The West End crowds were exceptionally silent, impressed by the organisation and colourful simplicity of the spectacle.

The festivities reached their height in the evening when a throng of women in white filed on to the Queen's Hall platform. Each held a tricolour to raise as the leaders appeared. A moment later Mrs Pankhurst wearing purple silk walked on to the platform closely followed by Christabel in a pale green dress. The applause was deafening and as the leaders stood there, people cheered, clapped and cried. 'It was a night of hero worship,' said the *Daily News*, 'and Christabel Pankhurst was the heroine.'

Christabel spoke optimistically of the future: '1908 has transformed the political situation as far as our movement is concerned. It has paved the way for the great doings of the coming year. The New Year will bring votes for women.'

Then Christabel spoke on the material implications of women's suffrage:

One has a good deal of time for meditation in prison. We used to read the paper and think of what we had read, and I noticed this one thing—it is very extraordinary just to see how the world is moving on—how the conditions are changing. I noticed that in the two months in which we were in prison, airships came out of the region of theoretical and problematical things into being something quite practical; they are to be as useful to us as motor-cars, or even more so. Now a thing like that—and there are sure to be other things in the air—a thing like that means that the world is going to be a far different place in future from what it is today.

We in this country still have to readjust ourselves if we are to hold our own in the world in future. We women want to take a share in saving our country. I think all men of generous and pure mind and heart will be with us in this fight. I call on the men who are here tonight to join forces with us to help us to overcome the Government which at the present moment is the greatest obstacle in the path of human progress.

Chapter Four: A Flourishing Movement
1908–09

A MUSHROOMING OF SUFFRAGE SOCIETIES—LADY CONSTANCE
LYTTON JOINS A DEPUTATION—THE PRINCE'S RINK EXHIBITION
—SUFFRAGETTES VERSUS CABINET MINISTERS—AMBUSHES IN
THE WEST COUNTRY.

As soon as the Press began to discuss and publicise the motives behind the Suffragette Movement, many professional people suddenly became aware that the principles corresponded with their own inherited ideals, and new suffrage groups formed rapidly.

The Artists' League was the first of these societies, and its members were essentially suffragist in their leanings. In designing posters and propaganda, they worked in the outmoded nineteenth-century tradition of William Morris and his Socialist followers who had visualised the twentieth-century world as a place of inspired men partnered by gentle goddesses. It was hard to equate the 'new woman'—the brash, daring young woman of the popular picture papers—with any Pre-Raphaelite vision, and only a certain section of writers and actors seemed to realise that the woman of the day was in all probability the forerunner of the 'ideal partner', and should be recognised as such.

Johnston Forbes-Robertson, the actor-manager, spoke for women's suffrage on every possible occasion. In February 1909 he said:

> We may talk about a highly organised society when all the bars in front of women are swept away, when every calling, every trade, every profession that they can follow is open to them. Every person is the better for having responsibility, man or woman. Give them that, and I can imagine such a development, such an arrival at a simplicity of life—not complexity—as will leaven the whole world.

Forbes-Robertson and his wife, Gertrude Elliott, were largely responsible for founding the Actresses' Franchise League in December 1908, and many distinguished actresses became members, among them Ellen Terry and her daughter Edith Craig, Mrs Langtry, Lillah McCarthy and the Vanbrugh sisters. Although as professionals they pledged to be strictly neutral regarding suffrage tactics, the militant policy was clearly the one they supported. It was paradoxically men in the theatrical world who took the initiative to convince, encourage and help their actress colleagues to fight.

85

'I had been in the Suffragette Movement from the beginning,' says Lewis Casson, 'and in 1904 I was at the Court Theatre and a great friend of Shaw and Laurence Housman.' Casson met his future wife, Sybil Thorndike, in 1908, and before long he asked her what she was doing for the movement.

When he found that I knew nothing about it, he was full of shame for me and proceeded to instruct me. Wherever Lewis went he spoke for the Suffragettes, and in three weeks' time, I was taking the chair at one of the Suffragette meetings in Manchester. I had never taken the chair at a meeting before; I don't think that I had ever made a public speech, I was terrified—but got along fairly well— bad grammar—but he was there. I didn't know him very well; really I'd only just met him.

The majority of members of the Franchise League were classical actresses, but the society was open to anyone connected with the theatrical profession, including singers and musicians; Kitty Marion was a red-headed variety artiste, and Vera Holme played 'chorus and understudy' in Gilbert and Sullivan at the Savoy. Under a cover of flippancy, Vera Holme took the suffrage question very seriously:

They used to tease me about being a Suffragette. Rutland Barrington used to sing:

> The policeman's lot is not a happy one—
> Happy one.

and he used always to stand in front of me and sing it. Workman— he was second in command—also used to tease me. He would say, 'How much will you give me if I say "Votes for women?" ' and I used to say, 'I'll give you a week's salary.' 'Ho! Ho! can't be done for that!' We used to have this private conversation up at the top of the stage.

A Women Writers' League was founded by Cecily Hamilton in 1908, and among its earliest members were Mme Sarah Grand, Beatrice Harraden and Olive Schreiner. Even gymnastic teachers formed a group and other organised bodies built up suffrage unions within their own societies. The Rev. Claude and Mrs Hinscliff founded a Church League in 1909, its object being 'to establish equality between the sexes and thereby to improve the general well-being of the community'. The league was open to all members of the Church of England and branches were rapidly established all over the country. The Liberal women formed a 'Forward Suffrage Union' aimed to concentrate the activities of the Liberal women on their own enfranchisement, and all suffrage societies including the Conservative women, the Men's League for Women's Suffrage and the International Suffrage Alliance started to hold large meetings in London and the provinces.

On January 2, 1909 Mrs Despard and members of the Women's Freedom League held a symbolic burial of the Women's Enfranchisement Bill in Trafalgar Square. Every day a picture or mention of some suffragist activity appeared in the national Press and in the confusion of enthusiastic efforts the militants saw a danger that potential W.S.P.U. recruits might come under the influence of other societies whose policies they considered damagingly compromising.

In a *Votes for Women* editorial—'Wanted, More Officers'—Mrs Pethick Lawrence appealed for new supplies of young women to train in W.S.P.U. methods of organisation:

> I say to you young women who have private means or whose parents are able and willing to support you while they give you freedom to choose your vocation: 'Come and give me one year of your life to bringing the message of deliverance to thousands of your sisters . . . Put yourself through a short course of training under one of our chief officers in London and then become one of our staff organisers.'
>
> It may be that some girl will read this and say: 'Oh, I wish I were fortunate enough to be in an independent position—but I must work for my living.'
>
> Well, if you feel like that, write, or better still, come and see me or some other member of the committee. Every would-be organiser has to undergo a training and testing of three months and during that time a sum to cover board and lodging expenses is paid to her.

Meanwhile every opportunity was made to show friendliness towards the other societies and to include them in the militant programme. The new session of Parliament was to open on February 16, and the Women's Freedom League felt that it was now their turn to make a mass protest. They organised a national campaign, and members from all over the country were expected to assemble in London following the reading of the King's Speech.

For this reason, the W.S.P.U. Women's Parliament was not to be held until a week later, but before the opening of the new session at Westminster they once again took advantage of making a protest when the Cabinet Council met at Downing Street on January 25. Five women, among them Mrs Pankhurst's sister, Mrs Clarke, were arrested for trying to get into the Prime Minister's house, and during the next two weeks 'the knocking on the door' was cited at mass propaganda meetings all over the country as a symbolic reminder to women of their position.

There was no mention of votes for women in the King's Speech on February 16, but in their new programme the Cabinet proposed an elaborate Electoral Reform Bill which might possibly include women, but which would, if carried further, postpone the consideration of a separate women's Bill. The Suffragettes were not taken in. Mrs Blathwayt, a member of the Bath W.S.P.U., writes in her diary: 'We all know the Universal Suffrage Bill is a trick of Asquith's against the women, but the female Liberal Society will not see it.'

The Women's Freedom League met at the Portman Rooms on February 17 to discuss the situation and they decided to send a deputation to Downing Street on the following morning. Next day strong cordons of police were on duty and the few Freedom League protestors were completely outnumbered. Both at Downing Street and at the House of Commons, where they later tried to present petitions, the women met with instant rebuff. The arrests were swift and Mrs Despard and some twenty of her followers were taken into custody.

Before the re-opening of Parliament, Cabinet Ministers were subjected to persistent questioning. During a visit to Newcastle on February 4 and 5, Churchill had been waylaid by Suffragettes at every stage of his two-day itinerary. Now Liberal meetings were banned to all women and elaborate measures were taken to protect Cabinet Ministers wherever they went. In spite of the precautions, Suffragettes would still be present to question Ministers on public occasions, and the possibility of a Suffragette intrusion caused suspicion and unease at every Liberal gathering.

It was planned that a W.S.P.U. deputation should go to Parliament on February 24 and, on February 2, Mrs Pethick Lawrence wrote to Asquith asking him to receive the women. Asquith forwarded the correspondence to the Press, and replied to Mrs Pethick Lawrence that he had nothing further to add to the statements he had already made and that, in the circumstances, he did not think that any advantage would be gained from receiving the deputation.

In order to advertise the fact that they still intended to go to the House of Commons on the twenty-fourth, some of the younger members of the W.S.P.U. decided to make use of a post-office innovation. On February 23 Jessie Kenney went into the West Strand Post Office with

Elspeth McClelland and Daisy Soloman. 'I want to send a human letter.' The form was duly handed out, and she completed it, addressing her two companions to 'The Right Hon. H. H. Asquith, 10 Downing Street, S.W.' When she had paid the threepenny charge, a telegraph boy was called and the party set out. The two women walked briskly along the Strand on either side of the messenger. Daisy Soloman carried a placard bearing the address, while Elspeth McClelland held a still larger board printed with the message: VOTES FOR WOMEN—DEPUTATION —HOUSE OF COMMONS—WEDNESDAY.

When they arrived at Downing Street they were stopped by the three policemen on duty. The boy showed his way-bill and he was allowed to go forward to Number Ten, but the Suffragettes were told to wait. The messenger rang the bell, handed his note to the butler who opened the door, and he was asked inside.

A few moments later the door re-opened and the butler came out: 'You must be returned.' 'But we have been paid for!' they protested. 'Well then, the post office must deliver you somewhere else. You can't be delivered here.' 'But the express letter is an official document and must be signed according to the regulations.' 'It can't be signed, you must be returned, you are dead letters,' said the butler firmly, and went back into the house leaving the women to return to Clement's Inn.

While Mrs Drummond was waiting to see the result of the 'human letters', she met Churchill on his way to the House. As she greeted him, he waved her off: 'Woman, I don't want to have anything to do with you. I will give you in charge.' A short exchange of words followed, and a man in the street, seeing the situation, came up to ask if Churchill wanted help. 'Excuse me,' interrupted Mrs Drummond, 'this is a private conversation between Mr Churchill and myself.' 'Your agitation has done very well up to now, but I advise you not to go too far,' warned Churchill. 'That's a big admission for you to make,' retorted Mrs Drummond as they reached the entrance to Palace Yard. 'Good day, Woman,' said Churchill and went on his way.

It was generally known that Mrs Pethick Lawrence was going to lead the deputation on the twenty-fourth—no future engagements had been planned for her, and it was a foregone conclusion that she would be imprisoned.

After long consideration, Lady Constance Lytton decided that she, too, should offer herself for imprisonment. She was still not a W.S.P.U. member, and when she finally enrolled and was accepted for the deputation, she dared not tell anyone. Even her mother had no idea where she was going when Lady Con left her family home at Knebworth on February 24. She had been unable to say good-bye to her mother and, at King's Cross Station, she wrote a long letter to Lady Lytton begging her forgiveness.

Lady Con lunched at Clement's Inn with the leaders, 'but I had a cracking headache and felt quite dazed.' During the afternoon she was taken to lie down upstairs in the Pethick Lawrences' flat, while Elsa Gye —one of the most enthusiastic of suffrage workers—was summoned to partner and assist Lady Con on the deputation. They had supper together at headquarters—Lady Con was scarcely able to eat—and as soon as the meal was finished they left by cab for the Caxton Hall.

In the taxi Lady Constance began to realise that she had no idea how to play her part. 'What does one have to do?' she asked her experienced companion anxiously. 'Oh, you needn't bother about what you'll do,' Elsa Gye reassured her. 'It will all be done to you. There is only one thing you must remember. You must on no account be turned back. If the police become too violent you can cut matters short and get arrested instantly by creating a breach of the peace. Pretend to make a speech, or collect a crowd round you.'

At the Caxton Hall the members of the deputation were seated on the platform, but Lady Con was not among them. Although she was wearing a regalia which signified that she was one of the volunteers, she was anxious not to be recognised at this stage, and she had even dressed her hair in an early Victorian style so as to avoid identification. She sat with Elsa Gye in the body of the hall until the women on the platform were ready to leave and as they filed down two by two she unobtrusively stepped into the line with her partner.

As they started out, Lady Constance began to consider what might happen if the rest of the deputation were refused admittance and if she alone, because of her position, should be allowed to pass. What sort of speech should she make? Ideas about the lot of the superfluous spinster and working women—washerwomen—flashed through her mind. Out in the grime of the foggy February evening, Lady Con noticed all the white shirts and collars dotted in the dense crowd—the work of women who had no means to justify their existence . . . Her thoughts were abruptly cut short, for the procession was being gradually hemmed in by police.

My companion and I kept together. Very soon all breath seemed to have been pressed out of my body, but remembering, 'Don't be turned back,' I tried to hold my ground even when advance was out of the question. Miss Gye, however, soon realised the situation and pulled me back, saying, 'We are not yet in Parliament Square; let's try another way.'

We soon got clear of the police and found ourselves in a friendly crowd, but I was already so incapacitated by the breathlessness I could not lift my chest and head. But for the assistance of my companion and an unknown man and woman of the crowd I should have been unable to get any further. Miss Gye and I eventually got separated and lost sight of one another. My two stranger friends in the crowd, however, not being marked by badges, were always returning to my help.

I was during most of the time physically incapable of speech—I only twice was able to express myself in words, on both occasions when I was lifted off my feet and relieved of the toil of dragging my own body. First when the crowd wedged me up against a policeman, I said to him, 'I know you are only doing your duty and I am doing mine.' His only answer was to seize me with both his hands round the ribs, squeeze the remaining breath out of my body and lifting me completely into the air, throw me with all his strength. Thanks to the crowd I did not reach the ground.

Twice again I was thrown and the concussion on reaching the ground was painful and straining. When seized for the throw, there is a feeling of wrenching throughout the body. A German lady had managed to keep near me, and three times, after each of the 'throws', she came to my help and warded off the crowd while I leant up against some railings or against her shoulder to recover my breath. Several times I said to her, 'I can't go on; I simply can't go on.' She answered, 'Wait for a little and you will be all right presently.'

Flashes of vivid light and the sound of a slightly muffled explosion came from time to time. It was only towards the end of the day that I realised that they were the photographers' flashlights.

Slowly and persistently Lady Con gained ground, edged her way through the last groups of police and found herself at the Members' Entrance. 'No crowd was near and only two policemen stood at either side of the gate. They did not seem to be noticing me. I straightened my back to assume as much of a normal appearance as possible and I passed through the gate.' Instantly her arm was seized. Two policemen took hold of her and led her gently away. She closed her eyes and her head fell forward.

When they halted, Lady Con looked up to find she was standing in front of a doorway over which was a blue lamp with the words POLICE STATION printed on it. It was a tremendous relief to go inside and meet other members of the deputation who had also been arrested. Soon Mrs

Pethick Lawrence was brought in. All the prisoners were taken up to the billiards-room and now, for the first time in her life, Lady Constance experienced a feeling of genuine comradeship.

The usual trial and imprisonments followed. Lady Con was put in the hospital at Holloway on account of her 'heart condition', and Mrs Pethick Lawrence was placed in the same wing for no apparent reason. There were already a number of Freedom League prisoners in Holloway serving time for their part in the deputations of February 18, but Mrs Despard's case had been remanded for a week. One afternoon, soon after her arrival in prison, Lady Con says that the Freedom League women in the hospital were in a state of great excitement. The prayer card at the head of one of the spare beds was altered to one of Roman Catholic prayers and they took this to mean that Mrs Despard would be coming in. She arrived late that evening, and as soon as she caught sight of Mrs Pethick Lawrence, Mrs Despard came forward to greet her. Just as they were about to shake hands, a wardress intervened and angrily forbade them to touch one another.

Only five days later Mrs Despard was released. 'I am absolutely in excellent health,' she told the Press. 'I have never been in better health in my life.' Both Mrs Despard and Lady Constance Lytton had been sentenced to a month's imprisonment and the situation was plainly causing embarrassment to the Government. There had been considerable comment in the Press over their treatment and that of Mrs Pethick Lawrence. The *Manchester Guardian* asked: 'Why has she been sentenced to two months while Mrs Despard, in identical circumstances, had been given only half that time?'

The Suffragettes felt that something might be gained at this point by sending out another deputation immediately. Probably as an inner political move on the part of the leaders, a group of Lancashire women was chosen to go to Parliament. Recently there had been a feeling in Manchester of an exclusion from the national campaign. Mary Gawthorpe, the chief organiser for Lancashire, wrote to Isabel Seymour of the 'joyous combat which once was and which ought to be'. She longed for a by-election as a relief from the incessant driving stress and strain of unavoidable provincial poverty and the ever abominable money problem on the top of a steadily accumulating mass of speaking and organising. Mary Gawthorpe ends her letter: 'I'm off to the cannibal islands very shortly before I become too stringy and stale to be digested!'

Mrs Pankhurst spent a week in Lancashire travelling all over the county to rouse enthusiasm for the deputation and her tour, reported as a record of triumphs, ended on March 24 with a great meeting in the Manchester Free Trade Hall. Volunteers for the deputation came forward at the meeting and among the women were three graduates: Dora Marsden and Rona Robinson of Manchester University, and Emily Wilding Davison, an Oxford graduate who also had a London degree. Later, Margaret Smith, another London B.A., joined the volunteers. Mrs Saul Soloman, sixty-four years old, a renowned social worker and widow of a former Governor-General of Cape Colony, was chosen to lead the deputation.

On the afternoon of March 30 a Women's Parliament assembled in the Caxton Hall and Mrs Pankhurst saw the deputation on its way. On this occasion the police had orders to force the deputation back but not to make arrests. Mrs Saul Soloman was actually allowed to pass through the cordons and she was received at the House, but she was refused an interview with the Prime Minister.

Meanwhile the Lancashire women were soon dishevelled and muddy. Bruised and panting for breath, they kept pushing forward and trying to pass behind the crowd of spectators unnoticed. 'The women squeak like rabbits,' commented an M.P. as he watched the scene from a window of the House of Commons. The newspapers on the following day showed pictures of the battle, where the women for the first time looked wild and undignified. The Suffragettes who were eventually arrested were charged with assault on the police.

On April 20 the Houses of Parliament Bill came up for debate in the House of Commons. Its object was to penalise anyone who was considered guilty of disorderly conduct within the Palace of Westminster while either of the Houses was sitting. The debate soon proved that the proposed 'Brawling Bill' would in no way secure the dignity of Members, for they would be called to give evidence every time a Suffragette was tried for breach of its terms. 'The Bill must have been drafted somewhere in the neighbourhood of Clement's Inn,' said an Irish M.P. 'Instead of taking away the chance of advertisement which has been offered to certain propagandists, it offers them a better chance than ever!' The idea was speedily shelved, but it had already received publicity and the Suffragettes immediately seized the opportunity to defy the introduction of any such measure.

On the afternoon of April 27 Mrs Bertrand Russell, Theresa Garnett, and three other W.S.P.U. speakers went to St Stephen's Hall and while Mrs Russell tried to enter the Central Lobby, the other women chained themselves to the selected statues of men who had fought for liberty— Lord Somers, Walpole, Selden and Lord Falkland. The chained

Suffragettes then began to lecture on the reasons for their protest while M.P.s and visitors flocked into the Lobby to watch the demonstration. A large crowd had gathered before the police finally managed to break the chains with pincers and free the women. No further police action was taken in this case and as soon as the Serjeant-at-arms arrived the women were allowed to go.

Since the grille episode, the public galleries in the House of Commons had been closed. Now, in a face-saving announcement on May 3, the Speaker stated that the galleries were to be re-opened, but that each visitor must sign a pledge on entrance. The Ladies' Gallery was to be confined to relatives of Members of Parliament.

The Suffragettes still hoped to win their struggle by peaceful means, and a great procession and a public meeting at the Aldwych Theatre on April 17 were planned to celebrate Mrs Pethick Lawrence's prison release. Mrs Drummond and Jessie Kenney usually worked out the order of the programme and made arrangements with the police for such occasions, but Mrs Lawrence herself always devised the pageantry.

In her absence W.S.P.U. members planned the features of this demonstration to include all the tributes that they felt Mrs Lawrence would most appreciate. Her prison companions from the deputation of February 24 followed her carriage, the Esperance Girls' Club marched in the procession and also a group of loyal friends and admirers from the Actresses' Franchise League. There were contingents of small children with flowers to present and a group of older girls all in white, but the *pièce de résistance* was a Joan of Arc, inspired by the current beatification of the saint in Rome. Elsie Howey, a clergyman's daughter and a keen horsewoman, headed the procession as Joan—Mrs Lawrence's great heroine. Dressed in armour and bearing an oriflamme in the colours, she rode on a huge white charger leading the lines of women through the West End towards the Aldwych. 'All the winners! All the winners!' called a bystander seeing a woman in white come along the kerb with her pile of *Votes for Women*.

As a further tribute to Mrs Pethick Lawrence, Mrs Pankhurst suggested that members should present her with a new car. It was an Austin, painted and upholstered in the colours with white wheels and a green body lined with a narrow purple stripe.

Mrs Pethick Lawrence took her first drive with Muriel Thompson— the 1908 winner of the Gold Bracelet for Driving—but later Vera Holme became the permanent chauffeur. 'Mrs Pethick Lawrence wanted me for the job,' says Vera, 'but Mrs Pankhurst thought I was very giddy and she wasn't at all for having me because I used to act the galoot in the office.' Later, Mrs Pankhurst revised her opinion after Vera had safely accomplished the hazardous journey to Scotland with her. 'In some places you didn't know when you were on the road and when you were off,' Vera says. 'The lights used to go down and if you went up a little rise in the road, you couldn't see anything.'

Vera Holme used to drive the leaders to their important engagements and on one occasion she took Christabel to address a meeting in Forest Hill. Christabel was invited to dine beforehand with Lady Sybil Smith.

Lady Sybil heard that the chauffeur had come and she thought I was an ordinary chauffeur. I had gone past the fanlight in the front door when Lady Sybil's chauffeur came up and thinking I was a chauffeur too, he caught me by the arm: 'Like to bring the bugger round to the yard, mate?' 'No—er!' I said, 'I think not.' Just at that moment Lady Sybil came out in her white dress and said: 'Come in, Miss Holme, and have some dinner.' Her chauffeur nearly went dotty. I must say the chauffeurs were always awfully nice to me and the maids used to get into the most frightful state of joy thinking a man was coming when they saw me.

The Prince's Skating Rink in Knightsbridge was taken from May 9 to 25 for the W.S.P.U. 'Woman's Exhibition'. The Pethick Lawrences had already started planning the show before the New Year and when Mrs Pethick Lawrence was imprisoned, one of her sisters, Dr Marie Pethick, took over as exhibition secretary and Sylvia Pankhurst was asked to organise the décor.

Sylvia embarked on an ambitious scheme, designing murals to cover every wall of the exhibition hall. She rented a workshop above a large stable and took a studio in the Fulham Road where there was space to carry out the project. Her assistants—seven ex-students from the Royal College—worked all day and night to complete the twenty-foot-high canvases. The three women were paid thirty shillings a week and the men, at their own request, tenpence an hour. The style of the decorations with their herald angels was in the tradition of Sylvia's teacher Walter Crane, using a realistic type of symbolic art for social propaganda.

A Suffragette drum and fife band had been in training for many weeks, and the public was able to see the bandswomen for the first time when they marched from Kingsway to Knightsbridge to advertise the exhibition. Led by Mary Leigh as drum-major, young musicians wore smart military uniforms in the W.S.P.U. colours. In order to become

...ghly proficient, the twenty-nine members went through a course
...drill under the direction of military non-commissioned officers.

A threepenny programme of the exhibition gave a comprehensive
account of the work of the movement with biographies of the leaders and
a foreword by Mrs Pankhurst:

> It has always been deemed women's part to raise funds which
> make it possible for political or philanthropic work to be carried on,
> although it normally happens that the women who have worked to
> raise the funds are not consulted in any way as to how the money
> raised shall be spent . . . This exhibition is intended to help a
> movement to give women power to work out their own salvation—
> political, social and industrial.

Among the special exhibits were two replica prison cells. A Suffragette
prisoner could be seen scrubbing, bed-making or stitching in the smaller
second-division cell, while a political prisoner—a man—sat in comfort
in the other cell which was well furnished and twice the size.

The Y.H.B. produced a remarkable exhibition of photographs. In the
September of 1907, when the Suffragette forces divided, an article in the
Daily News had described Mrs Pankhurst's followers as 'the younger,
more hot-blooded members'. This had inspired Mary Home, the
W.S.P.U. 'clippings' girl, to form a society of 'Young Hot-Bloods'—
Suffragettes under thirty prepared for 'danger duty'. Now, at the
Prince's Rink, the Y.H.B. showed a history of the movement as seen
through the eye of the Press photographer, ever present to record a
Suffragette spectacle.

Short, one-act suffrage plays were given by the Actresses' Franchise
League and each day there were orchestral recitals and morris-dancing
displays by Mary Neal's child dancers. Among the many other side-
shows, the best West End palmists were available for consultation but,
at Mrs Pankhurst's request, they were soon replaced by another
attraction. Quite possibly, their visions of the Suffragette future were too
full of foreboding to be comfortable.

Edith Garrud, the first British woman jiu-jitsu instructor, came to
give a demonstration some time after the exhibition had opened. A tiny
woman, she always worked in partnership with her husband and he did
all the speaking. 'He talked about the scientific side of judo,' she says,
'all its better ways—what it was for.' A side hall at the exhibition had
been put at their disposal and Mrs Garrud was already there awaiting
her husband's arrival.

At the last moment this boy came running round. 'Boss can't come,
ma'm,' he says, 'he's got a thundering bad attack of indigestion.'

It was really fright; he was frightened to death to speak. Anyway Mrs Pankhurst was very near and she said, 'Mrs Garrud, do it yourself. Work, and talk about it while you're doing it. I think we shall understand.' I said: 'I don't believe I can be heard.' 'Yes you can! You look up the hall, see someone right at the end and, if they're just looking at you, that's enough—talk to them. Your voice'll reach them and it'll go all round the hall.' Well we did the show and I was inundated for signatures afterwards.

Among the stalls, one of the most popular was the ice cream soda fountain, sponsored by a wealthy American supporter, and the first of its kind in England. The millinery stall, run by Kensington members, attracted more attention than any other. Many of the best hat-makers in London contributed to the stocks and Pethick Lawrence bought models for his wife, Christabel, and the Clement's Inn staff. When the grand total of five thousand, six hundred and forty-four pounds raised by the exhibition was counted it was found that the millinery stall had taken the highest single amount.

During the exhibition there had been a slight lull in militant activity, but the W.S.P.U. intended to send another deputation to the House of Commons in June, and now they employed all their by-election tactics in a nationwide campaign. Wherever a Cabinet Minister was due to hold a meeting, a group of Suffragette speakers would arrive in the district a week earlier to work up sympathy for their cause and anti-Government feeling.

Augustine Birrell, Secretary for Ireland and the local Bristol M.P., was billed to take the chair at a meeting in the Colston Hall on Saturday, May 1. Mrs Baldock, Vera Holme and Elsie Howey (who had so recently ridden as Saint Joan), arrived from London to augment Annie Kenney's west of England staff and together Vera and Elsie managed to rent a house exactly opposite the Colston Hall stage door. 'We were rather afraid when it came to fetching the keys because we were both young, but Mrs Baldock was a woman of a certain age, so we got her to go with us to the pub where they advertised the room.'

For a week the Suffragettes held meetings in every part of Bristol. On the Friday before the Liberal rally, every copy of *Votes for Women* was sold out and they had to send to London for more. The Press came and they were up all night.

As no women were officially allowed inside the hall, Mrs Baldock and some Bristol members installed themselves with a megaphone in the rented room, and prepared to make a disturbance from there while the meeting was in progress.

Elsie and Vera managed to get into the hall on the Saturday afternoon, and they climbed up to a narrow platform behind the top of the organ pipes. Before the meeting the building was searched. 'We could see the police right down on the floor of the auditorium with bull's-eye lanterns looking into every cranny, but they never thought of looking where we were,' says Vera; 'and when the meeting started, we could hear from the hall the hullabaloo going on outside across the way.' In 'An Organ Recital' (tune, 'The Lost Chord'), written by Vera immediately after the episode, she describes what happened when Birrell rose to speak:

> Seated one day in the organ
> We were weary and ill at ease;
> We sat there three hours only,
> Hid, midst the dusty keys.
> We knew not if they'd be playing,
> And to us what would happen then,
> But when we heard Mr Birrell,
> It was then we protested—then.
>
> Our voices rang out from the twilight,
> But nowhere could we be found;
> They looked from the floor to the ceiling—
> The stewards came searching round.
> We asked for votes for women,
> And that justice should be done;
> But Birrell he could not answer,
> And the audience made such fun!
>
> He said he had come from Asquith
> And to him they must give ear;
> But a voice rang out still louder,
> Making our question clear.
> It may be that Mr Birrell
> Daren't speak in that hall again,
> And it may be, never in Bristol,
> Until the vote we gain!

Elsie Howey told the story at the local W.S.P.U. 'At Home', on the following Monday: 'The stewards ran all about, but it never entered their heads that women would climb ladders. When they found us after about ten minutes, they came up, and we immediately went down with them because it would not have been secure to try a scuffle where we were.'

On every important occasion Cabinet Ministers were now attended by a strong police escort. Asquith was to speak on May 21 at Sheffield where the Suffragettes had recently won great popularity at a local by-election. Elaborate precautions were taken for the protection of the Prime Minister and to the annoyance of the Liberal women, men only were to be admitted to the meeting. The drill hall where Asquith was to speak had been barricaded and forty policemen guarded the station on his arrival. The *Sheffield Daily Telegraph* reported:

> The methods for conveying Mr Asquith from the station to the hotel were highly successful but not particularly English. The railway officials rigged up a platform adjacent to a sort of back door, and from that Mr Asquith was smuggled to the hotel as if he were a bale of contraband goods. Time was when a British premier was proud to face the people—but now! It was surely a little undignified for a British prime minister to be making unexpected entrances and mysterious exits like a trap-door artist in a Christmas pantomime.

For several weeks the Suffragettes had been persuading the townspeople to help them force a way into the hall on the day of the meeting. Now thousands of people clamoured against the police barricades. The evening was hot. Asquith had been smuggled into the meeting and his speech was dull and uneasy. The noise outside drowned his words and the audience was inattentive. Every moment—at the slightest cough—they expected a Suffragette interruption. The heat became unbearable, and men in shirt sleeves left their seats to go in search of cooling air. But they reached the exit only to find that the doors had been locked and barricaded against the mob breaking in.

Outside the crowd cheered the Suffragettes and plied them with cold drinks and soda water as they tried unsuccessfully again and again to get past the army of police. Before the meeting ended an area was cordoned off to enable Asquith to leave the hall in safety and he finally drove away, 'muffled to the ears', with the blinds of his motor-car closely drawn.

During the Whitsun holiday Asquith held a house-party for some of his colleagues at Clovelly Court in Devon. Elsie Howey, Jessie Kenney and Vera Wentworth, a former shop girl, also travelled to Clovelly for the week-end. In church on Sunday Mrs Asquith passed a note to her husband drawing his attention to the presence of the three well-known young Suffragettes, and throughout the rest of the service he kept glancing uneasily in their direction. After the final prayers he hurriedly left the church by a side door.

In the evening all the Clovelly villagers turned out at the station to see the Suffragettes depart. But at Bideford, twelve miles away, the girls left the train, deposited their luggage and returned on foot to Clovelly, arriving at two o'clock in the morning. They found their way into the gardens of Clovelly Court and painstakingly decorated the rhododendron bushes with three-inch *Votes for Women* discs, inscribed on the reverse side, REMEMBER SHEFFIELD, RELEASE PATRICIA WOODLOCK (undergoing three months' imprisonment for her part in the March 30 deputation) and RECEIVE OUR DEPUTATION ON JUNE 29.

Chapter Five: The Start of Violence 1909–10

THE 'BILL OF RIGHTS' DEPUTATION—MARION WALLACE DUNLOP AND THE HUNGER STRIKE—HERBERT GLADSTONE ORDERS FORCIBLE FEEDING—THE SUFFRAGETTES RETALIATE—LADY CONSTANCE LYTTON AS JANE WARTON.

It is the right of the subject to petition the King, and all commitments and prosecutions for such petitions are illegal. This passage from the Bill of Rights was quoted at every meeting, and written out on all the handbills which advertised the Suffragettes' thirteenth attempt to present a petition at the House of Commons. The deputation of June 29 was to be larger and more highly organised than any previous one, and it was preceded by a massive campaign to work up public support. 'The General [Mrs Drummond] went round telling us to hold six meetings every night and make things go,' says Grace Roe who had just been made an organiser.

Such was the public sympathy for the movement that a popular paper souvenir had been printed to commemorate the deputation. It showed the leaders in a border of violets and quoted the Bill of Rights, with an extract from a speech of Mrs Pankhurst's asking the support of men on the evening of June 29. Perhaps in anticipation of a national uprising, the Press hardly mentioned the suffrage question. 'A casual reader might be led to imagine that the educational side of the work was being only intermittently carried on and that militant protests were the only activity of the Suffragettes,' said Pethick Lawrence. 'The movement at the present time is responsible for over one thousand meetings a month in different parts of the country, and it is exerting far more influence on the life and thought of the people of the country than any other political question.'

Marion Wallace Dunlop, an artist and authoress, assembled the words from the Bill of Rights on a large rubber stamp and on June 22, a week before the deputation, she went to St Stephen's Hall intending to print the passage on the wall in violet ink. She had just time to impress her stamp before it was knocked from her hand by a policeman. She was taken to Inspector Scantlebury's office, the stamp was confiscated, her name and address were taken, and a detective escorted Miss Wallace Dunlop off the premises. 'Is the notice legible?' she asked as they parted. 'Well, it's only a smudge really.' Determined to succeed, Miss Wallace Dunlop went again to St Stephen's Hall two days later with a new stamp and this time she was able to print her inscription quite clearly on the wall before being arrested.

She was charged with wilful damage and sentenced to one month's imprisonment in the second division. Being refused political prisoner treatment, she decided to go on hunger strike and on Monday, July 5 she began her fast.

I threw a fried fish, four slices of bread, three bananas and a cup of hot milk out of my window on Tuesday, that being the only day I really felt hungry. They threatened all the time to pump milk through my nostrils, but never did. They kept my table covered with food, which I never touched. I only drank water. My pulse was felt many times in the day and I laughed at them all the time, telling them I would show them the stuff the Suffragette was made of; and that they would either have to put me in the first division or release me.

After she had fasted for ninety-one hours, the Home Secretary sent an order for Miss Wallace Dunlop to be set free.

On June 28, the night before the deputation, the Government gave a reception at the Foreign Office in honour of the King's birthday. The husband of a Suffragette had been invited with his wife to attend the reception, but she persuaded him to pass on the tickets to the W.S.P.U.

Theresa Garnett had just returned to Clement's Inn after campaigning in the provinces and she was sitting in the outer office awaiting new orders when Christabel came into the room: 'Oh, Theresa, we've got this ticket. Now you could do it—if anyone could get away with it, you could.' 'Well, I haven't got an evening dress, I don't even possess one,' said Theresa. Una Dugdale, who had three sisters, happened to overhear this conversation. 'If you come home with me we can dress you. You're just about Daisy's size.'

So I went home with her and they dressed me up beautifully—pale blue spotted Indian muslin, with a blue velvet cape. One of the sisters even lent me her pearls, and I looked very, very 'all there', complete with a fan. They found me a husband, Charles Pantlin, a very nice young boy just down from Cambridge, and we went in a hansom cab to the Foreign Office.

When we got there we parted, I to take off my cape and he to get rid of his hat. Then we met in the hall. On each of the lower steps of the staircase stood a detective and on the bottom step, the House of Commons detective himself, who knew me well. I thought, 'Oh lor! I'm sunk at the very beginning.' However, I made a little play with my fan as we went by, gazed up adoringly at my nice-looking

husband, and we got up to where the reception was being held. We
didn't want to be received and have the man shout out the name on
our ticket, so we managed to get into the room by edging round.

All the cream of Society was there, and we walked about and
identified various Cabinet Ministers. There was John Burns, who
had so recently stood up in Trafalgar Square with a red scarf round
his neck, protesting that he would never lay down his arms till the
streets of London ran knee-deep in the blood of the aristocracy.
There he was, in his cocked hat, buckled shoes, silk stockings, silk
trousers, and all the rest of it.

A string orchestra played, and in between whiles they had to
change their music. I decided to act. My husband deserted me, for
he was going to take part in the 'smash up' the next day, and he
didn't want to get identified with me now. I got up on a window
ledge behind a bank of flowers, and waited for the music to stop.
Then I began talking and there was absolute silence. How long it
really was I don't know, but it seemed to me ages. I got quite a lot
in, and then there was a patter of detectives. Up they came running,
headed by Inspector Jarvis. 'My God! How did you get in?' 'Well,
I saw you there on the bottom step, and I was afraid I wouldn't,' I
replied.

Then he lifted me down off the high ledge and took me by the
arm. He didn't hurry me at all, but walked me down the room, and
the guests parted on each side to let us through. As I walked by, I
bowed to right and left, saying, 'You will see that we get votes for
women, won't you?' There wasn't a sound.

Downstairs I was charged with disturbing the peace, and I said:
'But you know, there was no disturbance of the peace, and if you
insist on making this charge, I shall subpoena John Burns;' and I
recited the names of all the other cabinet ministers I had seen. They
kept me for a while until the people had dispersed a bit, and then
they let me go. The next day, a newspaper said: 'A Suffragette
disguised as a lady got into the Government reception last night.'

Every Suffragette of standing was asked to join the 'Bill of Rights'
deputation, as the imprisonment of women of class clearly caused
embarrassment in political circles. Hundreds of rank and file members
had already offered themselves and in order to accommodate them, a
manoeuvre was devised whereby demonstrators could approach the
House and some of the Government offices from a strategic base other
than the Caxton Hall.

On the evening of June 29, before the appointed hour of battle, small groups of volunteers assembled secretly in some thirty different offices in the Westminster area. Each team of seven or eight women was under the supervision of an organiser, who gave instructions and kept up morale. Some Suffragettes were to attempt to get into the House and as it was rumoured that they would receive rough treatment, several wore hockey dress, with an added home-made, papier mâché corset as armour underneath the thick sports jersey. Other groups were to make an attack on Whitehall and each woman was issued with a striped denim dorothy bag containing stones wrapped in brown paper and tied with string. The dorothy bags were attached round the waist under the skirt and at the signal for the 'smash up', the stones could be reached through a placket pocket.

On June 29 Mrs Blathwayt wrote in her diary:

This is the terrible night when Mrs Pankhurst is going to lead the deputation from the Caxton Hall, which Asquith says he will not receive. It is a very anxious time for all. Asquith was asked in Parliament if he would be responsible for tonight, but he would not answer.

Just after half past seven Vera Holme, in riding habit and tricolor sash, came cantering from the Caxton Hall with a message for the Prime Minister. Hundreds of yelling youths ran after her and her horse pushed its passage through the crowd in front, which scattered on either side. At St Stephen's Church she was stopped by a cordon of police; she handed her document to a mounted inspector who dropped it and told her to go away. As she made the return journey to the Caxton Hall, admiring crowds cheered and clapped.

Pressmen saw the deputation appear: 'By the side of Inspector Isaacs came the frail undaunted figure of Mrs Pankhurst, nervously followed by the white-haired Mrs Saul Soloman wearing a black mantle and a bonnet.' The seventy-six-year-old headmistress, Miss Neligan, walked behind, followed by the other five members of the distinguished deputation—the Hon. Mrs Haverfield, Mrs Mansel, Mrs Corbett, Miss Maud Joachim and Miss Catherine Margesson. As they marched swiftly towards the House of Commons, a way was ceared for them through the dense cheering crowds. They finally arrived at the steps of the Strangers' Entrance, to be met by Inspector Scantlebury and Inspector Jarvis. A letter from Asquith was handed to Mrs Pankhurst. It was a note expressing regret that he could not receive the deputation. Mrs Pankhurst read it out loud to the women, dropped it and demanded entrance. Inspector Jarvis began to push her away. Mrs Pankhurst foresaw the usual struggle. 'I had to take into account that I was accompanied by two fragile old ladies who could not possibly endure what I knew must follow. I quickly decided that I should have to force an immediate arrest.' Mrs Pankhurst slapped Jarvis's face. 'I understand why you did that,' he said, but he did not arrest her. She struck him again and then she was taken in charge.

Soon the main attack began. The stone throwers left base and each made her way to the specified area in Whitehall where she was to break a window. Ada Wright was one of the volunteers:

> To women of culture and refinement and of sheltered upbringing the deliberate throwing of a stone, even as a protest, in order to break a window, requires an enormous amount of moral courage. After much tension and hesitation, I threw my stone through the window of the Office of Works. To my relief, I was at once arrested and marched off by two policemen, the tremendous crowd making way for us and cheering to the echo, all the way to Cannon Row Police Station.
>
> Of the nightmare walk, I remember Laurence Housman suddenly detaching himself from the crowd, cheering louder than anyone else. Slapping me heartily on the back, he shouted out, 'Well done!' and waved his top hat in the air.

Laurence Housman had just been thrown out of St Stephen's Hall for making a speech: 'Fellow citizens, outside this House the people's right of petition is being violated. Women are being treated in a way that no decent government would allow.'

Other Suffragette teams swarmed out of the offices just as the sun was setting and made their way towards the House. The crowd watched, terrified, as the women stood their ground fearlessly under the rearing police horses. The Suffragettes were pledged not to give in until arrested and by the end of the evening one hundred and eight prisoners had been taken.

The next morning they all appeared for trial at Bow Street. Many had come dressed for court in smart, fashionable gowns of purple, white and green, with large picture hats, and the policemen had some difficulty in recognising and identifying their battered prisoners of the previous evening. The women were charged with obstruction, assaulting the police, and doing malicious damage. As test cases, the first taken were those of Mrs Pankhurst and the Hon. Mrs Haverfield. They pleaded that by the Bill of Rights and also by the terms of the Tumultuous Petitions Act, they were legally entitled to petition Asquith as a representative of the King. The magistrate was uncertain on this point and all the cases were adjourned until further advice could be taken.

The cases of the fourteen stone throwers were heard separately at Bow Street on July 12. Gladys Roberts of Leeds, a former solicitor's clerk, was sentenced to one month in the second division. On the day of her trial she started to keep a diary in shorthand:

> We left Bow Street at about 4.30. Mrs May [a pillar of the Clement's Inn staff] and Mrs Leigh stayed to the last, teaching us songs. There were eighteen of us in black Maria. The atmosphere and the jolting were indescribable. A regalia, floating from the end of an umbrella, was held through a hole in the roof all the way.
>
> On arriving at Holloway, we were taken into the corridor outside the reception cells. Our names were called and we answered. Miss Wright then asked to see the governor. The wardress, who had tow-coloured hair and was very disagreeable, fetched the matron who wanted us to answer to our names again. We refused and asked once more to see the governor. At last he was sent for. After hearing from Miss Wright that we intended to rebel against all the second-division rules, the governor said he would let us keep our clothing and bags until he communicated with the Home Secretary, if we went quietly to our cells, and on the understanding that we were not allowed to go to chapel or exercise.
>
> I am in bed which is not so bad, and it's about 2.30. Delightful to be able to rest at last.
>
> *Tuesday, June 13.*
> ... Breakfast just arrived which consists of another lump of that horrible brown bread and tea. I read *Votes*, and tried to eat some of the bread, but failed. To my joy, I found scratched on that bit of tin curved at one end, called a knife:
>
>> Glorious Christabel.
>> Courage! brave heart, victory is sure,
>> Help comes to those who work and endure.
>
> A wardress has just been in and removed my knife. This does not matter as I have my own old hedger ...
>
> I hear Miss Garnett in the distance. On her way back from the lavatory she knocked at each door and yelled, 'Votes for women' ... I find that by putting my chair against the pipes under the window and standing on the back of it, I can see more outside ... I saw a lot of prisoners in brown dresses filing into what I take to be the laundry. Also prisoners carrying rubbish to the ash pit, and others wheeling barrows of dirty clothes ...
>
> I have been having conversations with Miss Spong in the next

cell. I can't make Kathleen Brown hear. Miss Spong says it's 10.15. How slowly time passes! I have stuffed my peephole with paper. When the doctor came, the wardresses pulled it out, but I have put it back again. I wonder how long we shall be kept in close confinement. My tie is such a comfort and inspiration. It is delightful to have the dear old colours to look at when the walls seem so close in.

The governor has just been, accompanied by the matron. He says he duly reported our wishes to Herbert Gladstone last night, but he has not yet received any reply. The position is just the same. I asked for a form of petition. The governor smelt rather of spirits; he looks rather worried . . .

The Suffragettes had prearranged the course they would follow if political prisoner treatment was not forthcoming.

. . . Finished dinner. I mounted my chair with shoe in hand. We all knocked through to each other. I smashed three panes . . . Wardresses came running. One white with rage, with several others to back her up, burst into my cell. 'Uncover your inspection hole.' 'Uncover my what?' 'Your inspection hole,' pointing to the peephole. 'No,' I said. 'No, I won't.' 'Then we shall—that is what we are here to do;' and with that she pulled out the piece of paper and flung it down into my drinking water. 'Every time you cover it up, it will be uncovered!' Bang goes the door. Another half minute and they come: 'What is your name?' Then one sees it on the card outside the door and they retire.

All is quiet now. Oh for a good square meal fit to eat!

A wardress brought a petition form and pen and ink and blotting paper . . . I've finished my petition and pulled in my belt to the tightest hole. Theresa Garnett peeped in my peephole as she passed. Just going to read—What's the matter now? It was a wardress to count the number of panes I had broken. Read until tea came—or is it supper? Another knife with 'Votes for women' scratched on it. I scratched on the other side:

> Asquith's reign has passed away,
> Winston Churchill's had his day,
> Suffragettes have come to stay,
>   Therefore give them votes.

Just as I finished it, the wardress came for the knife. Tea consisted of the usual loaf. I could only manage a few crumbs—it's so vile— my fat will soon be reduced!

A few minutes ago, someone in a cell lower down called three cheers for Mrs Pankhurst, then Christabel, then Annie Kenney. I can't make Kathleen Brown hear me . . .

Wednesday, July 14.

I hear Theresa Garnett in the distance. We are all greatly excited. Theresa has been able to make a woman in one of the adjoining gardens hear, and has told her to send word to Clement's Inn and the Press.

I waved my tie out of a broken pane to a woman at a window. Her husband came, and they brought the baby and held it up for us to see.

Christabel has been and two photographers. We all stuck something out of our windows. The drum and fife band is coming to-night and other visitors.

A magistrate has been to see Miss Spong—one of those who were about to try us for mutiny. He told her that he knew that we were right, but that he would have to punish us. We were all taken down separately. My bag and hat were taken from me by six wardresses. I told the magistrates I was not sorry for breaking windows, and that I did not intend to comply with any second-division rules, so was sentenced to seven days' close confinement, and was brought down to this cell, with nothing in it except a block of wood fixed to the wall for a chair and a plank bed and pillow . . . unbreakable opaque windows, and double iron doors—God help me to stick it! I can hear the others singing, thank goodness!

They have brought us a pint of cocoa and a lump of the usual bread. Hunger strike commences. The drum and fife band is coming at eight o'clock. I wonder if we shall hear it. We seem to be buried alive.

Thursday, July 15.

I heard a bell this morning so I dressed. Wardresses came. 'Any applications?' I asked for the governor and the doctor. I lie on the bed—I feel so weak—breakfast has just been put in. I said I didn't want any. God help me! I wonder if those outside are thinking about us. I am a coward. A day of reckoning will come for this Government. No sunshine can get into this cell and at night there is a gas jet burning over the door. Always a dull light. However, my room at Stamford and Metcalfe where I sat for four years was not much lighter than this.

I have seen the doctor. He argued with me about the unreasonableness of our conduct . . . The chaplain came. He was rather nice. He asked if there was anything I wanted. I said I wanted a good many things, and I supposed we would not be allowed a library book . . . He said he was very sorry to see us here, and I couldn't keep back a few tears when he had gone. I feel so weak. A wardress brought in a Bible, Prayer Book and Hymn Book. I read the marriage service over. I thought it would get my blood up, so I read Paul's opinion on the duties of a wife.

I suppose Mother and Father are enjoying the sea air at Bridlington. Thank God they don't know where I am. The bang of the double doors is terrible. It seems strange to think of all whom we love going about their business in the normal way while we—Oh, I do feel blubbery. I expect it's because I'm losing my strength. I'm not usually given to weeping, but I feel I should like to have a jolly good cry.

I hear knocking on the walls, and all the prisoners are shouting that they have not eaten their food. Neither have I. Dinner consisted of an egg and potatoes and a pint of milk and (oh, awful temptation!) a boiled onion. I am getting disinclined to write even.

The governor's been. I asked if yesterday's proceedings were to be considered as Herbert Gladstone's reply. He said that the visiting magistrates were a separate body, and acted on their own initiative. Herbert Gladstone had not replied. I expect the visiting magistrates get their orders from Gladstone as I saw my sentence was written down before I was tried.

Friday, July 16.

The wardress said to me this morning, 'Get your clothes on. We shall want to take your bed out.' I wonder if they will. Miss Carwin didn't have hers all day yesterday. Part of the process seems to be to degrade us by not allowing us to wash properly. This morning I have had only my drinking can of water to wash in. May Gladstone's downfall be speedy!

. . . I saw through the peephole, which was accidentally left open, Mrs Holtwhite Simmons go out of the cell opposite looking ghastly. I wonder if I look likewise. Fifty-four hours without food! God help me to hold out! I feel so choky when I think of the world outside.

Saturday, July 17.

I can't get up this morning. The cleaner came and swept out my cell. She smiled at me and it made me so weepy. The doctor has been and tried to persuade me to give up the hunger strike by saying that I was not so robust as the others. What would my mother and father say, and so on. I had to make a fool of myself after he had gone.

It is now seventy-two hours since I tasted food. The governor and matron have just been to say that Herbert Gladstone had written that he has fully considered the petitions, but sees no reason why he should take action in the matter which proves he could, if he would.

Tremendous excitement—Mary Allen has just come down to the cell next to mine. She broke more windows when she heard Herbert Gladstone's reply. It has quite bucked me up.

There has been a butterfly in my cell all day. It beat itself against the window all night and made such a noise until I got up and put it in a paper bag.

Sunday, July 18.

Had a fairly good night, but dreaming of food all the time. I feel more cheerful today. I've had quite long talks with Mary Allen through the wall. We've beaten Miss Wallace Dunlop's record! Dinner time today will be ninety-six hours without food . . .

Monday, July 19.

I had rather a bad night. The bed, I was sure, must be stuffed with stones, and my poor bones ached terribly. At a little after twelve o'clock, just after dinner had been thrust in, the hospital matron and two prisoners with a carrying chair came for me and carried me to the hospital. They put me to bed and gave me a hot-water bottle and brought me jelly, milk, and bread and butter, which of course I refused. The doctor came and talked and talked, but I wouldn't budge. Then he came and asked me where I wanted what was left of me to be sent at the end of the month. I said I did not think that there would be any to send anywhere. I gave him Clement's Inn and Miss Jones's address.

At 6.20, the governor came with the matron and said: 'Are you feeling miserable?' I said: 'Not at all, I'm very comfortable.' He said: 'Are you still obstinate?' 'Yes.' 'Well, I have some news for you—you are to be released.'

He told me to be very quiet and move about slowly, and he would send a wardress to dress me and also some brandy in a beaten egg. He said he would send to Miss Jones and see if she could take me. As soon as he had gone, I got up and waited, and at about 7.20, after the matron had brought my bag, a wardress came for me and I was taken in a cab to the Joneses.

At about eight o'clock, the drum and fife band came, and they fetched Mrs Leigh in to see me, and then Mrs Lawrence and

Christabel came just as I was put to bed. I was never so happy in my life.

The cases of Mrs Pankhurst and the Hon. Mrs Haverfield were heard again on July 9 and Lord Robert Cecil acting as defence made a strong plea that in view of the constitutional issue involved, the case should go before a higher court. The magistrate agreed, on the understanding that Mrs Pankhurst made no further attempt to send a deputation to Parliament until the case was decided. The agreement was to hold good until the end of 1909 and meanwhile all the women charged with obstruction were remanded *sine die*.

As the W.S.P.U. was now bound by an undertaking, the Women's Freedom League pursued the right to petition. A letter was sent to the King's secretary, Lord Knollys, asking for an audience with the King, but the women were referred back to the Home Secretary, and when interviewed, Gladstone expressed his regret over the present impasse, and added that in his opinion the eventual outcome would be satisfactory to women. Unsatisfied, the members of the Freedom League decided to try passive resistance and to wait outside 10 Downing Street and the House of Commons whenever Parliament was in session, until Asquith consented to receive a petition from them. At Downing Street there were intermittent arrests; and women who actually attempted to approach the Prime Minister were punished with terms of imprisonment lasting up to three weeks. Mrs Despard and Mrs Cobden Sanderson were both arrested, but their case was finally suspended on the same grounds as that of Mrs Pankhurst.

From July 5 until October 8—the end of the Parliamentary session—relays of Women's Freedom League members were on continual picket duty outside the House of Commons. The Press commented from time to time on the miraculous way in which Asquith seemed to evade the guards. When Mrs Raoul de Vismes had attained a record of five hundred and fifty-eight hours on duty, the *Daily Telegraph* wrote of her: 'For seven hours at a stretch, by day and by night, there has stood at the gate of the House a tall, slender lady dressed in a simple grey costume, and often accompanied by a splendid silver Russian boarhound.' She told a reporter:

When first I went on duty, I scarcely felt that I would be strong enough, but somehow the strength came to me. I was enthusiastic and my feeling was intensified by a sight I happened to see one night. It was bitterly cold and, in one of the alleys not far from the House,

I found in serried, double rows, some fifty homeless men stretched on the ground fast asleep. Standing upright, rocking on her feet though fast asleep, was a little woman, pitifully thin, and clad in rags of desperate poverty. So much self-respect she had preserved that she would not stretch herself on the ground. She had taken up her stand just a little way off from the rows of sleeping men and there, with arms folded, she held herself as erect as she could. To me, she seemed the type of pitiful humanity, and I thought to myself: 'If she can stand the long night through, in the driving rain, I can!'

I have learnt at the gates of the House a new sense of things, more keen than I ever could have touched, if I had led my ordinary, sheltered life.

The policemen have been most kind to us, and the London cabmen have shown us the utmost courtesy. You could not believe how many times at night a cabman has walked his horse beside us, when he thought there was the least danger of anything in the way of rudeness being shown to us.

When all the hunger strikers were released, they recounted their experiences in detail. Their descriptions of the Holloway punishment cells—underground and damp—caused embarrassment to Gladstone who was now persistently questioned in Parliament about the prison conditions. In answer to Keir Hardie and other Members, the Home Secretary denied that there was truth in the women's reports, but nevertheless, having made this statement, he soon afterwards paid a visit to Holloway. From prison officials he gathered evidence—not about the conditions, but about the behaviour of the Suffragettes in prison; and very shortly a further charge was brought against Theresa Garnett and Lilian Dove Wilcox for kicking and biting wardresses. Both women denied the charges, which arose from the struggle there had been when wardresses attempted to strip them forcibly and take them to the punishment cells.

'Now, sir,' said Theresa Garnett in court on August 4, 'I have dressed myself today exactly in the way in which I was dressed that day in Holloway, and you will notice that I was wearing this portcullis brooch on my left side.' Theresa here unbuttoned and took off the coat she was wearing. 'I suppose you could bite as well in one dress as in another,' said the magistrate. 'I have already told you that my dress was torn. You will see that it is torn close to the brooch. I think it exceedingly possible that the wardress who tore my dress received a wound in the finger from the brooch.'

The 'biting' charge was dismissed, but both prisoners were found guilty of assault, and they were sentenced to a further period in prison. Still weak from their first hunger strike, they again refused food, which was now much more difficult. They had continual fainting fits, and they were both released within a few days.

Now the W.S.P.U. felt even more convinced that some action must be taken to improve conditions in Holloway. Keir Hardie asked endless questions in Parliament and finally prevailed on Gladstone to visit the punishment cells. Accompanied by Mary Allen, the two ministers and some colleagues made a tour of inspection on August 13. Although no public report followed, a change was soon noticeable in the aspects of Holloway life about which the Suffragettes had most complained.

Every Liberal rally was now a battleground. Suffragette disturbance of meetings resulted in imprisonments and further hunger striking. Mrs Blathwayt, closely following the west of England campaign, writes on July 31:

> Vera Wentworth and Mary Phillips were arrested at Exeter and imprisoned for a week, and it is said that they are going through the hunger strike as the fourteen have done. The crowds were with them outside Lord Carrington's meeting. All resisted the police and two working men were arrested.
>
> ... Annie Kenney expects to be taken soon herself. We do not know whether the militants are right or wrong. Several were arrested—women, and men too—for breaking up Lloyd George's meeting at Limehouse. One man defender was seriously hurt and was taken to hospital.

On August 6 Mrs Blathwayt writes: 'They say Mary Phillips was released when she took to fainting. Annie had a fearful time at Poole from the mob, her cloak being torn to pieces; and a large stone hurt her head. They thought there the women were opposing Churchill in the Tory interest.'

Many of the electorate believed that votes for women were now only a matter of time and they began to speculate as to how the measure would affect current politics. The women would surely be anti-Liberal. In the *Bath Herald* a writer asked what the outcome would be when Balfour (the Conservative leader), who was highly strung, came into power and received the attention of the ladies.

On September 5 Elsie Howey, Vera Wentworth and Jessie Kenney again disturbed the Sunday peace of the Asquith family circle. On this occasion the Prime Minister was staying at Lympne Castle in Kent. The

Suffragettes confronted him after church in the morning and waylaid him in the afternoon, just as he had finished a game of golf with Gladstone. In a scuffle on the steps of the golf club the ministers, unprotected, lashed out with fists. In the evening, the Suffragettes approached the castle by boat, climbed the wall and while the family was at dinner, they shouted through the dining-room window: 'Mr Asquith, we shall go pestering you until you give women the vote.' Then they smashed the window with stones.

> How we got down off the wall and scrambled over the fences and through the ditches, I don't know [says Jessie]. We heard a commotion behind us in the castle grounds, and a man's voice on the terrace cried out: 'There they go, down the steps!' We got quietly away into our boat and looked behind us. The glare of lanterns, yellow, red, and green, flashed about the castle grounds and voices called. But they never thought of casting the light on the canal, and looking for us there, and we got away.

On September 9 Mrs Blathwayt writes:

> This morning I posted the following letter to the Secretary at 4 Clement's Inn: 'Dear Madam, With great reluctance I am writing to ask you that my name may be taken off the list as a member of the W.S.P.U. When I signed the membership paper, I thoroughly approved of the methods then used. Since then, there has been personal violence, and stone throwing which might injure innocent people. When asked by acquaintances what I think of these things, I am unable to say that I approve, and people of my village, who have hitherto been full of admiration for the Suffragettes, are now feeling very differently.'

Later on, Mrs Blathwayt says that the colonel, her husband, wrote to Christabel expressing something of the same views. The Blathwayts had always held open house to the Suffragettes. How could her husband be again seen driving Elsie and Vera, Mrs Blathwayt said. 'They seem to have behaved very badly.' On September 10 the Blathwayts received a long reply from Christabel. 'She writes very sweetly, but she thinks their methods right and she appealed to my husband as a soldier.' The colonel wrote back to Christabel asking to what limits she would go, to gain victory. If stone-throwing failed, would she resort to bombs? 'I know some of her followers would,' said Mrs Blathwayt. 'Scotland Yard sends detectives now with Asquith wherever he goes.'

On September 17 Christabel wrote in *Votes for Women*:

This is war—and the absurdity of arguing that Mr Asquith's holiday must not be marred by Suffragette protests is apparent if we compare it with the argument that an army must not attack the enemy if he is playing cards. If he had left to us the choice of battle-ground, we should elect to pursue the conflict with him at great public meetings, and at St Stephen's, but since he refuses to meet us at these, the appropriate places, we are compelled, and we are resolved, to meet him at any other place in which he can be found.

This extract was part of a long article, 'Militant Tactics to Date', in which Christabel forecast a change in Suffragette methods.

On the evening of September 17 Asquith was to address a meeting at the Bingley Hall, Birmingham. In spite of precautions—wooden barricades and padded glass—two women broke some windows of the hall by throwing stones from a house opposite. Another Suffragette made to smash one of the barricades with an axe as she led on the sympathetic crowd.

At a recent Liberal meeting in Dundee, Isabel Kelley, in gymnastic costume, had emerged through a skylight. Now, to prevent such tactics, two huge American fire escapes had been set up on either side of the Bingley Hall, and hundreds of yards of fire-hose lay along the roof. In defiance, Charlotte Marsh and Mary Leigh climbed on to the roof of a neighbouring factory, and from there proceeded to shower down missiles on the roof of the Bingley Hall while the meeting was in progress. In anticipation of an attack, the glass roof had been covered by a thick tarpaulin and the women's ammunition proved ineffective and soon ran out. They gathered a further supply by dislodging slates from the factory roof with the aid of small axes.

On arrival at Birmingham Station, Asquith left the platform in a lift usually reserved for mail bags, and as soon as he alighted he was motored to the safety of his hotel. His journey to the hall by a devious route was without incident, but his meeting was ruined by interruptions. At least twenty men among the audience had come to protest on the Suffragettes' behalf and at every apt moment they broke into the Prime Minister's speech. One by one the demonstrators were thrown out, and each time the proceedings were suspended until the stewards had completed the removal.

As Asquith left the hall, long after the scheduled time, to address an overflow meeting in another part of the city, a shower of slates from the factory roof came rattling down on to his waiting car and shattered a window and one of the lamps. The fire-hoses were turned on, but the

Suffragettes behind a chimney stack refused to move. Even when hit by volleys of bricks and stones, they still remained on the roof until three policemen finally reached them and dragged them down by the fire escape. Soaked, bleeding and exhausted, they were led off to the police station in stockinged feet. Their shoes lay abandoned on the wet and slippery tiles.

Before Asquith's train left Birmingham, an iron bar and stones were thrown at one of the carriage windows, and two more Suffragettes were arrested. Altogether nine women were convicted for their part in the Birmingham protest—Mary Leigh and Charlotte Marsh receiving the most severe sentences, four and three months' hard labour.

Bernard Shaw, with typical prophetic insight, commented on the changing face of militancy in his *Press Cuttings*, described as, 'A topical sketch compiled from the Editorial and Correspondence columns of the Daily Papers during the Women's War in 1909'. The play was produced at the Court Theatre on July 9, but it was banned by the censor. A Prime Minister character called Balsquith may alone have been enough to prevent authorised performance. Witty and amusing, the play hits hard at everyone concerned in both sides of the suffrage question.

The scene is set in the future—1912. Civil war reigns, and the curtain rises on a War Office interior. A voice is heard from outside: 'Votes for women!' The stage directions say: 'The general starts convulsively, snatches a revolver from the drawer and listens in an agony of apprehension . . .' At the conclusion, women are given votes, but not before the militant woman and the working woman are accepted by the army as assistants, and the society butterfly is put in her place. Each man meets his match, and it is in fact the forces of nature that ultimately triumph.

The Bingley Hall demonstrators were imprisoned in Birmingham's Winson Green Gaol and, for a week, they carried out a campaign of protest and hunger strike. On September 25 it was announced in the *Daily News* that the authorities at Winson Green had decided to resort to artificial means of feeding. There were also tales in the Press of solitary confinement and handcuffing.

Horrified, Mrs Pankhurst and Christabel immediately travelled to Birmingham with a solicitor, intending to take legal action on the prisoners' behalf. At the prison, they were told that communication with the Suffragettes was forbidden and that until the prisoners themselves formally requested legal representation, no solicitor would be allowed to see them. A week had elapsed before it was possible for the imprisoned

Suffragettes to instruct an adviser to take proceedings against the authorities for unjust assault.

Meanwhile, the forcible feeding process was condemned and its danger and horror were widely publicised. Speaking at a drawing-room meeting, Mrs Pankhurst said that most of the Suffragettes had been given food pumped through the nostrils, but it was known that Mary Leigh, Charlotte Marsh and Patricia Woodlock were being fed by the stomach pump. Medical experts had advised the union that resistance to the use of the stomach pump would cause serious after effects which might result in death. 'Whenever I sit down to eat,' said Mrs Pankhurst in a trembling voice, 'I think of these women.' But it was too late to turn back:

> The women who are in this movement have gone steadily forward, never taking a step that was not forced on them. Last week I was appealed to by the Liberal Press to call a halt to our agitation, I should be cowardly indeed were I to listen to this appeal.

When Keir Hardie raised the forcible feeding question in Parliament, Members roared with laughter. He wrote to *The Times*:

> I was horrified at the levity displayed by a large section of the Members of the House. Had I not heard it, I could not have believed that a body of gentlemen could have found reason for mirth and applause in a scene which, I venture to say, has no parallel in the recent history of our country.

Keir Hardie went on to state that a man died from forcible feeding in 1872. 'I would not envy the Home Secretary or Government responsible for such a result.'

H. N. Brailsford and Henry Nevinson also wrote to *The Times* announcing their resignation as leader writers in the Liberal-supported *Daily News*. 'We cannot denounce torture in Russia and support it in England, nor can we advocate democratic principles in the name of a party which confines them to a single sex.'

The strong reaction against forcible feeding failed to move Gladstone. He denied in the House that the operation was in any way dangerous, and the general public were prepared to believe his statement. When Keir Hardie pronounced in Bristol that 'Manhood must revolt at the treatment of the women in Birmingham Gaol,' Mary Blathwayt was at his meeting and could only comment afterwards: 'He is a sweet old man, but looks tired and overworked and ought to be in bed.'

On October 1 Mary received a circular from Christabel asking her, in one day, to collect signatures from as many doctors as possible to certify that forcible feeding was attended by grave danger. Mrs Blathwayt tells how Mary spent all afternoon and visited the bulk of the Bath doctors sending in her message. 'Numbers were out, and some not in favour, and none of them owned the danger. One doctor showed her the rubber apparatus now in constant use. The old instrument used to be very bad. So Mary got no signatures,' writes Mrs Blathwayt, 'and we are thankful that there is not the suffering described.'

It was not until Laura Ainsworth's release on October 5 that any definite facts about the prisoners' treatment became public. Laura was a teacher and the daughter of a school inspector. As a stone thrower, she had been taken to Winson Green on Wednesday, September 22 and for three days she took no food. Then on the Saturday morning, she was taken to the matron's room:

> There were two doctors and six wardresses in addition to the matron. The prison doctor said, 'I have orders that you are not to be released. I have to do everything in my power to feed you. I am going to commit a technical assault, and I take full responsibility for my action.' He then asked, 'Will you take food or not?' 'No,' I said emphatically. Whereupon, I was sounded, and my pulse taken. Afterwards, I was placed in a chair, my head was held back by the wardresses, and one of the doctors opened by mouth by inserting his finger between the teeth at one side. Milk was poured down my throat by means of a feeding cup. While this was being done, both my mouth and nose were held. I was then put to bed. Afterwards, the governor asked me if I had any complaints to make, and when I complained of this treatment, he simply referred me to the visiting justices.
>
> At six o'clock on the Saturday evening, the two doctors returned. I again refused to take food out of the cup, and resisted their efforts to make me take it. Then they tried to force tubes into my nostrils. There seemed to be something sharp at the end of these tubes, and I felt a sharp, pricking sensation. Owing to an injury received before going into gaol through someone hitting me on the nose with a stone, it appeared the nasal passage was closed. One of the doctors said: 'It's no good. We shall have to use the tube.'
>
> I was raised into a sitting position, and the tube about two foot long was produced. My mouth was prized open with what felt like a steel instrument, and then I felt them feeling for the proper passage. All this time, I was held down by four or five wardresses. I felt a choking sensation, and what I judged to be a cork gag was placed

between my teeth to keep my mouth open. It was a horrible feeling altogether. I experienced great sickness, especially when the tube was being withdrawn.

After these facts had been made public, Mrs Blathwayt wrote:

The forcible feeding is stirring people's feelings, and the papers are taking it up. A large number of eminent physicians have signed about the danger, and Keir Hardie always asks a number of questions in the House. One they cannot answer satisfactorily is about the disinfection of the rubber tube. Mr Masterman who answers for Gladstone may be put down as one of the brutes of the country.

Soon a poster was circulated, depicting the forcible feeding operation in gruesome detail, and on October 29 Laura Ainsworth armed herself with one of these, before going to a Liberal reception at which the Prime Minister was present. While Asquith stood unattended by a fireplace examining a picture, Laura approached, and producing her poster, she flourished it at the Prime Minister. 'Why did you do this to me?' she said. Asquith made no reply, the poster was snatched away, and two detectives led Laura from the room and took her downstairs.

As soon as the Bingley Hall protest was over, the Suffragettes prepared to demonstrate on another official occasion—Lloyd George's week-end visit to Newcastle, three weeks later. The Chancellor was to make an important Budget speech at the Palace Theatre on Saturday, October 9, and during the two weeks beforehand, the Suffragettes held endless meetings in the city and suburbs. Early in the morning the women would address the miners on their way to the pits. At midday they spoke in the shopping centre, and a full programme was organised for the afternoons and evenings.

Two days before Lloyd George's meeting, the barricades went up, and every likely building was searched for Suffragettes. But the Newcastle demonstration differed from the Birmingham one in its extremely purposeful planning. A dozen volunteers had been accepted to carry out the protest, and on the night before the Liberal rally, they met with Christabel in a Newcastle lodging-house, only a few hours before their demonstration was due to begin. It was a remarkable gathering of highly sensitive women; Lady Constance Lytton, Emily Wilding Davison and Ellen Pitfield were all later to martyr themselves for the cause. Among the other volunteers were Jane Brailsford, Kitty Marion, Dorothy Pethick, a younger sister of Mrs Pethick Lawrence, and Winifred Jones. Brailsford had accompanied his wife to the meeting: 'They faced grimly and without visible emotion, every nauseating physiological detail of the torture they were facing. Each horror was realised and calmly discussed, and beyond these, the moral pain—the violation of a forcible operation.'

Winifred Jones leaned forward and asked many questions: would the wardresses be disagreeable—would they pull down her hair and take out her tortoiseshell combs? Lady Constance felt that this pretty, fair-haired young woman had not the look of silent, unhesitating determination which gave inflexibility to the others. Mrs Pethick Lawrence had recently met Winifred Jones at a bazaar. She wore a big hat, and looked as remote as possible from stone throwing. Lady Con felt that she ought to get her out of it, and she discussed the matter with Christabel later when they were alone together at the hotel. 'Of course, if she does not feel up to it, let her stand aside,' Christabel said. 'One cannot tell how one is going to feel, she has never done anything before.'

Later on the Friday evening the Suffragettes held a public meeting in the Drill Hall. Among the audience of four thousand was a clamouring mob of students with bells, whistles and rattles. Squibs were thrown before the meeting started, and very soon Christabel abandoned any attempt to address the entire assembly and, lowering her voice, she delivered her words to the front rows and the Press, so that a report of her speech and the announcement of the demonstration appeared in all the morning papers. Shortly after midnight the first part of the protest took place when four of the chosen women broke the windows of the Liberal Club.

'I have often tried to patch up from various sources a mental picture of militant actions,' writes Brailsford. 'I have seen men do brave things on the battlefield—hot-blooded and angry—but I never could have imagined the cold and lonely bravery of this women's war. Each of the twelve did at the appointed moment precisely what she had pledged herself to do.' Brailsford was watching Winifred Jones on Saturday afternoon:

Inconspicuous and alone, she stood for a while quietly selling, or affecting to sell, *Votes for Women* outside the Palace Theatre where Lloyd George was to speak. The queues at the side doors were just beginning to form. In the front were two men only, presumably Liberal officials, and a group of curious children. Very quietly— the word is rather, 'shyly'—she drew a stone from her pocket and jerked rather than threw it at a yard's distance, through a pane of the glass door. One of the men seized her arm, a policeman came rushing forward—the deed was over, without a shout, or a cry, or a trace of excitement.

The Palace Theatre overlooked the Newcastle Haymarket, and an oblong space was strongly barricaded and guarded by police. It was here that Lloyd George was now due to arrive, and Lady Constance Lytton and Emily Davison stood in the crowd awaiting their turn to protest. Each carried in her pocket four or five stones wrapped in thin brown paper on which slogans were written. At any second they would see the Chancellor's car. Then they heard distant cheering—the crowd welcoming Lloyd George at the theatre entrance. He had come by another way. All was lost.

Suddenly, there was a stir in the crowd, and the police started to make a clearing and to open up the carriage way for an official car. The Suffragettes found themselves on the very edge of the crowd, and Lady Constance felt that she could wait no longer, that she must throw her stone. As the car drew near, she stepped out in front of it. 'How can you, who say you back the women's cause, stay on in a Government which refuses them the vote?' she cried, throwing her stone straight at the car. To avoid injuring the chauffeur or passengers, she aimed so low that she believed her stone had missed the vehicle. Unknown to her, Sir Walter Runciman was in the car, and her stone, wrapped in a paper inscribed, 'To Lloyd George—Rebellion against tyranny is obedience to God—Deeds not words', hit the radiator doing an estimated four pounds' worth of damage. Both women were immediately arrested and led gently away to the police station, Emily Davison feeling most upset that she had done nothing.

Several minutes later Brailsford watched his wife as she edged up to one of the barriers. With much diplomacy and cajoling she managed to move some children aside to avoid frightening them. Presently a large innocent-looking bunch of chrysanthemums was resting on the barrier. A few minutes later the flowers fell suddenly to the ground. Mrs Brailsford raised the axe she had hidden, and brought it down with a dull thud on the barricade. It was a symbolic revolutionary act—that, and nothing more.

Just before seven o'clock Kitty Marion and Dorothy Pethick entered the double doors of the General Post Office. Dorothy made sure that no one inside was standing near a window, and came out again as the town clock was about to strike.

I had two large stones in a big Burberry coat and at seven o'clock exactly, I threw the first stone. It hit the pane, but unfortunately I didn't throw hard enough and it only cracked it. The second stone I threw with all my might, and it went on the woodwork of the window and didn't do anything.

A little chap clumsily grabbed hold of me, very pleased to have got somebody. Then a policeman, who was evidently more experienced, came up to arrest me. 'Hold the lady properly, Bill,' he said. And the next morning he sent me in the Sunday papers.

We were all in the police cells that Saturday night. They wouldn't let us out over the week-end because Lloyd George was going to stay in Newcastle. I said to the others: 'He wants to go to the cathedral to pray for the fatherless and weary and all the desolate and oppressed; and the people who are trying to work for them, he prefers to keep in prison.'

The cells were filthy with just a urinal in the corner, and awfully dark with a high window. But oh, it was such bliss, after all those meetings, just to be able to lie back on the plank bed while they left us alone.

That night, all the drunks and disorderlies began to be shovelled in at about eleven o'clock: 'Hullo Sal! that you?' yelling to each other across the cells. 'You in now?'

On the Monday morning we were to come up for trial. The matron called us at about five o'clock. 'Come along honey, come along honey,' she said and we had to go out and wash in a corridor where there were just open basins. Lady Connie stripped to the waist, regardless of the policemen walking about, and gave herself a thorough good wash.

During the whole of the week-end in the police cells Mrs Brailsford had been mysteriously segregated in the matron's room. She was a much esteemed person, and besides being married to a prominent Liberal journalist, she had done remarkable relief work in Macedonia. Now, when they came up for trial, both she and Lady Constance were given comparatively much lighter sentences than the other women, and they were to be given second-division treatment, while all the rest were placed in the third division.

The prison matron was exceptionally considerate. Lady Con and Mrs Brailsford were placed in adjoining cells, their doors were left open, and they were only shut in by a barred gate. The matron would either accompany them at exercise herself, or she would allow them to walk unattended. On the first morning Lady Con and Mrs Brailsford noticed some broken windows. They shouted: 'Votes for women, Hurrah! Hurrah!' but were not sure of any response for they knew that some of the women had already been put in the punishment cells.

They had just returned to their own cells when there were hasty footsteps in the corridor, their doors were slammed shut and a terrible shrieking began. The noise continued for about half an hour and when it stopped, Lady Con heard steps coming towards her cell. Two white-jacketed doctors entered. 'You have been feeding our friends by force?' 'Well, yes. We were bound to have a food trial with one or two of them.' They then took her pulse, and after both had felt it, they left.

Determined to resist any attempt at forcible feeding, Lady Con stood in the corner of her cell when the doctors arrived to see her the next morning. With her arms crossed, and her fingers in her mouth and nostrils, she decided that the doctors would not be able to feed her without a struggle. The doctors had in fact come to test her heart and, later in the day, a specialist arrived from the Home Office for the same purpose. After examining Lady Con, he reported a chronic heart condition, and both she and Mrs Brailsford were released that afternoon, having barely served three days of their one-month sentence.

When Dorothy Pethick and the other women arrived in prison, they defied all the regulations:

> We refused to change our clothes. They asked us what was our name—'Votes for women'; our age—'Votes for women'; what was our religion—'Votes for women'. Our idea was to break the resistance of the prison staff, so they would say they couldn't do with us.
>
> The first time we were forcibly fed, they tried to take us down to the operating room and about six wardresses had to carry us, because we would not walk. We flayed out, and possibly hurt some of the wardresses as they flopped us down the stairs. Without being asked whether I would take food naturally, I was set on by the wardresses, flung violently into a chair, one wardress sat on my knees, and others held me down by the ankles, feet and head. The doctor was exceedingly rough. He said later: 'Of course I was not in the best of tempers. Miss Pethick was not the first I had to deal with.'
>
> They had an awful job to dig us back into our cells again, and after that they always brought the feeding equipment to us. We tried to break the process and make ourselves sick every time by putting our fingers down our throats, but it didn't always work.
>
> On the morning before my release, I had occasion to go to the reception room. It is in this room that incoming prisoners change their clothes and don prison uniform. Imagine my horror then, when near the window in an open basket tray (which had often been brought into my cell), I saw the tube lying open and exposed and

jug by the side from which the liquid was poured. We were still
being forcibly fed. There was only one tube used, and this is where
it was kept apparently in the intervals of use.

The prison doctors were careless and callous, and it was not until
within four days of my release, when the nasal passages were very
much swollen and inflamed, that the tube was dipped in glycerine
to facilitate its passage and relieve the agonising pain. They were
unnecessarily violent, and when the feeding was over, they just left
you in a kind of half sobbing condition.

One had a tight feeling like a band round one's head all the time.
The matron was very sympathetic, as far as she actually allowed
herself to show it. She once quoted to me: 'Be the day weary, be
the day long . . .' and she even brought me some scent and put
it on my forehead, because one did get a little bit swimmy.

There was an awful old chaplain. He had a long white beard
which swung in front of his greasy old waistcoat, and he stood over
me lying on the plank bed, and said how sorry he was to see me in
such a condition. I spluttered out at him: 'Oh well, the soul is more
important than the body.' 'Yes, but the body is the precious casket
in which is laid the jewel of the soul.' 'If the early Christian martyrs
had fought like you, we should not have even what Christianity
we've got left today,' I replied. 'Well,' he said, 'I counsel you—I
can only counsel you—with your magnificent physique to look
after your body. I know what a father feels like. I have (I think he
said) sixteen children.' 'I wonder if you know what a mother feels
like!' I replied. That's all he got out of me. But when he began
moithering on like this to Dora Marsden, she eyed him without a
word, until at last she said: 'If you're not out of my cell within half a
minute, you'll find yourself outside.'

I used to watch the sunset going down the side of the cell—a
streak of light—and I always had a very strong feeling of people
like Garibaldi, Mazzini and Joan of Arc with me. The night before
I was let out, the matron came in. 'It won't be long now,' she
whispered, 'only till tomorrow.' It was all she dared say.

On October 9—the same Saturday as the Newcastle protest—a peaceful
demonstration was held in Edinburgh where Suffragettes from all over
Scotland took part in a mass procession. Women pipers were trained for
the occasion, the Edinburgh W.S.P.U. arranged a series of historical
tableaux depicting famous Scottish women, and the Riding Academy
provided horses for several of the well-known Suffragette horsewomen
who came up from London. On horseback, 'General' Drummond

appeared again in public for the first time since the birth of her son, Keir. Crowds cheered and people waved from balconies as she led the procession through the centre of Edinburgh towards the Waverly Market—the covered fruit and vegetable market—where eight thousand people were expected to gather for a meeting. Mrs Pankhurst, Mrs Pethick Lawrence and Christabel were to speak. The processions had been held to rouse the spirit of women and the sympathy of the on-lookers, said Mrs Pankhurst, but the real business of the W.S.P.U. was to win the political enfranchisement of women. Whether by the pageantry, or the powerful speeches, the Scottish people were impressed and there was mass support for a Suffragette demonstration on the occasion of Churchill's visit to Dundee a fortnight later. The crowd joined with the women in an attempt to rush the barriers and five women, among them Adela Pankhurst, were arrested and imprisoned. They adopted the hunger strike, but so great was the feeling in Scotland against forcible feeding that in Dundee it did not take place.

On October 13 Mrs Pankhurst left England to carry out a lecture tour in the United States. Her son Harry was now seriously ill, and the main purpose of her journey was to raise funds so that she could afford proper medical treatment. Several months previously Mrs Pankhurst had placed Harry in an advanced agricultural college, hoping that he might make a career in scientific farming. Harry was an ardent disciple of early Socialism and believed in 'back to the land' ideals, but he was unsuited to rough farm labouring, and at the start of the training his health broke down. He contracted polio, and was brought to London to be cared for at the nursing home in Notting Hill of the faithful Suffragette Sister Pine, a former matron of St Bartholomew's Hospital. Harry was now paralysed from the waist downwards, and Sylvia was in constant attendance, but even at this critical stage, Mrs Pankhurst—ever optimistic—left for the States as planned.

The tour had been arranged with the help of Mrs Harriot Stanton Blatch, the daughter of the great American suffrage pioneer, Elizabeth Cady Stanton. Mrs Stanton Blatch had married an Englishman, she had known the Pankhurst family for many years and now, as President of the Women's Political Union of America, she was delighted to have the opportunity of welcoming her old friend to the United States. On October 20, Mrs Pankhurst disembarked in New York. 'Mrs Pankhurst has arrived, and America is characteristically disappointed,' said the British Press. The New Yorkers had pictured her as an Amazon with a cropped head, blue spectacles and a billycock hat. 'Can this pale, frail woman have terrified Mr Asquith and created an uproar in the

Commons? Why, she looks more like a quiet housewife going shopping.'

For her first appearance, on the platform at the Carnegie Hall, Mrs Pankhurst wore a violet chiffon velvet gown, lined with dull green silk and her hair was fashionably dressed. She made a strong impression on the American Press. ' "I am what you call a hooligan," she announced in a calm ladylike voice, and the audience was hers to play with. She made them laugh, she followed a laugh by bringing out sobs over the hall, and again she made those cool, refined, cultured women flush with indignation, just as she wished.' Americans always love to hear stories of how someone 'bested' someone else, and they enjoyed being told how Asquith had been forced to slide through a mail chute.

In Boston the American suffragists were waiting to meet Mrs Pankhurst when she alighted from the New York Express. A retinue of eleven cars was lined up at the station, each decorated in the colours, with the steering wheel muffled in violet and the axles smothered in purple bows. Although the Americans were at first taken aback by Mrs Pankhurst, they soon recognised her exceptional qualities and wherever she went she won admiration and sympathy.

Meanwhile, in England the forcible feeding continued, and the Home Secretary came under fire from all quarters, not only for introducing the operation, but also for his preferential treatment of Lady Constance Lytton and Mrs Brailsford. Gladstone denied that he was a 'respecter of persons', and when attacked by the Fabian Society, he argued in his defence that forcible feeding was not a seriously painful process.

Bernard Shaw, himself a Fabian, wrote to *The Times*:

It may be that Mr Gladstone is right on this point. I will, therefore, undertake to procure the co-operation of the Fabian Society in providing for Mr Gladstone a banquet which Sardanapalus himself would have regarded as an exceptional treat. The rarest wine and delicacies shall be provided absolutely regardless of expense. The only condition we shall make is that Mr Gladstone shall partake through the nose, and that a cinematograph machine shall be at work all the time registering for the public satisfaction the waterings of his mouth, the smackings of his lips and the other unmistakeable symptoms of luxurious delight with which he will finally convince us all of the truth of his assurances that the forcibly fed suffragist is enjoying an indulgence, rather than suffering martyrdom.

In spite of the terrifying prospect of forcible feeding, the Suffragettes continued to protest at every important Cabinet Minister's meeting. Emily Wilding Davison, who had failed to be imprisoned at Newcastle, was arrested at Radcliffe a fortnight later for breaking the windows of the Liberal Club during Sir Walter Runciman's visit to the town. She was imprisoned in Strangeways Gaol, Manchester.

Mary Leigh in Winson Green and Kitty Marion in Newcastle had both taken desperate measures to resist forcible feeding. Mary Leigh barricaded her door with the cell furniture, and warders with iron staves were successfully held at bay for three hours. Kitty Marion, in the same way, managed to hold out against the authorities for twenty-four hours, until they finally chiselled away the hinges of her door. Kitty Marion later gnawed a hole in her pillow, emptied out the stuffing, tore up the cell Bible, and in the early hours of the morning she broke the glass of the gas jet, lighted a spill of paper, and set fire to the heap she had made. She was already unconscious when discovered.

Emily Davison had been in prison for several days and was already undergoing forcible feeding when she was put temporarily in a cell where there were two beds:

Quick as thought, I put them down quietly lengthwise one touching the other. A space of about a foot remained which was filled by the stool, legs upward. The wedge was not absolutely firm, so I jammed in my two slippers and a hairbrush. I sat down on the only doubtful spot between the two beds, piled up the table and mattress to make weight, and my blockade was complete.

Emily sat quietly, smiling and refusing to move, while prison officials spent the afternoon imploring, threatening, and attempting to prize open the door with crowbars. They dared not break down the door for fear of crushing her.

The visiting magistrates happened to be in the prison at the time, and they were consulted.

There was an interval and then a voice called, 'Davison, if you don't get off those planks and open the door, we shall turn the hosepipe on you.' I sat perfectly calm. At last a ladder appeared at the window. Then followed a crash of glass. I looked round and saw the nozzle of a hosepipe. They took a long time to get it fixed in position, and when they had done so, the voice at the door gave me one more chance. Then came the deluge!

At first the stream shot over my head. I took hold of the bed boards and sat firm. Then they got the water trained full on me: the stream came straight at me, full force. I had to hold on like grim death. The power of the water seemed terrific, and it was as cold as ice. For an age it seemed to play on me, though it may have been only a quarter of an hour and my gasps for breath were getting more and more spasmodic. At last the operator halted for a moment, and a voice called out quickly: 'Stop! No more! No more!'

Then they determined to burst open the door. It was clear to me that if the door fell it would kill me on the spot. The thought in my mind was that the moment for the sacrifice, which we have all agreed will probably be demanded, was at hand and, strange to say, I had no fear. Those outside, however, had also realised the danger. They called out: 'If you don't move off that plank, you will be seriously hurt.' The door gave! I watched it, fascinated. As it lurched, however, hands seized it. The gap widened. A male warder rushed in and seized me, saying as he did so: 'You ought to be horse-whipped for this.' The bed board was taken up, the door opened, and the water (about six inches deep) rushed out into the corridor.

Emily was stripped by the matron and wardresses, wrapped in blankets and taken to the hospital. Here she remained—still being forcibly fed—until her release three days later. To her surprise, she found the hosepipe incident known throughout England and being brought up in Parliament.

Churchill was to speak in Bristol on Colston Day, November 19, and several of the best-known Suffragette speakers arrived some days beforehand to help Annie Kenney work up sympathy among the west country people. Three of the released Newcastle prisoners—Dorothy Pethick, Ellen Pitman and Kathleen Brown—came to stay in Bristol, and Elsie Howey and Vera Wentworth joined them. Mary Blathwayt took on housekeeping for the workers, and helped with the organisation of meetings and publicity. Thousands of handbills were distributed, giving details of the Bristol Franchise Riots of 1831, when one hundred thousand pounds' worth of property was destroyed.

The plans for the demonstration on the nineteenth were secret, but Mary, in any case, was always kept in the dark on militancy because her family condemned violent methods. However, on the day itself, she wrote in her diary: 'Last night at a little past one in the morning, Miss K. Brown arrived in a taxi. I heard the taxi and opened the door and let her in. Annie and Elsie Howey were up and about all night in the town.'

Theresa Garnett volunteered to take part in the demonstration. She decided to go to Bath, and from there she would later join the train on which Churchill was to travel. She carried out her plan, but couldn't see him anywhere so at Bristol she got out and made for the ladies' room which was exactly opposite:

I wondered, what to do now? Where is he? Why hadn't he come? There were a whole lot of policemen on the platform and they were keeping it pretty clear, so I stayed where I was, and after a few minutes another train came along which had been an express with no stops. Churchill had arrived with twelve detectives and he got out exactly opposite where I was hiding.

I had a riding switch. I had no intention of using it. I was only 'going through the motions', as they say in the Army. So I went out with the switch which I had kept up my sleeve and I said, holding it in my hand, 'Mr Churchill, what about votes for women?' Of course, they all pounced, and the detectives by that time had got up to me. One pulled me by my 'Merry Widow' hat, they got the whip and it was broken in two in the struggle.

I was charged with assaulting Mr Churchill. 'All right,' I said, 'I'll have him in court as a witness,' because I hadn't attempted to hit him. So they changed the charge to disturbing the public peace, and I was sentenced to a month in prison. While I was in prison, I heard that Churchill had asked for the whip as a souvenir, so I asked for it back, and the matter was taken up by a solicitor. When Churchill heard about this, they say he hastily returned it to the police. But the case was taken to court, and the magistrate said: 'I won't give the whip to either of them. It isn't Mr Churchill's property and if I give it to Miss Garnett, she will only put it in the window of their shop in Bristol and it will be used to ridicule a Cabinet Minister, so we will retain it.'

During Churchill's visit four other women were arrested for damage to public buildings and, throughout his speech at the Colston Hall, Churchill was continually heckled by young men who supported the Suffragettes. In Bristol, however, there was an equally strong group in opposition to the women, and these men were determined to attend the important Suffragette meeting which was to take place at the Colston Hall a few days later, on November 24.

Mary Blathwayt went to help decorate the hall in the morning and in the evening she saw the meeting broken up.

Annie Kenney was in the chair and Christabel was the speaker. Hundreds of students came. Mr Risely played something on the organ first of all, and the students sang, 'For he's a jolly good fellow'. The hall was packed with people. A woman was led out, bleeding at the mouth; someone had thrown down something from above which exploded as it struck her, nearly blinding her.

I arranged the literature on the table. The students tried to rush the platform, and we carried the literature away to a back room and took down the decorations. One girl's hand got knocked by a collecting box and bled a good deal. The students threw flour over Annie and Christabel and made their hair quite white. Not a word could be heard all the evening—people were making such a noise.

By the time Mrs Pankhurst returned from America in early December, the political state of the country was in upheaval. There were differences between the Commons and the Lords, involving the proposed Budget, and a general election was imminent.

Cabinet Ministers were severely hampered in their electioneering. During Churchill's tour of his constituency, in spite of the hundreds of pounds spent on measures for his protection, his meetings were still interrupted and all his election advertisements were covered with Suffragette, forcible feeding posters and 'Double-Face Asquith' propaganda bills.

Churchill was expected to lunch at the Queen's Hotel in Southport on December 4, but perhaps he had a suspicion that Mrs Duncan of Brixton was concealed in the luncheon room behind a curtain holding a portable hose full of water, for he gave up his lunch and went for a walk instead. Later that day Dora Marsden with two other Manchester members interrupted Churchill's meeting in the Southport Empire, by calling down at him through the roof.

Realising that it was impossible to ignore the women during his campaign, Churchill was now perfectly civil when unavoidably tackled by Suffragettes. The *Daily Dispatch* reported: 'Considerable comment has been aroused by the marked change of front of at least two members of the Cabinet, notably Lloyd George and Churchill, who have suddenly become solicitous that the ladies should be treated with every courtesy.'

During November Suffragette persistence had become more than just a personal embarrassment to Cabinet Ministers. On November 11 Lloyd George and his family attended a performance of *The Mountaineers* at the Savoy to hear C. H. Workman sing the 'Chancellor' and the 'Budget' songs, to which topical encore verses had recently been added. Just as Workman began: 'If I were Chancellor . . .' a banner inscribed, NO STOMACH TUBES, was let down from the balcony stalls by a group of Suffragettes in evening dress. 'Down with tyranny!' called a woman waving a feeding tube in Lloyd George's direction. The audience groaned. Again and again the chorus repeated the refrain against hisses and shouts, while Lloyd George sat gazing fixedly at the stage.

After the incident Christabel wrote a letter of apology to Workman, explaining that the protest was brought about by the presence of Lloyd George. She ended: 'Our friends have told me how greatly they enjoyed the performance and how exceedingly sorry they were to be obliged to intervene with their protest. They look forward to revisiting the Savoy under happier circumstances.'

Asquith and his wife, Churchill, and R. B. Haldane, the Secretary for War, were guests at the Lord Mayor's Banquet on November 10 when a protest occurred that considerably shocked the public. Amelia Brown and Alice Paul, an American Suffragette, managed to enter the Guildhall early on the morning of the banquet disguised as kitchen-maids. After hiding all day under some benches, they finally emerged when the guests were seated at table, and made their way to a staircase which led on to the public gallery. Just as the Lord Mayor was proposing a toast to the King, there was a smashing of glass and fragments from one of the stained-glass windows flew down on to the tables and the floor. Amelia Brown had thrown her shoe through one of the panes.

There was a rush for the roof. Firemen, police and guests in evening dress scrambled over dirty wooden beams expecting to find the women there. It was several minutes before a scarlet-uniformed officer with a sword discovered the Suffragettes standing by their window, keeping up a cry of 'Votes for women', while the band played the National Anthem to drown the call which was coming through to the guests. 'Mrs Asquith who sat at the right of the Lord Mayor looked frightened and angry, while her husband had an expression like that of the smile on a figure of carved marble.'

The women appeared before one of the aldermen at the Guildhall Police Court next day: 'I really don't understand how you hysterical creatures expect to promote the movement you are intent upon, by coming to the City and damaging our historic buildings. You don't seem to have any plea or justification for your conduct.' The women were sentenced to one month's hard labour and as soon as news of Alice Paul's imprisonment reached America, a deputation was formed to go to Washington for consultation with President Taft. Mrs Pankhurst said that the American men had been appalled by tales of British prison treatment. 'What are Englishmen doing?' they had asked. 'It couldn't happen in America. We wouldn't allow it.'

It was now an important moment to impress upon the British electorate that the women's demand was reasonable. On December 9—the day after Mrs Pankhurst's return from America—she spoke about the situation at the Albert Hall. 'Some men still look on the movement with a smile,' she said. 'There seems to be something inherent in men, that must be changed before they can realise that these things mean to women what they say they do. I am glad that the women of today stand on their own rights. That is the way of the younger woman,' but it was the work of the older woman, she said, to persuade men of the need for men and women to record their votes and choose their rulers together.

Rather than appeal for restraint in view of the election, the leaders tackled the situation by maintaining calm, and by impressing on all speakers and workers the importance of educational suffrage propaganda.

On the day that Mrs Pankhurst sailed from America, the Lord Chief Justice gave judgement against her in the case involving the right to petition. A fine of five pounds was imposed which Mrs Pankhurst refused to pay, but by the time she reached England the sum had already been settled anonymously. Mrs Haverfield was also fined, and the Government, unwilling to revive the outdated issue, dismissed the cases of the ninety-two other women who were expecting trial for their part in the Bill of Rights deputation.

On December 9 another important case was heard in the High Court. Mary Leigh, on her release from prison, brought an action for assault against the Home Secretary and the governor and doctor of Winson Green Gaol. The Court finally reached the decision that the authorities' treatment of Mary Leigh was justified, in that it had been necessary to safeguard her life. This ruling against her now set a precedent for the continuation of forcible feeding of Suffragettes in prisons all over the country.

The end of December was a weary time for the Pankhursts. Harry was now completely paralysed and although the family in no way allowed their personal affairs to interfere with the business of the movement, all the workers knew that there was no hope for Harry's recovery. When he died, no fuss was made, but *Votes for Women* of January 7 included a short message of sympathy, and the classified advertisements section was headed: 'DEATH—PANKHURST. On January 5, HARRY FRANCIS PANKHURST, aged 20, only son of Mrs Pankhurst.'

Sylvia says that at the funeral her mother was broken as she had never seen her. 'Huddled together without a thought for her appearance, she seemed an old, plain, cheerless woman. Her utter dejection moved me more than her vanished charm.' Too grief-stricken to face the situation, Mrs Pankhurst left Sylvia to arrange the placing of a stone on her child's grave. 'Choose something you like,' she said as she left to embark on the election campaign. 'And Sylvia, remember, when my turn comes, I want to be put with my two boys!'

On January 9 Mrs Pankhurst was about to visit Bradford and she wrote to the organiser:

> If you can arrange it, I would be grateful if Bradford friends would just behave to me as if no great sorrow had come to me just now. It breaks me down to talk about it although I am most grateful for sympathy. I want to get through my work and I know you will all help me to do it.

In spite of the forthcoming election, younger members of the W.S.P.U. continued to demonstrate on every opportune occasion. On December 10 Jessie Kenney, disguised as a messenger boy, tried to get into a Liberal rally at the Albert Hall, where Asquith was speaking. The police, knowing Jessie well, were suspicious when they noticed her unmanly hands, and she was soon recognised and hastily turned away when a tress of hair escaped from under her cropped wig.

A few weeks later a woman in disguise did in fact succeed in getting into a meeting of Asquith's at the Dome in Brighton. Bessie Newsam, wearing collar and tie, her husband's coat, cloth cap and boots, was admitted to the hall, and in the middle of the proceedings she stood up and called: 'What about the women, Mr Asquith?' Asquith stopped short, and the audience laughed and cheered.

It was the season for masquerading. Vera Wentworth and Elsie Mackenzie were discovered lying in wait for Lloyd George at the Albert Hall, Swansea, with housebreaking implements, a toy pistol, and a lantern of the most up-to-date variety.

When Asquith visited Liverpool just before Christmas, Selina Martin disguised herself as a match seller and Leslie Hall as an orange girl. Leslie Hall had a catapult and special missiles which she did not in fact use, for both women were arrested after Selina Martin had broken one of the windows of Asquith's car. Probably because it was Christmas time, the magistrate, when they were brought up for trial, remanded the women for a week on the pretext of making enquiries about them, but no bail was allowed and they were imprisoned in Walton Gaol.

Selina Martin's refusal to comply with any of the prison regulations so exasperated the authorities that in a fury they threw her on the floor and handcuffed her with her hands behind her back. Then, taking her by the legs and arms and pulling her by the hair, the wardresses dragged Selina, face downwards, to be forcibly fed upstairs. 'Does *that* hurt you?' asked the doctor as he forced a gag into Selina's mouth. When the operation was over, she walked alone to the top of the stairs, but then refused to return to the punishment cell. A wardress kicked her from behind, and others pulled her roughly some way down the stairs. Near the bottom they let go of her arms and, still handcuffed, she fell forward on her head. Helpless, she was picked up and carried to her cell.

All this occurred while Selina Martin was still on remand. After her trial, she was put into a canvas straitjacket, and her cell was continuously guarded. Nevertheless, she managed to scratch on the wall: 'Torture Chamber! No Surrender! Freedom's Cause till Death!' When the writing was discovered, her cell door was screwed back so that she was permanently overlooked by relays of wardresses.

The W.S.P.U. did everything possible to publicise the outrage and pamphlets were printed exposing the prison authorities, but Gladstone denied all allegations, and the Press showed little interest in the affair. The seasonal frivolities and the forthcoming election were foremost in the public mind; the wave of indignation about the treatment of prisoners on remand was allowed to pass, and after the women had been sentenced, their imprisonment was left to take its course.

'These are women quite unknown—nobody cares about them except their own friends,' said Mary Gawthorpe with tears in her eyes. She was speaking to Lady Constance Lytton who had come to Manchester to help with the election campaign. 'That was enough,' says Lady Constance. 'My mind was made up. The altogether shameless way I had been preferred against the others at Newcastle made me determine to try whether they would recognise my need for exceptional favours without my name.'

Following in the tradition of the Holloway protest marches, the provincial organisers arranged weekly demonstrations outside the prisons where women were being forcibly fed. 'These were not being held during the elections,' said Lady Con, 'but I told the Liverpool organisers that if they would have one more of these meetings on Friday, January 14, it was my intention to go in disguise, call upon the crowd to follow me to the governor's house, and insist upon the release of the suffrage prisoners.'

Lady Con joined the W.S.P.U. again, filling up the membership card as Miss Jane Warton. She chose the surname when an appreciative relative, a Mr F. Warburton, wrote to her after her Holloway imprisonment, and decided then that she would assume his name if ever the need arose. Now she felt that 'Warburton' sounded too distinguished, so she left out the 'bur' and made it 'Warton'. Her idea was to transform herself into the *Punch* version of a Suffragette, for she knew from experience that the prisoners who looked unprepossessing were the worst treated.

On the morning of the fourteenth Lady Con was in Manchester. She had her hair cut short and arranged in early Victorian style, and she bought an entirely new outfit of clothes to suit Jane Warton, spinster and seamstress. Each part of the disguise came from a different shop, and Lady Con even went to the length of buying name tapes embroidered 'J.W.' to sew on her underclothing to replace her own initials. Already in disguise, complete with pince-nez, purse and net bag, she left Manchester by train in the afternoon.

Only the local organisers knew her identity when she arrived in Liverpool. Some sympathetic members had been told that Jane Warton was going to make a protest and they were asked to give her a meal, and to escort her to the gaol where the protest meeting was to be held. Before leaving their house, Lady Constance gathered several stones from the garden and wrapped them in purple W.S.P.U. handbills.

All through the day I had been dogged by the nightmare thought that I should be too late. As we neared the place, a crowd of about two to three hundred were following the carriage in which were our speakers. It had been arranged that I should mix with the crowd, not join with the speakers, but at the end of the meeting should have my say from below. I passed the carriage to report myself to the organisers. Many of our members were standing around, but I think they did not recognise me, except for my voice later on.

The Press reported: 'Miss Flatman and Mrs Baines addressed the crowd, and then a delicate-looking woman came forward, and in a clear voice spoke in a way that much moved her audience.' Lady Con reminded the people how the men of Dundee had protested against forcible feeding. Could not Englishmen do the same? The Home Secretary has denied responsibility and asserted that it rested with the prison officials. She called on the men of Liverpool to put this to the test, and go with her to the governor of the prison to demand the women's release. The governor's house was a separate building surrounded by a small garden, and as Lady Con began to lead off in that direction, to her surprise, the crowd followed.

I shouted out to them: 'No violence, remember, but call for the governor, and refuse to be dispersed until you have secured the release of the prisoners.'

I took to running and urged on the crowd. The police then took hold of me. As for once it was my object above all else to get arrested and imprisoned, I began discharging my stones, not throwing them, but limply dropping them over the hedge into the governor's garden.

One stone happened to fall on the shoulder of a man who was passing.

Although he was not hurt, this accident was enough to constitute a charge against Lady Con, and the police marched her away to the station.

Elsie Howey and a Mrs Nugent recognised Lady Con's voice and they were determined that she should not go to prison alone. While her companion stood guard, Elsie Howey poked the staff of the flag she had been carrying through a window of the governor's house. They, too, were arrested and taken to join Lady Con. Mrs Nugent had assumed her name for the occasion, and she was in reality the wife of a town magistrate. She looked most distinguished and the police were obviously curious as to her identity. Anxious to divert all attention from Lady Con, the women played up to the situation, and addressed Mrs Nugent as 'Princess'. At midnight, however, the police were enlightened when her husband arrived in great distress to see her.

In the early hours of the morning the Suffragettes were taken out of the cell and lined up for examination in a room where several other women prisoners were waiting. As one by one they had to go before a policeman who noted down their particulars, Lady Con began to play her part:

It was the turn of Jane Warton. She walked across to the policeman, one shoulder hitched slightly above the other, her hair sticking out straight behind and worn in slick bandeaux on either side of her face, her hat trailing in a melancholy way on her head. The large, grey woollen gloves were drawn up over the too short sleeves of her coat; on the collar of it were worn portraits of Mrs Pankhurst, Mrs Lawrence and Christabel in small china brooches; her hat had a bit of tape with *Votes for Women* written on it, interlaced with the cloth plait that went round it, and eye-glasses were fixed on her nose.

'It's a shame to laugh at one of your fellow prisoners,' said the policeman behind the desk, hushing the other women, who had started to titter.

Next morning the prisoners were tried. Mrs Nugent was released, Elsie Howey was given six weeks' hard labour because of her previous convictions, and Jane Warton was sentenced to fourteen days' hard labour in the third division. After four days of fasting, Lady Con was forcibly fed, and this time there was no medical examination. 'The horror of it was more than I can describe.' The doctor who had handled Selina Martin so roughly knelt on Lady Con's knees to feed her. Wardresses held her down, and she was violently sick all over them.

It seemed a long time before they took the tube out, and as the doctor left, he gave me a slap on the cheek.

Suddenly I saw Jane Warton lying before me, and it seemed as if I were outside of her. She was the most despised, ignorant and helpless prisoner that I had seen. When she had served her time and was out of prison, no one would believe anything she said, and the doctor when he had fed her by force and tortured her body, struck her on the cheek to show how he despised her! That was Jane Warton, and I had come to help her.

Lady Con, unlike the other women, offered little resistance. On the second day of forcible feeding she said to the doctor: 'Unless you consider it part of your duty, would you please not strike me when you have finished your odious job?' The doctor gradually softened, but whenever the feeding took place, Lady Con was practically asphyxiated. On the third occasion, she had a shivering fit, and the doctor, alarmed, called in a junior colleague to test her heart. The junior listened for a moment through a stethoscope. 'Oh, ripping, splendid heart!' he exclaimed. 'You can go on with her.' When he had gone, the doctor pleaded with her: 'You are absolutely unfit for this kind of thing. How could your union send a woman like you?' Lady Con gave no reply, though the following day she told the doctor that her action was entirely unprompted.

On her first day in prison Lady Con had written on the cell wall with slate pencil, and dirt mixed with soap: 'Votes for Women', and a quotation from Thoreau's *Duty of Civil Disobedience*: 'Under a Government which imprisons any unjustly, the true place for a just man (or woman) is also in prison'. Opposite the bed she scratched: 'Only be thou strong and very courageous'. For this offence, and also for breaking the glass of her gas jet as a protest, Lady Con was called to appear before the visiting magistrates. She was reprimanded, and her own complaints to them were cut short. It was only later that she was able to explain to the governor that she suffered from a slight chronic heart disease, and that she had been fed by force without any tests being made.

She also spoke to the governor about the doctor's slapping her.

He did not hurt me, but seemed to wish to show his contempt. I do not wish to complain as of an insult to me personally; I am an abnormal-looking woman with short hair, and if a man has anything of the schoolboy left in him, it is understandable that he should consider me fair game for his contempt. He no doubt was irritated by his repulsive job, but this is hardly the mood for an official, and what he could do to one woman, of no matter what type, he might possibly do to another.

Within a week Lady Con lost strength. At each feeding the process was more painful, until at last she wrenched out the tube one day, and broke down, sobbing. From this moment, the attitude of the authorities changed. They were, in any case, beginning to suspect her identity. A report was sent to the Home Office, and the governor, hoping to discover who she really was, suggested to Lady Con that she should write to her mother. Upset by the idea, and in a great state of indecision, she finally decided to send a letter. She announced her intention of eating breakfast that morning so that she would have the strength to write, and she drafted a message to her mother on her slate, making no complaint, except of the pain of forcible feeding.

The letter was never sent, for on the same Saturday—January 25—the Press Association heard a rumour that Lady Constance was imprisoned in Liverpool and sent a message to her brother, Lord Lytton, asking if there was any truth in the report. He passed on the message to his sister, Lady Emily Lutyens, who received it on Saturday evening as she was dining. Immediately, Lady Emily telephoned the Home Office, identified the suspect Jane Warton as her sister, and left for Liverpool by the midnight train. She arrived at Walton Gaol at six o'clock on Sunday morning, and later the same day Lady Con was released.

For a day or two, she struggled to recover. With great effort, she wrote letters to the newspapers, and a report to the Home Office giving accounts of the treatment she had received as Jane Warton. One week after her release, she managed to speak at a Queen's Hall meeting, but on the following day, February 1, she fell ill. Her heart had been seriously affected by forcible feeding, and for six weeks she was confined to bed. No visitors were allowed, and even her correspondence was put aside.

Lord Lytton took up his sister's case, and both he and H. N. Brailsford wrote long letters to the Press and the Home Office, but now that the general election was imminent, there was little public interest in the matter. Gladstone denied that there was any foundation for Lady Con's allegations, and shortly afterwards he was relieved of all his Home Office duties on his elevation to the peerage, to serve as Governor-General of South Africa. By this means, Lord Lytton was completely prevented from challenging any of the Home Office authorities concerned in the Jane Warton episode.

Lord Lytton persevered in his efforts while a Liberal Government was re-elected to power. Winston Churchill had replaced Gladstone as Home Secretary, and in April, while staying with Lord Lytton for a week-end at Knebworth, he was persuaded to look through all the papers concerning Lady Con's case. He finally reached a decision when he came to the report of the letter on the slate, which gave no indication of the alleged treatment. ' 'Twould be hopeless,' he said, 'to bring forward any complaint with this letter in the background.'

Chapter Six: A Truce from Militancy 1910

THE CONCILIATION BILL—THE 'SUFFRAGETTE REST'—SUFFRAGE
SOCIETIES UNITE—'FROM PRISON TO CITIZENSHIP'—SUCCESS
ANTICIPATED—A SHATTERING CRITICISM OF THE BILL.

'The elections are going against the Liberals, and their sins come home
to them one after another,' wrote Mrs Blathwayt in her diary on January
24. The Liberals lost many seats and, among all the election results in
the newspaper, Mrs Blathwayt had just read of Lady Constance Lytton's
release. In their garden, in a prominent place overlooking the road, the
Blathwayts had displayed the W.S.P.U. election poster:

THE RIGHT DISHONOURABLE
DOUBLE-FACE ASQUITH—
KEEP THE LIBERAL OUT.

'Last night people coming home called out under our house: "Good old
Suffragettes!" and cheered three times, so we were not surprised to hear
this morning that both Unionists were in.'

Lord Lytton had achieved little success in taking up his sister's case, and
now he and Brailsford began to work on a constructive plan to bring the
women's suffrage question before Parliament as an inter-party measure.
They formed a conciliation committee—a group made up of thirty-
seven members from all political parties, but predominantly Liberal, and
Brailsford, the one non-parliamentary member of the committee, drafted
the Conciliation Bill. In order to satisfy the particular objections of all
parties, the Bill did not propose to give votes to women as John Stuart
Mill had advocated, 'on the same terms as men', but it was designed to
enfranchise about one million women who occupied premises for which
they were responsible. The single woman, whatever her class, was in the
group most likely to benefit by the terms. 'Christabel would agree to the
Bill if others do,' wrote Mrs Blathwayt.

In view of the conciliation proposals, Mrs Pankhurst and the Women's
Freedom League formally declared a truce from militancy a week before
Parliament reassembled. At the opening, on February 21, there was no
mention of women's suffrage, but the truce was held. The Suffragettes
were exhausted. At the end of 1909 militancy had reached a dangerous
point; anxiety was telling on the leaders and organisers and although
many of the militants were ready to fight on, the leaders were loth to

adopt the warlike measures they had pledged to use should a continuation of militancy be necessary. A period of comparative rest and peaceful campaigning would allow the Suffragettes to redeem their good name and gain support for the proposed Bill.

The eager militant forces were kept busily occupied. Organisers and workers all over the country were asked to raise funds and boost the sale of *Votes for Women* and suffrage literature. In the provinces and in every small town Suffragettes were advised by headquarters to hold drawing-room meetings, speak in small halls and school rooms, and anywhere out of doors where they could assemble an audience. At least once a week a prominent speaker or ex-prisoner would arrive to support the local organisers at a large public meeting. Handbills to advertise the event had to be printed and distributed, and on the preceding days it was the organisers' job to work up the meeting and secure a good attendance by rousing local enthusiasm. Bicycle parades became a very popular means of advertising. About a dozen men and women would set out on decorated cycles, heavily placarded with details of the coming meeting. They rode in file along the country lanes singing the Women's Marseillaise, and when they arrived at an open space or a village green, they would dismount, and from an improvised platform encourage the local people to come and hear the distinguished Suffragette speaker.

Mrs Pankhurst had travelled extensively throughout the election, and when it was over she continued to tour the country addressing two or three meetings each day. Her mother, Mrs Goulden, died in the Isle of Man on April 23, and the Press reported: 'Mrs Pankhurst was looking war worn. She bore the mark of sorrow too, after the recent loss of her only son and aged mother.'

The Pethick Lawrences realised that some of the other leading women were suffering from the strain of the past months, and they often invited speakers and workers to come and recuperate at Holmwood. In the *Daily News* an article appeared about their house, The Mascot, which was termed 'the unofficial headquarters of the W.S.P.U.'

Its unpretentious Dutch-like front hides a beautiful lawn and garden where M.P.s, tired work girls, ladies of fashion and Labour leaders have played and plotted. Bowling matches take place between leading Suffragettes and M.P.s, and the editor of *Votes for Women* keeps herself physically fit with the racquet. At the further end of the garden stands a high tree, up which has been built a platform where budding speakers can try their lungs amid romantic surroundings.

One or other of the two motor-cars especially kept by Mr and Mrs Lawrence at the service of 'The Cause' generally brings down from town at the week-end some of the most prominent of the Suffragettes. What Rapley, the chauffeur, does not know about the W.S.P.U. is not worth knowing, but if you attempt to draw him out, he has the habit of closing the discussion with the crushing phrase of, 'I don't think.'

After dashing about the country for election meetings Annie Kenney was so tired out that the Pethick Lawrences sent her to take a holiday with Christabel in Sark. Sylvia was still grieving for Harry, and in April Mrs Pethick Lawrence took her and Annie to Oberammergau where they actually stayed at the house of Anton Lang who was playing Christ in the Passion Play.

In spite of their disapproval of militancy, the Blathwayts still welcomed Suffragette visitors. The colonel had served in the Indian army and now, in retirement, he had become a keen scientist. His garden at Eagle House, Batheaston, lay on a steep grassy slope and as an expert on rare shrubs and trees, he decided to plant an arboretum of evergreens to commemorate the women who had fought and been imprisoned for the cause. From time to time he invited one or two of the best-known Suffragettes to visit Eagle House, and during her stay each prisoner would plant a species of fir tree, while the militants who had not been to prison planted hollies. To one side of the arboretum Colonel Blathwayt had built a large summer-house known as the 'Suffragette Rest'. The shelter was used as a place of retreat where Suffragettes could read or prepare work, and inside there was even a small platform where less experienced speakers could practise. As each Suffragette planted her tree, the colonel recorded the event with his camera. He was a skilled photographer and he also made careful portrait studies—full face and side view—of most of the women who came to stay.

Annie Kenney, as west of England organiser, spent much of her spare time at Eagle House and for three years she was virtually a second daughter to the Blathwayts. They did all her chores, Mary kept Annie's accounts, and the colonel would often assist her in historical research for her speeches. Annie's sisters were also welcomed at Batheaston, and visits by the Kenney family always enlivened the Blathwayt household. Regularly after dinner every evening there was singing and although the elderly colonel occasionally found Jessie and Annie 'very happy but a trifle wild', he would take the girls out for local drives in 'Bodo', his Oldsmobile. In the summer of 1910 Kitty and Jenny Kenney, teachers, spent several months at Batheaston. They arrived originally to convalesce from illness, but while staying at Eagle House they both had to undergo operations, and they were nursed back to health by the Blathwayts.

During the period of waiting before the Conciliation Bill was read in Parliament, the non-militant societies massed together their forces as never before, and everywhere women joined in propaganda work for the Bill. By the beginning of May, however, hopes for its being given a hearing began to fade. Parliamentary differences had arisen between the Lords and the Commons and there was talk of another general election.

Just when the situation seemed to have reached a complete impasse, a national crisis changed everything. On May 7 'muffled toll and flag half-mast', announced the death of the King. He had returned unwell from a holiday in Biarritz. 'It was bronchitis,' wrote Mrs Blathwayt, 'which seems to have been chronic, but the King was not laid up and didn't stay in bed, but went on with business to the last.' Immediately the two Parliamentary Houses were united, and temporarily, everyone became involved in the national situation. Mary Blathwayt hurried into Bath by tram and bought a black coat and skirt and when her mother went into town later, every draper's shop was filling the window with black things. Mrs Blathwayt bought some ribbon for her hat, but decided that her grey dresses would have to do. 'It is a good example to set,' she said.

Two days later, Mrs Blathwayt wrote: 'The papers are full of George V and Queen Mary. She seems very good and has simple habits, and thinks of the poor. Perhaps now something may be done for the women.' In any case the outlook for the Conciliation Bill was much more hopeful, as Parliament, having temporarily dropped its own contentions, was left with ample time for the consideration of other questions. The Bill was to be introduced on June 14, and a massive march of all suffrage societies had been planned to take place prior to that date, but because of the King's death the demonstration had to be postponed. There was now a prevailing feeling that the country should be united over national issues and when the conciliation proposals were made public, they gained an unforeseen measure of approval.

On June 14 when D. J. Shakleton put the Bill before the House, the Women's Liberal Federation were holding their annual council meeting in London. When they heard that the Bill had met with overall support in Parliament—that the vote on it had been carried unanimously without a division—they were delighted, and Lady Carlisle announced that a message would be sent at once to the Prime Minister to press for further facilities for the Bill. Mrs Wiles, the wife of the Member for Islington, was so anxious to deliver the message that she suggested that the council should go immediately as a body to the House, to show that they were in real earnest. 'You would be denied admittance,' said Lady Carlisle. 'If the council wishes to send any deputation, they will have to go after the Parliamentary work is done.' 'May we not forgo the lunch hour?' 'I have never been at a council meeting where the women were willing to forgo their lunch,' said Lady Carlisle. Mrs Stuart Brown settled the question by saying that a deputation in force would only come in contact with the police, tactics which the federation had continually deplored. Finally the Liberal women sent a message asking Asquith to receive a deputation, and this was acknowledged with a favourable reply. A date for their reception was given—Tuesday, June 21.

Meanwhile, the franchise demonstration that had been postponed was now to take place on Saturday, June 18. The W.S.P.U. planned to make this the greatest procession ever seen. In recent months there had been a gloom on public spectacles—even Ascot was 'all black'—but now that the period of full mourning for the King was over, the women planned to dress in white for their procession, and to carry bunches of garden flowers in the colours.

On the Saturday evening vast crowds assembled, and as the marchers formed up to go to the Albert Hall, the line of suffrage supporters stretched along the Victoria Embankment from end to end. Dressed in black, with a flowing white robe and a white plumed hat, Mrs Pankhurst strode at the head of a column of six hundred and seventeen women each representing a term of Suffragette imprisonment. They carried long wands tipped with silver-gilt broad arrows that glinted in the sun. Above them hung a great banner designed by Laurence Housman: FROM PRISON TO CITIZENSHIP.

The suffrage pioneers—white-haired old ladies—came next in the procession and following, between the forty bands, were one hundred and thirty more contingents from all nations and ranks of society. Upright and slender, carrying a sheaf of white lilies, Mrs Despard headed the Women's Freedom League. The graduates were led by Dr Elizabeth Garrett Anderson—the first woman to qualify in the medical profession, and also the first woman mayor. The array of caps and gowns astonished the onlookers who had no idea that there were so many 'clever women'.

Wearing the pink and green of the Franchise League, the actresses carried their rose-twined staves with theatrical panache and whenever the procession halted, the gymnasts marked time in perfect step. Beside these vivacious groups the sweated workers in their Sunday best looked emaciated and bedraggled. An American contingent was led by Miss M.

Roosevelt, a second cousin of the ex-President, and a section of the newly formed Men's Political Union walked behind another of Laurence Housman's banners: WE FIGHT THE GOVERNMENT THAT REFUSES TO GIVE WOMEN THE VOTE. Brailsford was among the men, and also A. J. Webbe, the cricketer, who had left the Middlesex versus Yorkshire match in order to be able to take part in the procession.

By nine o'clock the long file reached the Albert Hall, and the men and women poured into the decorated auditorium until every place in the house was taken. The leaders were seated on the platform with Lord Lytton at their side. Mrs Pankhurst rose. 'Victory!' she said, 'the Bill will go through,' and all were convinced. Lord Lytton was slightly embarrassed by the cheering women, but he said that to have contributed towards their hopefulness gave him more pleasure than anything that had happened to him since he entered public life.

'Money speaks,' said Mrs Pankhurst appealing for funds before the collection was taken. Esther Knowles, aged thirteen, was watching from the highest balcony.

Wearing a white dress, and the widest purple white and green ribbon sash I could get, I had marched in the children's contingent of the procession, in spite of my father's disapproval. I had sold *Votes for Women* outside the hall before the meeting, then I had helped to steward people to their seats in the balcony, and now I stood gazing down into the vast auditorium. The leaders on the platform looked like pygmies and the heads of the audience swayed like a field of summer grasses below me.

A huge scoring frame was erected on the platform and as soon as Mrs Pankhurst made her appeal the members of the audience began to fill in the 'promise cards' they had been given. A small pencil was attached to each card by a silken cord in the colours, and when the promised contributions had been written in, stewards collected the cards in batches and the pencils and cords flashed in the floodlight as Pethick Lawrence received them on the platform. He swiftly totted up the amounts, and the score was marked up on the frame with huge, white cardboard figures. As the total continued to mount higher and higher, so the suppressed excitement in the hall became more and more intense, and when at last the score of five thousand pounds was reached, such a tremendous cheer arose that I thought the roof would come crashing down on my head.

'Victory!' Mrs Pethick Lawrence was also certain, and Christabel alone among the speakers cast any doubt that the Bill would go through.

When Esther reached home late that Saturday night she found that her parents had quarrelled bitterly. 'For the first time my father had struck Mother because she had allowed me to join the demonstration.' Mrs Knowles supported the cause, but Esther was dedicated, and in spite of her father's opposition, she soon became the youngest worker in the W.S.P.U. general office. There were still many men in the country who, like Mr Knowles, were violently opposed to the idea of women having votes.

Asquith was to receive the Liberal Women's Suffrage Deputation on the following Tuesday and he had agreed to receive a deputation of 'antis' on the same day. On Monday morning at the Westminster offices of the Women's Anti Suffrage League, all the 'anti' forces were gathering. Miss Terry Lewis, the Chief Organiser, was asked what she thought about the glowing newspaper accounts of Saturday's demonstration. 'We think that people were more impressed with the picturesqueness of the procession than with its purpose,' she said.

On Tuesday, June 21 the Suffrage Deputation to Asquith asked him to arrange an early date for the second reading of the Conciliation Bill. 'There is undoubtedly a growing opinion in favour of the question,' he said smoothly, 'but I decline to give my own view. Although a number of Cabinet Ministers support the Bill, some are equally opposed to it, and I therefore leave it to the Cabinet to make the decision about giving further facilities.' Following the suffragists, the 'anti' deputation put forward their arguments. Women did not really want the vote, they said, and the whole Constitution would be upset if women had any say in Parliamentary affairs. 'You are preaching to the converted,' Asquith informed them as they began to set down further reasons.

On the Tuesday evening Mrs Blathwayt wrote: 'It does not look very hopeful about facilities for the new Bill, and the W.S.P.U. and the W.F.L. have threatened terrible militant methods.' On its introduction the Bill had been backed by such an overwhelming majority that there was no reason why it should not become law within the session if dealt with immediately. After a second reading it would have to pass through a committee stage. On the committee's report, a third reading could be taken, and the Bill had only then to be approved by the Lords. Time was no excuse. There was so little Parliamentary business that on several afternoons the House had risen early.

Two days later the conciliation committee asked in Parliament for a date for the discussion of the Bill, but Asquith would only commit himself so far as to say that the Government would give time before the close of the session. Suffrage societies were indignant. Lord Lytton said in an address to the constitutionals:

> The answer really in effect comes to this: 'We have for so long fallen into the habit of trifling with this question that we are all going to trifle with it a little longer.' If the discussion is given to us within the next fortnight our Bill will still be alive, and there will be time for the House of Commons to express their conviction. But if we are to be given the second reading at the end of the month, or some time in August, even supposing the Bill were to pass unanimously without a division, there would be no time to go any further; the whole question would be academic, would be absolutely worthless and a mere waste of time of the House.

On June 23, Mrs Pankhurst begged the Suffragettes to wait a little longer before taking immediate action. She still had hopes that friends in the House might persuade the Government to alter their decision. The *Daily Mirror* reported that there was a warlike atmosphere at the Suffragette At Home in the Queen's Hall on June 27: 'When Mrs Pankhurst mentioned the Prime Minister, the fat was in the fire and the good ladies hissed like cobras.' There seemed to be little hope, but Mrs Pankhurst still insisted on preserving a spirit of calm, and on June 30 Asquith announced that two days, July 11 and 12, would be set aside for the second reading of the Bill.

'For over a fortnight, Members have been bombarded with letters,' said the *Daily Mirror* on the eve of the second reading. 'The canvassing on both sides has been extraordinary. A prominent politician who has sat in the House for over a quarter of a century has received more correspondence on this subject than on any other since he entered public life.' The Suffragettes worked unceasingly to persuade Members who had voted for the Bill on its introduction to vote in favour again. There was a rumour that Lloyd George was not going to support the Bill but Suffragists believed this to be impossible—he had recently made so many protestations of his belief in women's suffrage.

On the first day of the debate Lloyd George spoke. He said that he disliked the Conciliation Bill because it excluded the majority of married women, who did not qualify under its terms as occupiers in their own right. He asked the Speaker to allow an amendment, saying that if it were not granted he would vote against the Bill. His request was refused.

It was an important debate in which many notable M.P.s took part. The main objection to votes for women was the fear of female dominance, and this manifested itself in witty as well as serious speeches.

Hilaire Belloc opposed the Bill: 'It is not true that men exercise tyranny over women; for their own good, and in the providence of God, it is a little the other way.' Also speaking against the Bill, Walter Guinness said: 'The methods of the Suffragettes have brought home to us that the granting of the franchise will be followed by a very far-reaching and regrettable alteration in the habits of the people.'

Another Member said that votes for women would overrule the marriage vow and bring discord and trouble into family life.

On the second day of the debate the Prime Minister's wife and Mrs Churchill were present to hear their husbands' speeches. Also among the guests in the House were Lady McLaren and her rival, Mrs Humphry Ward, the President of the 'antis'.

The debate was uneventful until Churchill rose to speak. 'Sir, I cannot support this Bill,' he began. His words fell icily on the listening assembly, and a gloomy silence filled the House. Churchill then proceeded verbally to tear the Bill to pieces, pointing out all its shortcomings. He described it as capricious and anti-democratic, giving an unfair representation to property as against person. 'And in any case, the denial of recognised political status to women as a sex implies a slur of inferiority.' He continued by citing all the inconsistencies he saw in the conciliation proposals. A rich man could set up his wife and daughters as 'occupiers', while the working man had no such opportunity. The majority of wives and mothers—responsible women—were excluded from the vote while inexperienced young girls of twenty-one, and spinsters living on man-made capital, were admitted. Churchill's crowning example was the case of the prostitute. She could vote unless she married and became an honest woman; but if she adopted a respectable life, she could only regain her right to the franchise by divorce.

The House filled to hear the Prime Minister. 'The very perfection of Mr Asquith's oratory is its limitation,' said the *Daily News*. 'It lacks the unexpected.' 'No suffrage measure will be satisfactory which does not give women votes on precisely the same terms as men,' said Asquith, and referring to the militants he continued:

> Those who take the sword shall perish by the sword. A cause which cannot win its way to public acceptance by persuasion, by argument, by organisation, by peaceful methods in agitation, is a cause which already, and in advance, has pronounced on itself its own sentence of death.

The Leader of the Opposition, Balfour, rose to speak next, but he was suffering from a bad cold and his voice was so husky that his brilliant defence of the Bill could scarcely be heard.

After Balfour, Lloyd George spoke again: 'I am all in favour of women's suffrage. It is a gigantic change—it will have very great results—it is a change of very great moment in the history of this country—it ought to be considered by a full committee of the whole House and when the House of Commons is perfectly untrammelled.' He then went on to say that he thought that the Conciliation Bill as it stood, without possibility of amendment, was an attempt to dictate to the House how the question should be solved. Several times he expressed his profound regrets for not supporting the Bill, and he ended his speech: 'I, with deepest reluctance, for the first time in my life, and I think the last, will go into the Lobby against the Bill.'

These powerful speeches of leading ministers put the proposals in a very unfavourable light. Philip Snowden in winding up the debate on behalf of the conciliation committee said bitterly: 'Ministers are always in favour of the general principle, but they always condemn the particular Bill.' Nevertheless, when it came to the ballot, those Members who were pledged to support the Bill kept to their word and in the face of fierce opposition the second reading of the Bill was carried by a majority of one hundred and nine votes.

After this success, a decision had now to be made as to whether the Bill should remain on the floor of the House for the committee stage or to be sent 'upstairs' to a standing committee, who could work on it independently and prepare a report for consideration by the whole House at a third reading. The Bill would have to take its place beside other Parliamentary business if kept on the floor of the House, and this course provided every excuse for delay. A vote was taken, and those Members who had felt bound to support the Bill at its second reading were now in a position where they could justifiably express their growing doubts about it. By a majority of one hundred and forty-five, Parliament decided that the committee stage was a matter for the whole House.

All hopes for the Bill faded, but the conciliation committee refused to accept defeat. They gathered every shred of evidence in favour of their proposals, and in a letter to Asquith, Lord Lytton asked that in view of undeniable Parliamentary support, the Bill should be given an immediate third reading. The Prime Minister had recently decided to prolong the Parliamentary session until the autumn, and there would now be ample time for further facilities for the Bill. Lord Lytton reminded Asquith of the promise he had made to the suffrage deputation on June 21, that if the House expressed the deliberate desire of dealing with the question, an opportunity would be provided. It was surely proof of Members' wishes that a large majority were in favour of the conciliation proposals despite the fierce opposition of Lloyd George and Churchill.

Asquith replied that when announcing dates for the second reading, he had said that the Government would be unable to afford further facilities during the session, and regarding his statement about providing an opportunity for the question if the House so desired, he said that his statement did not refer to time during that session, nor did it refer to the Conciliation Bill.

The W.S.P.U. leaders assumed a somewhat forced optimism to uphold the morale of their supporters.

This is a critical point in the future of the Bill [said Christabel] but we are confident of the issue. Another such crisis arose when the Prime Minister declined to fix an early date, or any date, for a second reading. After one week of agitation, he reconsidered his decision and appointed two days. Let us now repeat and redouble the effort which produced so great a result.

Another huge procession and meeting had been planned to take place on July 23, the anniversary of the Men's Franchise Demonstration in 1866, when the Hyde Park railings were torn down. The planning and timing of the manoeuvre were perfect but, following so soon on the June demonstration, it failed to excite the crowd with any novel spectacle, and the people watched in comparative silence.

Meanwhile, the Press had published a bitter exchange of words between Lord Lytton and Churchill. Speaking at a W.S.P.U. meeting at the Queen's Hall on July 18, Lord Lytton said:

I do not relish public controversy even with my political opponents, and the last person with whom I should choose to carry on such a correspondence is my old political friend. For the Home Secretary is the oldest of my political friends; he was the man who introduced me into the political world. He is a man with whom I have had the most intimate and personal relations from that day. We have sat together on the same platform when we belonged to the same party, and although changed circumstances have placed us on opposite sides of politics, it has never interfered with our friendship. I did genuinely believe that he had given us encouragement, that he wished well to our cause, and that so far as he could, he intended to help us, whereas his speech against the second reading of our Bill was not the speech even of a friendly critic, it was the speech of a man engaged in destructive work for the mere love of destruction. It was done without one word of regret for the doing of it, and it was that which roused in me such a feeling of indignation, and drove me to protest against his conduct.

The incident is closed, and for myself at any rate it is closed with a sacrifice greater than I like to dwell upon. It is a price which is extorted from us for our adherence to the cause which we believe in. Nearly all of you have had to pay a price of this kind, and because of the sacrifice you make in this cause, you will never be able to turn back from it.

The summer recess now obviated any question of the Bill being considered immediately. Throughout the rest of the summer and early autumn, the W.S.P.U. held peaceful demonstrations all over the country, but at the same time they publicly declared that if facilities for the Bill were not granted when Parliament reassembled, there would be a renewal of violence. Probably in anticipation of a fresh outburst of militancy, Churchill announced conditions for the preferential treatment of prisoners 'whose crimes did not involve moral turpitude'. Already hundreds of women had offered themselves for a fighting deputation.

Chapter Seven: Black Friday 1910–11

A VIOLENT OUTBREAK—THE DEATH OF MRS CLARKE—THE
GENERAL ELECTION AND A NEW TRUCE—NATIONAL CENSUS
RESISTANCE—CORONATION PROCESSION AND ARTISTIC AND
OVERSEAS SUPPORT—ASQUITH'S MANHOOD SUFFRAGE BILL.

Parliament was to reassemble for the autumn session on November 22.
On November 10, Mrs Blathwayt wrote in her diary:

> Tonight is the social and political meeting at the Albert Hall. All
> the different societies are holding big meetings this week to urge
> that facilities shall be given for the Conciliation Bill to pass ...
> There has been terrible rioting in Wales in the mines by the strikers,
> large forces of Metropolitan Police have been sent and then the
> military.

At Westminster, there was little thought for the Suffragettes or the
Welsh strikers. An overruling Parliamentary crisis had arisen between
the Commons and the Lords, which would, if unresolved, force yet
another general election. Asquith made an emergency journey to
Sandringham to consult with the King on November 11, and it was
generally expected that Parliament would be dissolved immediately.
'Now there is no chance of the Bill being considered,' wrote Mrs
Blathwayt, 'and all the suffrage societies are like hornets' nests let loose.'
The Suffragettes believed that if the Government wound up the
business of the session without making any promises about the future of
the Conciliation Bill, all would be lost, and negotiations would have to
start from the beginning again. It was imperative to extract a satisfactory
promise from the Prime Minister before the dissolution.

On Tuesday, November 15, Mary Blathwayt, now an organiser in
Bath, received a wire from Annie Kenney: 'Deputation to Prime
Minister tomorrow instead of 22nd. Go and see Mrs Moger and other
Bath member whose name was given. They must meet Caxton Hall
London 2.30. Very urgent. Annie K.' The following morning, however,
a letter arrived: 'All is put off until Friday as Parliament will not meet
again until then.' The King had returned to London from Sandringham,
and efforts were still being made to negotiate between the two Houses.
The Suffragettes decided that they could not risk waiting—already
electioneering had started and Mrs Blathwayt wrote: 'The dissolution
is expected any day, only Asquith will not say when.'

Some volunteers for the deputation had already arrived in London.

Jessie Kenney wrote to Isabel Seymour on the Tuesday, asking for help: 'If you could slip up to the office tomorrow I should be glad, as we have telegraphed to a great many people in the provinces, and some of them have started so will not get our second telegram. They will need mothering a little if they have to be in London till Friday.' 'Annie and Jessie are not allowed to go on the deputation,' said Mrs Blathwayt, 'as they are not strong enough, neither will they accept some very old women who have offered, nor any girl under twenty-one.'

On November 18, Suffragettes from all parts of the country gathered in the Caxton Hall. Those who were wearing little white satin badges inscribed *Deputation 1910* had volunteered for danger duty. The Cabinet was meeting at Westminster and the women's one purpose was to secure a future for their Bill before Parliament was dissolved.

Mrs Pankhurst addressed the audience:

> In quietness and assurance shall be your strength. You are acting legally in persistently endeavouring to see Mr Asquith. All your other kinds of effort having failed, you will now press forward in quietness and peaceableness, offending none and blaming none, ready to sacrifice yourselves even unto death if need be, in the cause of freedom.

After her speech, Mrs Pankhurst left the hall with the first contingent of distinguished women, among them Mrs Garrett Anderson, M.D., her daughter Dr Louisa Garrett Anderson, Mrs Cobden Sanderson, Mrs Saul Soloman, Mrs Hertha Ayrton the eminent scientist, Princess Sophia Duleep Singh, and Mrs Brackenbury and Miss Neligan, both ladies in their late seventies.

It was rumoured that Churchill had ordered that no arrests should be made on this occasion, and that the deputations were to be turned back by firm handling. The dignified group of women set off along Victoria Street accompanied by police, and cheered by people on passing buses. It was only when they approached Parliament Square that trouble began. Their escort of Westminster police deserted them and among the dense crowds and hundreds of police they noticed tough-looking men from the East End. 'We were not long in finding out what it meant,' says Hertha Ayrton.

> Before any of us could get into the House, we had to run the gauntlet of organised gangs of policemen in plain clothes, dressed like roughs, who nearly squeezed the breath out of our bodies, the policemen in official clothes helping them. When Mrs Pankhurst and Mrs Garrett Anderson had got through, it was still worse for

the rest of us. I nearly fainted and Louie Garrett Anderson succeeded in making them let me through. Mrs Saul Soloman was
seized by the breasts and thrown down. Women were thrown from
policemen in uniform to policemen in plain clothes literally till they
fainted.

The petitioners struggled through separately until finally all twelve
reached the steps of the Strangers' Entrance. Here they were surrounded
by a strong cordon of police, and left unmolested to observe the battle
for the next six hours. The Prime Minister received their request for an
interview, but he refused to meet the deputation, and the women only
succeeded in having a rather unsatisfactory talk with his private
secretary.

Meanwhile, Christabel was in her office at Clement's Inn with Jessie
Kenney.

Suddenly some members of the Men's Political Union came
rushing in [says Jessie]. 'It's terrible,' they gasped, 'this is not like
any other deputation we've had.' And they began to tell Christabel
—and Christabel went quite pale. 'They've brought up a lot of
police from the City, and they're bashing the women,' they said.
'Who is responsible for this? Inspector Jarvis our great friend is not
there, Superintendent Wells is not there.'

Casualties were brought back to the Caxton Hall where an ante-room
had been converted into a temporary hospital. As women came away
from the fight bruised and bleeding, fresh deputations set out. Ada
Wright was in one of the groups:

When we reached Parliament Square, plain-clothes men mingling
with the crowd kicked us, and added to the horror and anguish of
the day by dragging some of our women down side streets. There
were many attempts of indecent assault.

The police rode at us with shire horses, so I caught hold of the
reins of one of the horses and would not let go. A policeman grabbed
my arm and twisted it round and round until I felt the bone almost
breaking and I sank to the pavement, helpless. A contingent of the
United States Navy was in London at the time, and they lined up
outside Westminster Abbey and watched the proceedings. I was
continually tripped up by the police and thrown to the ground in
the sight of the American sailors. Each time I got up, and once more
made a show of advancing to the House of Commons only to be
thrown to the ground once again . . .

As I leaned against the railings after one of these episodes, a sense of the humiliation I was undergoing came over me. I wondered what my relations would think of me if they were to see me. When night came, I was mercifully arrested. After a long proceeding in the police station, we were bailed out and I returned to where I was staying at one o'clock in the morning. As I lay down, tired and exhausted, I said to myself with a shudder: 'What a sordid day!'

The next morning I found I had been photographed lying on the ground where I had been flung, and the photograph occupied the front page of the *Daily Mirror*. As soon as this became known to the Government, an order to have the picture suppressed was sent to the office of the newspaper, but they could not suppress the copies which had been sold. There were headlines: BLACK FRIDAY.

Mrs Blathwayt commented in her diary on November 19: 'The police had been instructed to avoid as far as possible making arrests, but over one hundred women were arrested, including some of high family ... It has caused astonishment that all the arrested have been tried and released.' Mr Muskett prosecuting said: 'The position has been considered by the Home Secretary who has come to the conclusion that no public advantage would be obtained by proceeding with the prosecution.'

In court, instead of being treated like political prisoners, the women were dealt with like naughty children. At first singly, and then in batches, they came before the bench and were discharged. Mrs Blathwayt writes:

The women call it a triumph, for formerly they got long terms of imprisonment for the same offence. *The Times* is down on Asquith for letting the women go. The strike in Wales is worse than ever, police are wanted there, and not for the Suffragettes, but Mrs Pankhurst is keeping the women in readiness until Asquith gives an answer.

Asquith had announced that he would make a statement on women's suffrage the following Tuesday, and meanwhile the Suffragettes felt that it should be made quite clear how much they were relying on him to produce some concrete proposals. During Monday afternoon Mrs Pankhurst went with a small deputation to the House, but she was denied admittance while Parliament was in session. Although it was a bitterly cold afternoon, the women waited outside St Stephen's entrance for two hours until Mrs Pethick Lawrence arrived with another group to relieve them. They, too, waited unsuccessfully until the House rose.

On Tuesday, the Suffragettes assembled again in the Caxton Hall to await the Prime Minister's statement. At Westminster, all parties were now anxious to wind up the session as quickly as possible so that the election campaign could begin. In less than an hour, the outstanding Parliamentary business was worked off, and the Prime Minister dismissed the suffrage question, as the W.S.P.U. had feared, with a non-committal statement.

Some three hundred women were assembled at the Caxton Hall and as soon as they heard how Asquith had dealt with their question they rose *en masse* and left the hall. Hearing that the House had risen, they set out for Downing Street carrying small purple silk banners on bamboo poles. 'It is my intention to go to 10 Downing Street or die in the attempt,' said Mrs Bowerman Chibnall. She tells how a nearby police-man replied by giving her a blow on the head. 'He caught me by the hair and flinging me aside said: "Die then!" I found afterwards that so much force had been used that my hairpins were bent double in my hair and my sealskin coat was torn to ribbons.'

As the women pushed forward relentlessly against the police, bamboo banner poles were seized and broken and the splintered sticks scratched dangerously. Suffragettes tried to approach the Cabinet Ministers re-turning from the House and 'Asquith had to be transferred to a motor to escape,' wrote Mrs Blathwayt. 'Birrell got hurt getting away and sprained his knee and is in bed, windows of official residences of Cabinet Ministers are broken, and Mrs Pankhurst is arrested.'

On November 24, Mrs Blathwayt wrote:

One hundred and seventy-six prisoners have been dealt with in two days and most of them discharged, including Mrs Pankhurst, as Churchill ordered that none should be tried except those who had committed acts of violence. The violent ones were fined, but chose to go to prison. None of the papers publish the names, but the Hon. Mrs Haverfield was fined for assaulting the police. She said it was true. She was determined to do something this time, as before she was fined for doing nothing. She used the worst threats about pistols etc. and she, I fancy, is capable of using them.

Mrs Clarke, Mrs Pankhurst's sister, was also among the imprisoned women.

Other suffrage societies strongly disapproved of the W.S.P.U. outbreak, and the conciliation committee was very upset by the incident. Lord Lytton, speaking at a suffrage meeting, said:

Conciliation and militancy cannot go hand in hand. What is so humiliating in this fresh outbreak is that it implies that the committee has failed, and we have not failed. The committee has accepted the Prime Minister's statement as an undertaking to grant facilities to our Bill in the next Parliament, and we are pledged to do our utmost to secure these facilities in the next session.

Now that the general election was imminent, the conciliation committee urged all women to canvass for Members who were pledged to support the Bill.

During the election excitement, the militant Suffragettes featured little in the news, except in connection with the security of Cabinet Ministers. As women were still banned from election meetings, the Men's Political Union began to champion the cause in public. The union was founded in 1910, by Victor Duval, and although most of its members had been in the movement since the early days of militancy, often planning and abetting Suffragette manoeuvres, they had always remained behind the scenes. They were men with strong political ideals—Liberals disillusioned by the Government, or Socialists. Many were young, all were ready to fight, and on Black Friday they had stood by the women in Parliament Square. Now the men were determined to avenge the way the women had been treated by the Metropolitan Police. Churchill was to blame, and during the election period Churchill and Lloyd George were the two ministers particularly sought out by the men for political attack.

Lloyd George bore with his interrupters, calling them 'the women's hirelings', but Churchill gave straightforward orders to have anyone who spoke for the Suffragettes removed from his meetings. Alfred Hawkins, a lifelong suffragist, had interrupted Cabinet Ministers' meetings and had been thrown out on several occasions, but when he heckled Churchill at Bradford he was literally attacked by the Liberal stewards. Hawkins, middle-aged and grey-haired, offered no resistance. 'Now you have got me out of the hall you needn't be so violent,' he said. But the stewards took no notice, and Hawkins was kicked savagely down a flight of stone steps where he fell crashing on his knees at the bottom. 'You've broken my leg. Haven't you done enough, you curs?' he cried as the stewards surrounded him again. 'No!' they shouted, and, lifting him up, they flung him out of the entrance hall on to the pavement outside.

Hugh Franklin was also turned out of the meeting, and afterwards he travelled back to London on the same train as Churchill. Police recognised him as a Suffragette supporter, and one of their detectives took a seat opposite Franklin in the same carriage. Churchill was in a nearby coach, and in order to reach the dining-car he had to pass through the compartment where Franklin was sitting. As the door opened for him to come by, Franklin jumped up, brandishing a horsewhip: 'Take that, you cur, for your treatment of the Suffragettes!' The detective grabbed Franklin by the throat and forced him back into the corner seat, while another detective wrenched the whip from him, and Churchill continued on his way to the dining-car. Franklin was tried at the Old Bailey the following week, and was sentenced to six weeks in the second division. Churchill giving evidence in court, referred to the members of the M.P.U. as 'money-fed supporters', an allegation which the Suffragettes hotly denied.

The Government took further elaborate precautions for the safety of Cabinet Ministers; 'but perhaps the most preposterous of all,' said *Votes for Women*, 'is the police protection accorded to Mr Churchill's baby. She is never allowed out of doors unaccompanied by detectives. Of course everyone knows that the Suffragettes wage no war on women and children and that Mr Churchill's baby would be as safe in the presence of a score of Suffragettes as she is in her own home.' As a token of their goodwill, the Wimbledon W.S.P.U. sent Diana Churchill a Christmas present—a doll dressed in the colours of the union, and carrying a *Votes for Women* banner.

The Suffragettes began to feel increasing bitterness towards Churchill himself. When the Suffragette prisoners were released from Holloway one month after Black Friday, many were still suffering from cuts and bruises, painful breasts and dislocated limbs resulting from the way they had been thrown about by the police. Two days after her prison release, Mrs Clarke was spending Christmas Day with the Pankhursts, when she complained of feeling tired and left the family party to go and lie down. When Mrs Pankhurst went upstairs to see her sister some time later, she found her dead. The following week, a second victim of Black Friday, Henria Williams, died of heart failure.

By 1911, another Liberal Government had come into power, and the prospect of votes for women again began to look hopeful. Sir George Kemp had won first place in the House of Commons ballot, and he was going to put forward an amended version of the Conciliation Bill. The country was immersed in elaborate preparations for the forthcoming coronation, an atmosphere of general goodwill prevailed, and suffragists believed that it was an opportune moment for women to be given the vote. Playwrights, musicians and artists, in an outburst of creative activity, were as eager to work for the suffrage cause as they were to glorify the new King and Queen.

Numerous one-act plays were written dwelling on the disadvantages of women of all classes because of their disqualification from the vote. The Suffragette was the heroine in every theme, often shown as an outcast from her family, who brings to light some social injustice and finally converts her disapproving relatives. Barker's Motion Photography Company of Soho Square even produced a film, *True Womanhood*, for showing in the cinematograph theatres. The script was written by Inez Bensusan who also took part in the film with Decima Moore, Auriol Lee and Ben Webster. Although it was virtually a play on screen, there were two outdoor scenes—a poster parade and an election meeting—where the production was taken beyond the limitations of the theatre.

It was at this time that Dr Ethel Smyth composed the 'March of the Women' which was to replace the Women's Marseillaise, as the Suffragette song. The music was played for the first time on Saturday, January 21 at a social evening at the Suffolk Street Galleries to welcome the Black Friday prisoners. The words of the song were written by Cecily Hamilton after the music was composed. 'And that is one of the most difficult things in the world,' said Dr Ethel. 'It is like asking someone to move gracefully in a strait waistcoat and handcuffs.' A special choir had been trained to sing the work and they did not find it easy to master the complicated intervals. Privately, the Marseillaise was the acclaimed favourite, but everyone had to learn the new marching song for the approaching mammoth suffrage demonstration on June 17, one week before the coronation. Many Empire visitors would be in London, and a large number of suffrage societies from abroad were expected to join the women.

Before the celebrations a national census in April provided an opportunity for passive protest, and the Women's Freedom League, under the guidance of Laurence Housman, organised a boycott. The idea of dodging the census appealed to militants and non-militants alike and many suffrage societies decided to join the protest. All-night ventures were organised throughout the country so that resisters could be away from home on the night of April 2 when the count was to be taken.

The organiser for Bath, Mrs Mansel, took an empty house in Lansdowne Crescent for some of the west of England supporters, and the local Press gave the protest considerable publicity. As early as March 10 a 'Census Ditty' appeared in the Bath *Chronicle and Argus*:

> Not till we've got the vote, then I don't mind,
> I'll help the census,

But while we're trodden down by all mankind
   It discontents us.
If we but get our votes, our threats we'll cancel;
If not, no census for Mrs ——

'Tis our design obstruction to promote;
Though our proposal every franchised man cursed,
I'd not give way—'No Census if no Vote.'
That's quite the final word of Mrs P——.

What, fill a census paper? No not me
(And I am only one among the many).
I'll burn the blessed thing; just wait and see,
I am dear Sir, yours truly A—— K——.

On the morning after the protest, Mary Blathwayt wrote in her diary:

I got to 12 Lansdowne Crescent before ten o'clock last night. A little crowd of people were standing in the next doorway to watch us go in. I took a nightdress etc. with me, and had a room to myself on the first floor and a bed. Everyone else slept on mattresses. There were twenty-nine of us. Mrs Rogers came over from Bristol and recited, but left us again at midnight. Grace Tollemache played the violin and Aethel accompanied her on the piano. Mrs Forbes Williams gave a lecture on clairvoyance but did not stay all night. We sat up till two o'clock this morning—breakfast at eight o'clock.

Marian Lawson, a brilliant and enterprising member of the Women's Freedom League, spent the whole night on roller skates at the Aldwych Skating Rink. 'We were very tired the next morning, but we were so pleased to have diddled the Government about a few names on the census. It didn't really make any difference!'

The event did cause enough stir to merit a disapproving article from G. K. Chesterton in the *Illustrated London News*:

Somehow I think the Suffragettes are unlucky in the particular shape which their protests assume. It always seemed to me that, quite apart from morals or manners, the punching of policemen was bad tactics from a military point of view. The tactics were bad because they were not female and did not use the natural weapons. A woman putting up her fists at a man is a woman putting herself in the one position which does not frighten him. Every other attitude or gesture, every turn of the head or hand, is capable at times of shaking him like a dynamite explosion. He is afraid of a woman's tongue and still more afraid of her silence. He is afraid of her endurance and still more afraid of her collapse. He is afraid of her sanity and insanity, of her laughter and her tears. The only part of her he is not afraid of is her deltoid muscle.

There seems to be the same ineptness about the selection of the census as a weapon of protest. It is the sort of thing that annoys men but does not annoy them enough.

During the first months of 1911 suffrage societies grew and flourished as never before and the National Union of Women's Suffrage Societies prevailed on many town and borough councils to sign a memorandum in favour of votes for women. On May 5 the amended Conciliation Bill passed its second reading by a majority of two hundred and fifty-five votes and following this triumph, the Lord Mayor of Dublin agreed to take advantage of an ancient privilege permitting him to plead at the Bar of the House.

The Burgesses and Aldermen of Dublin signed a petition asking for immediate further facilities for the Conciliation Bill, and the Lord Mayor travelled to London to present the document. Suffragists from all societies joined in the colourful midnight welcome on May 12 when Alderman Farrell and his wife arrived at Euston with their infant son. After the Parliamentary ceremonial some hours later, the suffragists organised a public dinner—a unique occasion where the leaders of every important society were momentarily united in an atmosphere of friendliness and rejoicing.

In spite of the Government's persistent refusal to give assurances on the future of the Conciliation Bill, the W.S.P.U. still upheld an optimistic front for the sake of their supporters. Before the women's great demonstration on June 17 Lord Lytton wrote to the Prime Minister asking him to clarify the Government's intentions and on the eve of the Suffragette coronation procession, Asquith, perhaps fearing an outrage so near to the royal celebrations, answered Lord Lytton to the effect that full facilities would be given for the Conciliation Bill in 1912.

'One of the nicest and most successful things the Suffragettes have ever done was their picturesque and poetic procession on June 17, 1911,' says Yoshio Markino, the Japanese artist and writer:

A certain gentleman was willing to offer one window of his office at Northumberland Buildings to anyone who was anxious to see the procession. Did I care to go there? I was delighted to accept this offer.

The window of the question was on—I forget which—five or six stories high. There I could see the whole view . . . the square being crowded more and more every minute. The boys began to ride on the back of the Nelson lions and some to climb up the street lamps. I have never seen the crowd from such a height! Nothing but hats and hats, which were waving like the oatfields on a breezy day.

Suddenly I heard the band playing the Marseillaise march just underneath our window. I saw the procession was coming. Those two Suffragettes both sides of me seemed awfully excited. 'There, that is Mrs Lawrence! That is Mrs Pankhurst! Where is Christabel? There she is!'

Only a minute or two later, the head of the procession was proceeding far towards Haymarket. They gave me some deep impression which I cannot express with words. Whole crowds of the spectators seemed to me only one dark mass or pattern (though I knew each of them might be quite important individuals), and there those most dignified white souls were marching on! By the way, I very much regret that I could not see either their faces or the designs of those innumerous banners, which I was told were most artistic things. For through that window I could see only their backs. It lasted until 7.30 p.m., or for three hours duration!

Was I tired to watch them all? Never! Nay. I was fascinated by every one of them. Each of them looked as fresh and interested as the first one. Why was that so? I have seen other kind of pageants very often—such as the Lord Mayor's Show, or many historical ones. In these cases the performers generally have no fixed mind. Some of them are joking, while others are in quite absent-mind, or they want only to show their beautiful costumes or their clever make-up. What I mean is that each one has each soul, or perhaps no soul at all.

The Suffragette procession was entirely in different nature. There were some forty thousand women, but they had only one spirit—that was the faith in votes for women. No wonder why we, the spectators, have received some unusually strong impression from them!

Support for women's suffrage had increased at a phenomenal rate. Mrs Pankhurst spent the first six months of 1911 on a campaigning tour of the country, and much of the growing enthusiasm was due to her personal effort. She had a new chauffeur for this period. Aileen Preston had advertised for a post, after being the first woman to qualify for the Automobile Association Certificate in Driving, and she was accepted by the W.S.P.U. 'My family were livid,' she says.

They thought I was going straight into the dark arms of Hell—to be going to that dreadful woman, as her chauffeur! It was an awful blow, but I thought it was the most wonderful job. At a pound a week it was wealth!

The car was a Wolseley—a presentation from Miss Dodge, a wealthy American friend. I was used to driving rather light small cars, but this was a pantechnicon, and I quailed at the look of it. We were very, very heavily laden with an enormous amount of literature piled on the top which I had to reach by climbing up a little ladder.

We would start off at about half past ten in the morning and then we'd have a puncture. Mrs Pankhurst never got out of the car, she never moved from her papers, so I used to jack her up with the car. I took that for granted. She was always absolutely absorbed in working out her speech for the next meeting or reading some book on social welfare. In my mind all the time was, 'Mrs Pankhurst's got to be there.' That's all that mattered. Her meeting was the only thing that mattered, and we always got there in time.

During the early summer Aileen Preston often drove Mrs Pankhurst down to Ethel Smyth's country cottage in Woking:

It was a wonderful trip. Dr Ethel would improvise, and keep Mrs Pankhurst perhaps an hour or an hour and a half, perfectly happy just sitting in her drawing-room, playing to her. I used to wait outside on a little bench, under an open window and listen, with the nightingales literally within a few yards from me in the woods.

On October 4 Mrs Pankhurst left for another lecture tour in America. Just at this time the *Standard* decided to promote the suffrage cause, and each day an entire page was given over to 'A Woman's Platform'. It included articles by leaders of suffrage societies and reports of any outstanding suffrage activities. There was a detailed description on October 5 of Mrs Pankhurst's departure:

As Mrs Pankhurst left for the States, there was an informal but enthusiastic 'God speed' at Waterloo. A large purple, white and green flag floated in front of the engine and many of the visitors bore the colours of the movement. 'We mean to have the vote next session. Prospects have never been so bright,' said Mrs Pankhurst. 'The Prime Minister has given us the most definite promises that full facilities shall be given to the Bill, and we are going to make the most of them.'

Once again all hopes were smashed. On November 7 Asquith announced that the Government intended to introduce a Manhood Suffrage Bill which would enfranchise all men. If this were successful, it would invalidate the conciliation proposals which were based on existing franchise laws. 'Torpedoed!' as Lloyd George put it, the Bill was doomed and Mrs Pethick Lawrence sent out a circular on November 15:

> We have come to a very grave crisis. The Government now proposes to exploit our long national struggle for political freedom in order to give votes to all men. If they pass this Manhood Suffrage Bill through Parliament next year, the position of the womanhood of the country will be one of complete political subjection to men as the ruling caste . . .
>
> Hundreds of women have already volunteered to take, on Tuesday next (November 21), such action as may be necessary to protest against this outrage upon the honour of women. In their name and in my own, I call upon you to join us.
>
> We must have a thousand women on this deputation. Garibaldi with his thousand set a nation free. Remember, if we have a thousand, it will be impossible for the Government to punish any.

A postscript followed: 'The Prime Minister has just consented to receive a suffrage deputation. The interview is expected to take place this week—but whenever it takes place and whatever statement the Prime Minister may make, we shall meet in the Caxton Hall on November 21, prepared to take any action which may be necessary.'

The proposed interview took place on November 17 at Downing Street. Some thirty women from various suffrage societies made up the deputation and the W.S.P.U. representatives, Mrs Pethick Lawrence, Lady Constance, Christabel, Sylvia and Annie Kenney, arrived after all the others heralded by distant cheering. When the Prime Minister entered, the ladies rose silently. The meeting was calm, and all the leaders were able to speak freely. Amid general laughter, Maud Arncliffe Sennett delivered a totally feminine speech on behalf of the Actresses' Franchise League. 'Our Bill was like a little bird that laid a little egg. By bringing in your great manhood measure, you have—you have robbed our hen roost.'

Beaming, Asquith finally made his reply. 'I am not convinced. You may think it deplorable, but that is the fact and I have colleagues—a minority—like minded!' In reply to muffled protests, he continued: 'Get rid of me by all means if you can, but at the moment I am head of the Government and I am not convinced.'

Militancy was resumed. On the evening of November 21 Suffragettes left the Caxton Hall armed with stones. After the usual attempts to reach the House, an organised window-smashing operation was carried out. Two hundred and twenty-three arrests were made, and next morning all London's glaziers were at work repairing broken windows of Government offices in Whitehall, and replacing panes in shops and post offices along the Strand.

Chapter Eight: The Argument of the
Broken Pane 1911–12

WINDOW SMASHING IN THE WEST END—THE LEADERS ARRESTED
—PRISON ATROCITIES—A HATCHET THROWN AT ASQUITH IN
DUBLIN—THE PANKHURSTS AND PETHICK LAWRENCES SPLIT
FORCES.

The window smashing of November 21 left the public momentarily speechless. They had been wooed to believe in votes for women. They had also believed in Asquith's promises. When the first shock was over, the militants were gently condemned by their fellow countrymen, but from the States Mrs Pankhurst sent a sympathetic message from the American people: 'It cannot be possible in the face of the progress of the women's movement all over the world, and after the rigorous and devoted struggle that has been carried on by Englishwomen, that a responsible Government could have the effrontery to do such injustice.'

Since the Conciliation Bill had been killed, the ultimate question arose as to whether or not women should be included in the Manhood Suffrage Bill. Rarely had any issue so divided the country. The 'antis' were markedly concerned and rallied all their forces to take a petition to Asquith. If women were to be included in the new Bill, they argued, at what rank could the line be drawn? Asquith reassured them that in his opinion votes for women would be a disastrous mistake, and he encouraged them to pursue their ideals, although he said that he personally was bound to stand by the Cabinet. The Cabinet, however, was completely undecided on the question. There was talk of a substitute Bill being introduced, the Conciliation Bill was put forward again and Cabinet Ministers were persistently questioned and heckled by men until eventually questions were banned altogether at some Liberal meetings.

On January 16, at the height of the political wrangling, Mrs Pankhurst returned from America. Since the New Year, Clement's Inn had been inundated with letters from women volunteering for the next protest and at the first great W.S.P.U. meeting after Mrs Pankhurst's return, a date —March 4—was announced for the demonstration and Mrs Pankhurst spoke:

If the argument of the stone, that time-honoured official political argument, is sufficient, then we will never use any stronger argument
. . . Why should women go to Parliament Square and be battered

about and insulted and, most important of all, produce less effect than when they throw stones? After all, is not a woman's life, is not her health, are not her limbs more valuable than panes of glass?

Meetings were held all over the country to work up support for the protest, and the Suffragettes were quick to interpret as incitement a remark made by C. E. H. Hobhouse, the Member for Bristol, at an 'anti' meeting in his constituency: 'In the case of the suffrage demand there has not been the kind of popular sentimental uprising which accounted for the arson and violence of earlier suffrage reforms.' Even now Mrs Pankhurst wished to negotiate peacefully and twice she wrote to Asquith asking him for an interview, but he refused to see her. The authorities were therefore informed that the proposed demonstration would take place, and while they were busy arranging security for March 4, on March 1, without warning, the Suffragettes stormed London's West End.

Mrs Pankhurst herself opened the proceedings:

Late in the afternoon of Friday March 1 I drove in a taxi-cab, accompanied by Mrs Tuke and another of our members, to 10 Downing Street. It was exactly half past five when we threw our stones, four of them, through the window panes. As we expected we were promptly arrested.

At a quarter to six precisely, the next part of the manoeuvre started in Piccadilly. It was one of the busiest periods of the day, the half hour before the shops closed. Suddenly women who had a moment before appeared to be on peaceful shopping expeditions, produced from their bags and muffs, hammers and stones. 'From every part of the crowded and brilliantly lighted streets came the crash of splintered glass,' said the *Daily Mail*. 'People started as a window shattered at their side; suddenly there was another crash in front of them; on the other side of the street; behind—everywhere. Scared shop assistants came running out to the pavements; traffic stopped; policemen sprang this way and that; five minutes later the streets were a procession of excited groups, each surrounding a woman wrecker being led in custody to the nearest police station.'

At six o'clock another contingent made an assault on shops in Regent Street and the Strand, and fifteen minutes later Oxford Street was attacked. Mrs Garrud's jiu-jitsu school was just off Oxford Street, in Argyle Place, and six of her Suffragette pupils were taking part in the stone throwing.

The raid went from Tottenham Court Road to Marble Arch [she says], but on one side of the road only. And do you know, the other side of the road were most indignant to think they'd been left out. 'Shop after shop said: '—Spoiled our trade! Instead of them all coming in here, they've gone in there to see what happened!'

Mrs Garrud's gymnasium was one of the bolt holes after the raid. She had taken up some of the floor-boards and covered over the gaps with heavy tatemie mats.

They came back to the school because it was easy. They came straight in and turned those mats up. I made them strip off their outside clothes and give me their bags with their stones and any other missiles they had left. All went under the floor-boards and back went the mats.

They were all in their jiu-jitsu coats working on the mats, when bang, bang, bang on the door. Six policemen! I looked very thunder-struck and wanted to know what was the matter. 'Well, can't we come in?' said one of the policemen. I said: 'No I'm sorry but I've got six ladies here having a jiu-jitsu lesson. I don't expect gentlemen to come in here.' He said: 'Are they pupils?' I said: 'Yes, pupils.' So it ended up by one old man coming in and having a look round. He didn't see anything, only the girls busy working, and out he went again.

About two days after—it was the year when the big muffs were worn—I went along Regent Street looking in at Liberty's, when all of a sudden a great big police hand came down on my muff. 'Let me see what you've got in there, madam.' I looked at him: 'What do you mean?' 'You know what I mean!' I said: 'Here it is then,' and showed him the muff. Of course there was nothing in it, but he did find a pocket there. 'Yes, of course there's a pocket. I wouldn't have a muff without one, I must have something for my gloves and my handkerchief and my key.' 'You don't put your things in there with a bag hanging on your arm.' We had such an argument and quite a little crowd collected. When it was all over, he walked off with apologies. Then the manager came out and said: 'Well done! Come in and have a cup of tea.' I said: 'Well now, what do you know about it?' He said: 'Nothing, only I know who you are.'

There were so many arrests after the raid that the court had to sit for the whole of Saturday and even by the end of the day, only thirteen of one hundred and twenty-one cases had been heard. Mrs Pankhurst, Mrs Tuke, and their accomplice, Mrs Marshall the wife of the W.S.P.U. solicitor, came before Mr Curtis Bennett on Saturday morning. Mrs Pankhurst spoke in her own defence:

If we had the vote, we should be constitutional, but since we have not the vote, we learn our lesson, a lesson that has been given to us. I hope this will be enough to show the Government that the women's agitation is going on ... What happens to us does not matter, but what comes of what happens to us matters very much. The individual will disappear, but the cause is going on.

On the morning of Monday, March 4 the Suffragettes raided Knightsbridge. It had been assumed that their demonstration would take place in Parliament Square that evening, and already extra police were on duty in the Westminster area and every property owner in the vicinity was taking precautions against attack. No one suspected that there would be another Suffragette coup, and police forces in the Knightsbridge area were totally inadequate for dealing with the situation. Onlookers stood by, helplessly watching pane after pane being smashed, until soldiers from the Knightsbridge Barracks arrived on the scene to assist in making arrests.

Nine thousand police were on duty in central London on Monday evening and vast crowds gathered to witness yet another assault on Parliament. They were disappointed. There was no 'Great Demonstration'. Many of the stone throwers—'Mrs Pankhurst's bold bad ones'— had already done their work, and the militants who remained had been organised to take part in a manoeuvre outside the immediate area of the House. After attending an afternoon meeting at the London Pavilion, about one hundred and fifty Suffragettes made their way in small groups to the Gardenia—a vegetarian restaurant near Covent Garden—where they were briefed. As the groups re-emerged one by one from the restaurant, each was followed by a detective to an appointed window. Again stones were thrown and women were arrested.

Dr Ethel Smyth had spoken at the Pavilion meeting and directly afterwards she went to Berkeley Square and smashed a window at the house of Louis Harcourt—a Cabinet Minister who had incensed her by re-marking that he would give the vote to women if they were all like his wife.

At 9.30 on March 5 detectives arrived at Clement's Inn to arrest the Pethick Lawrences and Christabel on a charge of incitement. The Pethick Lawrences were taken away immediately, and police returned to the offices later to search the building and remove a vast quantity of papers. They also confiscated several articles that the printer was about to include in the next issue of *Votes for Women*, among them Christabel's leader in which she justified window smashing:

The greatest conflicts of history, however worthy their purpose, have been made up of actions which brought death to human beings and devastation to property. The Suffragettes are happy indeed in knowing that not only is their object as great as that of any soldier or militant reformer—but that their action has been infinitely less harmful to life and property . . . Over and over again have cabinet ministers jeered at our militancy in consequence of its restraint. They have derided what they call the policy of pinpricks and contemptuously asked why we did not use real violence. Finally has come Mr Hobhouse's challenge, his incitement to violence.

Where the leader should have appeared in *Votes for Women*, a dramatic blank was left, headed 'A Challenge' and signed 'Christabel Pankhurst'. Christabel herself had vanished, and readers could but wonder what 'A Challenge' meant. The Press was full of ideas on Christabel's whereabouts, and the picture papers showed interesting photographs of possible country-house hiding places, with their handsome Suffragette owners and children posing outside.

Unknown to all but a few close friends, Christabel was in France. Her escape had been prompted by a flash of insight. When she heard of the warrant for her arrest, she suddenly realised that it was essential for the survival of the union to have a leader out of the reach of Government authority. She took no further advice, and on March 6, in disguise, she left the country.

Annie Kenney had been secretly appointed to follow Christabel as Chief Organiser, but even Annie received no word from Christabel for three days. However, Christabel's flight had not disrupted her own command of the movement, and her new manifesto, 'Broken Windows', was already circulating in London by the week-end.

Our very definite purpose is to create an intolerable situation for the Government, and, if need be, for the public as a whole. 'Government property,' say the critics, 'you are justified in attacking, but not private property.' Militant suffragists would, of course, be glad if an attack on Government property were sufficient to attain their purpose. More dramatic measures have been proved to be essential. That is why private property has now been attacked.

West End firms called a special meeting—'Creative Man as against Destructive Woman'. In the course of considering how a recurrence of window smashing could be prevented, there were many sore comments and declamations, but the suggestion of votes for women by Miss Atherton of the Fine Arts Society was received with howls of disapproval. Many commercial enterprises did in fact trade on the broken windows. Evelyn Sharp who now edited *Votes for Women*, had a penchant for the

Victorian type of witticism, and she included such remarks as: 'The Suffragettes are believed to have remarked as they walked down Oxford Street, that they were taking *Liberty's* on the way.' 'A huge window poster of a shipping agency in Parliament Street announced today— "We are sending people where women have the vote. Avenging angels please pass over!" '

Most of the active members of the union were in prison, and for a period militancy ceased. A strong intellectual set under Evelyn Sharp worked at headquarters taking over the Pethick Lawrences' editorial role, and they produced a *Votes for Women* that contained much copy, but little direction for workers and organisers. Annie travelled to Paris via Le Havre every week-end to report to Christabel, and returned to London again on Sunday fully briefed on future policy, and with Christabel's leading article. Annie, as a character, was submerged in the new part, and her great support was Rachel Barrett who held the office in her absence. A devotee of the Pankhursts, Rachel joined the W.S.P.U. in 1907 and gave up her studies and her teaching post in Wales to become a provincial organiser. She already knew Annie well from working with her in Bristol in 1909.

During the general lag in activity, the office girls at Clement's Inn had nothing to do, and they wondered daily whether they would be sacked. Esther Knowles, still the youngest of the staff, spent hours on the office roof, trying out a new box camera. Apathy spread to the provinces, and organisation flagged.

On the north Norfolk coast Suffragette forces were assembled for a by-election campaign, but gossiping and sun-bathing had become the order of the day. Grace Roe, as organiser for the eastern counties, had been sent by Annie Kenney to back up Margaret West, the local organiser. Evelyn Sharp had been in the constituency and was highly impressed with Margaret West as a speaker, and now Grace found that two sets of instructions were coming from headquarters. Grace was receiving daily letters of criticism from Annie of the ways things were *not* going and Westie was getting flattering letters saying how calm and capable she was.

One week before the election took place Grace had a sleepless night: 'I realised I must *act*, that nothing worse could happen than lose that election while the leaders were on trial. When I came down in the morning, the Brackenburys were awaiting me and they both had the same thought: "G.R. must take complete charge." They were ready to back me to the hilt.'

The organisers were given twelve hours and told that unless they started work at once, they would be sent back to London. This was enough. The women pulled together immediately, and only three probationers were sent away. Meetings were held everywhere and at the poll on May 31 the Liberal majority was vastly reduced—a triumph for the Suffragettes at this critical period.

The stone throwing had given rise to a strong undercurrent of prejudice against women in general, and just at this time Sir Almroth Wright, M.D., F.R.S., brought out his 'Unexpurgated Case against Woman Suffrage'—a deliberate attempt to stir up a sex war by proving that every woman was mentally deranged on account of her physical system. Suffragists of every creed rallied in support of the militants, to uphold the status of womanhood, and to prevent a schism in the ranks that had campaigned together with such strength. Speaking at the London Opera House on March 15, Granville Barker said: 'I have never been one to believe in the possibility of a sex war, but during the last year there has been sown in the suffrage movement the seed of hatred between women as women and men as men, and God forbid that such a curse should ever come!'

The prison sentences after the window smashing ranged from two weeks to six months. Holloway was full, and a large number of women were sent to Winson Green and Aylesbury Gaols. Prison life became a farce of inconsistencies. The Suffragettes were denied certain privileges while their less reasonable demands were considered, and the authorities generally ignored the many tricks and ruses that were devised to annoy them. 'There were so many of us that they couldn't do much about it— just blink the eye at a lot of things,' says Gladys Roberts. She had been sentenced to three months in Holloway for breaking post-office windows in the King's Road, Chelsea, but this was very different from her first imprisonment:

> We had associated labour and we all sat in the body of the hall and were allowed to do needlework or knitting—convicts' clothing. We used to put embroidery on the convicts' knickers! As a matter of fact we did very little that was really useful. If we knew that anyone was leaving prison, then we tried to smuggle letters out. The day before Mrs Marshall left, she went round the yard in a red dressing-gown saying that she was a pillar-box. The sleeves were turned inside out to that letters could be slipped in.

Dr Ethel Smyth had been put in an adjoining cell to Mrs Pankhurst, and the matron leniently allowed them to spend more time together than was officially permitted. One day Thomas Beecham came to visit his fellow musician. 'I arrived in the main courtyard of the prison,' he says, 'to find the noble company of martyrs marching round it and singing lustily their war chant while the composer, beaming approbation from an overlooking upper window, beat time in an almost Bacchic frenzy with a toothbrush.'

Pethick Lawrence was detained in Brixton Gaol, and his wife in Holloway, pending preliminary enquiries at Bow Street Magistrates' Court. Mrs Pankhurst was also implicated in the conspiracy charge, and all three leaders were brought out of prison to appear before the Director of Public Prosecutions while their part in the affairs of the union was examined, and the confiscated W.S.P.U. papers were minutely scrutinised. Mrs Tuke, ill and quite unfit for prison life, was soon acquitted when it was ascertained that she was merely an official in the organisation. Finally on April 4 the leaders were released on bail to prepare for their case in the High Court and Pethick Lawrence took advantage of the break to make a secret journey to Christabel in France to discuss the future of the union.

The conspiracy trial took place before Lord Coleridge on May 15—the Attorney General prosecuting, Pethick Lawrence and Mrs Pankhurst speaking in their own defence, and Tim Healy, K.C., the eminent Irish politician, appearing for Mrs Pethick Lawrence. 'This is a great State trial,' said Healy. 'It is not the women who are on trial. It is the men. It is the system of Government.' Nevertheless, Sir Rufus Isaacs had said in his speech for the prosecution that the political question was irrelevant, and after a hearing lasting a week, in spite of their impressive sincerity, the leaders were found guilty.

The charge against Pethick Lawrence was mainly based on the fact that he had stood bail for the Suffragettes. 'He was ever ready to take root in any police station, his money bag between his feet at any hour of the day or night,' says Ethel Smyth. Pethick Lawrence deplored violence, but he sided firmly with the Suffragettes: 'It is not merely a woman's battle. It is not merely a battle for women—it is a battle for the good of the people of this country. It is because of the men who have stood in the battle that a sex war has been prevented.'

Although the jury recommended leniency in view of the leaders' undoubtedly pure motives, they were each sentenced to nine months in the second division, and Pethick Lawrence and Mrs Pankhurst were ordered to pay the costs of the prosecution.

It was an astonishing sentence. Immediately the jury organised a petition for a remission or reduction of the terms. There was a public outcry that the leaders were not being treated as political offenders and, within hours, Pethick Lawrence was transferred from Wormwood Scrubs—a prison offering no first-division facilities—to Brixton. The new Home Secretary, Reginald McKenna, granted some immediate minor concessions, but the prisoners remained in the second division and their status was not vitally changed.

Protests poured into the Press from all over the world: '*C'est avec indignation que nous venons d'apprendre le jugement qui inflige à Mrs Pankhurst et à Mr et Mrs Pethick Lawrence un emprisonnement de neuf mois.*' A supporter wrote from India: 'My blood boils at the treatment which the noble women in prison are receiving. I have seen much of the subjection of women in the East, but nothing here equals civilised England's methods of breaking a woman's spirit.' Telegrams and letters from abroad preceded an international memorial to the Prime Minister signed by some sixty distinguished professionals, among them Madame Curie, George Brandes, Upton Sinclair, Hermann Bahr, Selma Lagerlöf and Romain Rolland. In England, Keir Hardie led a protest in Parliament and memorials were sent to the Home Secretary from universities and learned societies all over the country.

Meanwhile Parliament momentarily settled the women's suffrage question. The Conciliation Bill, lamely brought forward again on March 28, was finally voted out by a majority of fourteen, and on June 17 when the Manhood Suffrage Bill was introduced, it was made quite clear that women were not included in its terms.

Under pressure from all sides, the Home Secretary transferred the leaders to the first division on June 10, but the other eighty-one Suffragette prisoners were still kept in the second division. Nearly one hundred M.P.s protested and when no change was made, a prearranged hunger strike began in Holloway on June 19. Word reached Pethick Lawrence in Brixton, and he too began a fast.

On Saturday forcible feeding started. 'Holloway became a place of horror and torment,' says Mrs Pankhurst. 'Sickening scenes of violence took place almost every hour of the day as the doctors went from cell to cell.' Violet Bland describes the wardresses as transformed into inhuman brutes and fiends. Women barricaded their cells, and officials battered the doors down with crowbars, blocks and wedges. 'The barricading was always followed by the sounds of human struggle and suppressed cries of the victims' groans,' says Emily Wilding Davison. Emily threw herself over the prison staircase. 'The idea in my mind was that some desperate protest must be made to put a stop to the hideous torture, and one great tragedy might save others.' She was seriously injured and taken to the prison hospital where forcible feeding continued.

On June 22 Mrs Pankhurst was lying in bed, very weak from starvation, when she heard a sudden scream from Mrs Lawrence's cell, then the sound of a prolonged and very violent struggle:

> I knew they had dared to carry their brutal business to our doors. I sprang out of bed and, shaking with weakness and with anger, I set my back against the wall and waited for what might come. In a few minutes they had finished with Mrs Lawrence and had flung open the door of my cell. On the threshold I saw the doctors, and back of them a large group of wardresses. 'Mrs Pankhurst,' began the doctor. Instantly I caught up a heavy earthenware jug from a table hard by, and with hands that now felt no weakness I swung the jug high. 'If any of you dares so much as to take one step inside this cell I shall defend myself,' I cried. Nobody moved or spoke for a few seconds, and then the doctor confusedly muttered something about to-morrow morning doing as well, and they all retreated.
>
> I demanded to be admitted to Mrs Lawrence's cell, where I found my companion in a desperate state. She is a strong woman, and a very determined one, and it had required the united strength of nine wardresses to overcome her. They had rushed into the cell without any warning, and had seized her unawares, else they might not have succeeded at all. As it was she resisted so violently that the doctors could not apply the stethoscope, and they had very great difficulty in getting the tube down. After the wretched affair was over, Mrs Lawrence fainted, and for hours afterwards was very ill. This was the last attempt made to forcibly feed either Mrs Lawrence or myself, and two days later we were ordered to be released on medical grounds.

Mrs Pankhurst and Mrs Lawrence both left prison on Monday, June 24, and on the same day George Lansbury, the Labour Member for Bow and Bromley, questioned McKenna in the House about the situation. He was told that there were still seventy women and one man in prison. Out of these, fifty-two prisoners were refusing food and forty-seven had been fed by force. Lansbury asked leave for the House to be adjourned so that there could be a discussion on the matter, but his motion was defeated.

The next day Tim Healy appealed to Asquith on behalf of the Suffragette prisoners, but the Prime Minister remarked complacently that any woman could get out of prison immediately, on giving an undertaking. Incensed, Lansbury left his place and advanced on the Premier. 'You will go down in history as the man who tortured innocent women,' he shouted. Having made his initial protest, Lansbury returned to his place to continue: 'You murder, you torture and drive women mad, and then tell them to walk out. You ought to be ashamed.' Asquith ordered him to leave the House for the day, but Lansbury went on addressing the Prime Minister. After the Speaker had called on him three times to withdraw he rose and walked across the Bar and out of the Chamber.

'Militancy has broken out again!' A new outburst of window smashing took place on June 27, and now messages were attached to the missiles: 'A woman's protest against the Government that tortures women!' 'A protest against forcible feeding. Release our women!' 'A warning to the Government. More to follow until they get votes for women!' The protest was probably in anticipation of the debate on the Home Office vote next day which was to be entirely devoted to forcible feeding. Before the question came up in Parliament, the Lytton family made public that Lady Constance had suffered from a serious heart condition since her treatment as Jane Warton, and that she had recently collapsed and was only slowly recovering from total paralysis. During the debate McKenna justified the treatment of the Suffragette prisoners and pleaded for Members to support his present refusal to make concessions. In the case of Lady Con, McKenna backed his predecessors, but at the same time he exposed facts which had previously been denied. This brought a strong warning from Lord Lytton in *The Times* that the Home Office was not to be trusted.

By the end of June many of the hunger strikers had already been released, and they told horrifying stories of the prison atrocities. Suffragettes felt bitter resentment, and the pestering of Cabinet Ministers was no longer a light-hearted matter. When the King and Queen were visiting Llandaff, accompanied by the Home Secretary, an unprecedented and most dramatic scene occurred. The royal party was passing along a narrow passage approaching the cathedral, when suddenly Helen Craggs sprang over the wall and confronted the Home Secretary: 'Mr McKenna, you are a traitor to all the women in the country.' The procession was held up, police rushed to arrest her, and she was removed. No subsequent action was taken and when Helen returned to Cardiff, she saw the whole town placarded with bills announcing: 'A Suffragette Attack on Mr McKenna'.

Helen, the daughter of Sir John Craggs, had been the 'titled Suffragette incognito', at the North-West Manchester by-election in 1908. It was there that she and Harry Pankhurst fell in love, and later she had been at Harry's bedside throughout the last weeks of his life. Only a fortnight after the Llandaff episode, Helen Craggs was discovered, on the night of July 12, in the grounds of Louis Harcourt's country house at Nuneham Park near Oxford, and she was arrested and charged with attempted arson.

Twice before, at times of crisis, women had tried to hasten on the end, by arson. In December 1911 Emily Davison had fired a letter-box; and during the stone throwing of 1912, Ellen Pitfield, dying from incurable injuries received on Black Friday, tried to set light to the General Post Office in London. No one had taken a lead from either of these incidents, but the Nuneham Park episode opened a new era in militancy.

Women in Ireland had already protested against Asquith's proposed Home Rule Bill because it made no provision for votes for women, and on Thursday, July 18, when Asquith visited Dublin, *Votes for Women* reported:

> Prime Minister leaves Paddington by stealth, goes by train to Wolverhampton, creeps into motor-car guarded by detectives, reaches Holyhead, is safely smuggled on board a specially chartered steamer, and reaches Kingstown at 8.30 p.m. where he is greeted on a megaphone by Irish suffragists in a yacht. Surrounded by a posse of police he manages to reach a special (armoured?) train in safety, and is conveyed to Dublin under cover of darkness. The same evening, an attempt is made to fire the Theatre Royal, in connection with which Miss Gladys Evans is arrested. Later, as the Prime Minister is driving to the Gresham Hotel, a hatchet is dropped into his carriage. The woman who throws it is badly knocked about but not arrested.
>
> Next day the Prime Minister scarcely emerges from the Chief Secretary's Lodge, which is guarded as though in a state of siege, until the evening, when he drives to the Theatre Royal through dense lines of police, and addresses a packed audience of detectives and Home Rulers at 8 p.m. Five men who remind him of the existence of women are ejected with serious brutality. Earlier in the day three women suffragists are arrested and charged with conspiracy.

The three women were arrested in connection with the firing of the Theatre Royal. Although all Dublin was talking about the hatchet—it was said that John Redmond, the Irish political leader, had been hit and wounded by it—the incident was treated as rather a joke, and no charge was made at the time. The *Dublin Evening Mail* reported that Margot Asquith had picked up the hatchet and taken it back to the hotel, where she had displayed it.

Immediately after the Dublin episode, the W.S.P.U. said in a manifesto: 'The leaders of the Women's Social and Political Union have often warned the Government that unless the vote were granted to women in response to the mild militancy of the past, a fiercer spirit of revolt would be awakened which it would be impossible to control.'

Gladys Evans, Mary Leigh and Mrs Baines came up for trial in Dublin on August 6. Mary Leigh made a brilliant and moving speech in in her own defence. 'This is not the time or place to pay compliments,' said the judge, 'but this lady is a very remarkable lady, of very great ability, and of very strong character.' Mary Leigh had to be tried twice, as the first jury failed to agree on a verdict, but she was eventually found guilty and sentenced to five years' penal servitude. Gladys Evans received a similar sentence, and Mrs Baines was given seven months' hard labour.

Because they were denied political rights, they adopted the hunger strike and Mrs Baines was released within a few days in a dangerous condition. The other two women were fed by force, although the measure was against the principle of the Irish authorities. Scientists at the British Association Conference in Dundee condemned the operation at a meeting on September 6. Sir Victor Horsley said that quasi-scientific statements in defence of forcible feeding had been read by the Home Secretary to the House of Commons, but the authors had concealed their names. Professor Halliburton of London expressed his view that forcible feeding—even of criminals—would not be tolerated if statesmen really knew what it meant. The horror and disgust of it, quite apart from the physical injury which so often resulted, was a punishment which recalled the worst days of medieval cruelty.

The W.S.P.U. had several times challenged the Government to impose long imprisonments, but the Dublin sentences of five years were quite unexpected and thought to be out of all proportion. Immediately Grace Roe was sent to Dublin to organise a campaign on behalf of the prisoners. Thousands of leaflets with heavy black edging were distributed, and donkeys paraded the streets placarded with mournful notices saying: THREE WOMEN ARE FACING DEATH IN MOUNTJOY PRISON. After a few days Grace began to find these so depressing that she had some tricolour bills printed, and the next week the donkeys toured the city with a black poster on one side and a coloured on the other. The young men of Dublin, however, seemed to prefer the original dramatic black.

On September 8, a demonstration was held in Phoenix Park. The three platforms were decorated with the W.S.P.U. colours, and black flags bearing the uncrowned harps and shamrock. The spectacle attracted thousands of people. Only Sylvia Pankhurst was bothered by hecklers, and for the most part the huge audience was genuinely impressed. Grace Roe interviewed the Lord Lieutenant and his Under-Secretary, Sir James Dougherty, but it was clear that they did not hold authority in the case of the English prisoners.

Mary Leigh's release was announced on September 20. 'This is victory indeed,' wrote Laurence Housman. 'It is no petty advantage over an enemy, but the triumph of one great spirit over all the forces of law and physical force.' He dedicated a verse to 'Mary Leigh, August 9–September 20':

> They took a living soul away,
> And shut it from the breath of day;
> They bound the feet, they bound the hands,
> They fenced it round with iron bands;
> Into the mouth they forced the bit,
> Bridled and bruised, and tortured it.
>
> 'Five years,' they said, 'here shall you be,
> O Soul, in your captivity!
> Five years of weariness and pain
> Before we let you out again.'
> Five years! And scarce five weeks are run—
> She looks on freedom and the sun.
>
> 'Basis of Government.' Brute Force,
> Has had its fling and run its course.
> The utmost that it dared to do
> Was done! flesh shrank till bones showed through—
> Yet still within that house of clay
> The spirit lived and won its way.
>
> She won because she had the will
> To die—she whom they dared not kill!
> Possession gave them their nine points:
> This tenth has pierced their harness joints.
> They fought with backs against the wall:
> One poor weak body beat them all!

Referring to Mary Leigh's release, Bernard Shaw said:

The other day we had challenged the Government to starve Mrs Leigh to death. The way the suffragists had really beaten the Government was by the old oriental trick of starving on your enemy's doorstep. If your enemy was certain that he was in the right, and that public opinion was on his side, he had no hesitation in letting you starve. But when it turned out that your enemy was not prepared to let you starve, it meant that the person on the doorstep was in the right. That was what the Government appeared too stupid to realise.

Suffragists were still prepared to hope that there would be an amendment to include women in the Manhood Suffrage Bill, and Lord Haldane, Sir Edward Grey and Lloyd George were among the cabinet ministers to encourage this thinking. The Suffragettes made it their business to find out where each of these statesmen was spending his summer holiday, and none was left in peace. Lloyd George was spending some days in Marienbad with Sir Rufus and Lady Isaacs and two Suffragettes had a light-hearted encounter with them in the town, after which Lloyd George received an elaborately purple, white and green wrapped present—a green phial tied with purple ribbon, and a white tumbler for taking the waters. Later, a gloxinia arrived at his hotel with *Votes for Women* delicately pasted on all the leaves. A note tied to its white and green basket said: 'Give votes to women and the flowers to Lady Isaacs.'

These were the last frivolous reminders. On September 5 Lloyd George was subjected to constant interruption when he opened the National Eisteddfod at Wrexham. He lost patience: 'I remember little eisteddfodau at which prizes were given for the best hazel walking-stick. One of those sticks, by the way, would be a rather good thing to have just now.' As interrupters were thrown out, the crowd fell on them, tearing off their clothes and snatching out lumps of their hair. 'Being thrown to the wild beasts is nothing to being thrown to an infuriated mob,' said Kitty Marion. 'The former might tear you to pieces, but would draw the line at indecent assaults, and so do I!' Similar scenes occurred two weeks later at Lloyd George's native Llanystumdwy where he was opening a new village institute.

Since the beginning of July the leaders had been out of the country. Soon after her release, Mrs Pankhurst went quietly to join Christabel in France and it was at this time that Christabel's whereabouts became public. The Pethick Lawrences—Mrs Lawrence very shaken by her prison experiences—travelled to visit her brother in Canada.

Just before their return the Government placed bailiffs at The Mascot, and threatened a sale of the property to pay the costs of the conspiracy trial. Immediately Annie Kenney, Rachel Barrett and Charlotte Marsh went to Holmwood with a group of friends and speakers, hoping to stir up local sympathy before the Lawrences came back.

On September 27 a cable was received at Clement's Inn: 'Greeting to all: returning on *Campania* ready for the fight: no surrender: unitedly—Pethick Lawrence.' The Lawrences were unprepared for all that awaited them. Not only was the Government claiming costs, but the West End firms had also started to take proceedings for damage to their shops. However, these were minor upsets beside the fact that the Pankhursts now wished to pursue the militant campaign without them. The Lawrences were prepared to sacrifice everything for the cause, but the Pankhursts realised that to pursue militancy as they intended would involve Pethick Lawrence in personal ruin. Christabel risked a journey to London, only protected from recognition by thick fog. There was a heated meeting between the leaders at which Annie and Mrs Tuke were present, and the decision to part company was made.

All the leaders were to appear at a great Albert Hall meeting to celebrate their return on October 17. Instead Mrs Pankhurst appeared alone, and the following notice was issued:

GRAVE STATEMENT BY THE LEADERS

At the first reunion of the leaders after the enforced holiday, Mrs Pankhurst and Miss Christabel Pankhurst outlined a new militant policy, which Mr and Mrs Pethick Lawrence found themselves unable to approve.

Mrs Pankhurst and Miss Christabel Pankhurst indicated that they were not prepared to modify their intentions, and recommended that Mr and Mrs Pethick Lawrence should resume control of the paper, *Votes for Women*, and should leave the Women's Social and Political Union.

Rather than make a schism in the ranks of the union, Mr and Mrs Pethick Lawrence decided to take this course.

Although there had been signs of change—the headquarters was moving to spacious new premises in Kingsway—no one had suspected such a division in the leadership. W.S.P.U. members, devoted to both parties, were thrown into a state of distress and confusion. Both sides seemed equally powerful and although *Votes for Women* remained with the Lawrences, the Pankhursts now brought out a new Union paper, *The Suffragette*, which promised to be as helpful to members as *Votes for Women* had been in the past. Only the strong personalities were able to decide which to follow, and those who could not withstand the conflict left the movement altogether.

Punch divided the Suffragettes into 'Peths' and 'Panks'. An intellectual group joined the 'Peths', and they continued to uphold the Pankhursts' ideals and to support the movement through *Votes for Women*. The paper was widely read, and since the editors were no longer themselves engaged in warfare, they were able to write with a detachment that helped to justify militant policy to the public. The 'Panks' became a vivacious group, fearless and quick in action. The days of amusing ruses and pageantry were over, and all had now to be prepared to take vital risks.

Chapter Nine: Through Property we shall Strike the Enemy 1912-13

THE CROWN JEWEL CASE SMASHED—A BOMB AT LLOYD
GEORGE'S HOUSE—MRS PANKHURST SENTENCED TO THREE
YEARS' PENAL SERVITUDE—THE GOVERNMENT RAIDS W.S.P.U.
HEADQUARTERS—GRACE ROE, CHIEF ORGANISER IN DISGUISE.

At the Albert Hall meeting on October 17 Mrs Pankhurst called on the
Suffragettes to join her in new militancy:

> The only recklessness the Suffragettes have ever shown has been
> about their own lives and not about the lives of others. It has never
> been, and it never will be, the policy of the Women's Social and
> Political Union recklessly to endanger human life. We leave that to
> the enemy. We leave that to the men in their warfare. It is not the
> method of women. No, even from the point of view of policy,
> militancy affecting the security of human life would be out of place.
> There is something that Governments care far more for than human
> life, and that is the security of property and so it is through property
> that we shall strike the enemy.
>
> Be militant each in your own way. Those of you who can express
> your militancy by going to the House of Commons and refusing to
> leave without satisfaction, as we did in the early days—do so. Those
> of you who can express militancy by facing party mobs at Cabinet
> Ministers' meetings when you remind them of their falseness to
> principle—do so. Those of you who can express your militancy by
> joining us in our anti-Government by-election policy—do so. Those
> of you who can break windows—break them. Those of you who can
> still further attack the secret idol of property, so as to make the
> Government realise that property is as greatly endangered by
> woman suffrage as it was by the Chartists of old—do so. And my
> last word is to the Government: I incite this meeting to rebellion.

The W.S.P.U. had never taken unprovoked action, and the first
occasion for an outbreak was the defeat of Philip Snowden's Women's
Suffrage Amendment to the Irish Home Rule Bill. On the night of
November 5, following the debate in Parliament, there was a window-
smashing raid in the West End.

There was a faint hope that George Lansbury might still save the
situation. Ever since his outburst in the House in June, he had

championed the suffrage cause with increasing enthusiasm. Sylvia Pankhurst had given him every encouragement, bringing him into the Suffragette Movement as a speaker, and at the same time accepting him as a party politician who could use his influence. Mrs Pankhurst and Christabel had always been against this policy, but Lansbury had set out to persuade the Labour Party to vote against the Government on every question until a women's suffrage measure was introduced, and when his party refused, Lansbury resigned. On November 11 he announced his intention to seek re-election on the votes-for-women issue, and at once suffragists and Suffragettes flocked to his constituency of Bow and Bromley.

Apart from genuine supporters, there were anti-suffrage and anti-Lansbury canvassers at work. Lansbury had become an embarrassment to many of his party, and the Labour agent himself was carrying on a subtle policy against his candidate. Throughout the campaign, Lansbury had the full support of the East End working women, and he was always followed by crowds of children chanting election songs, but at the poll on November 26 he was defeated by seven hundred and fifty-one votes.

The news was greeted with dumb disappointment and there was a total lack of post-election enthusiasm. Instead of attending the Unionists' victory firework display, most of the crowds went to hear Lansbury speak at the Bow Obelisk.

I have come out to fight an issue that is rather new in English politics. I have come out and defied not merely Liberals and Tories, but the political Labour Party, that party which has used all the influence it could to confuse the issue. Now Mr Blair has won this seat by seven hundred votes. That means that a large number of Liberals—Liberals remember—preferred a Tory to a Labour man and Socialism. I want to say quite deliberately that rather than sit in Parliament at the mercy of the Liberals, I would prefer to be outside. I shall go home tonight remembering that better men than I, and better women, have had to endure much more than I have had to endure in losing a seat in the House of Commons. After tonight I shall rise up refreshed and strengthened, not merely to earn my own living but also to do what one can to inspire people to revolt against their abominable conditions.

Lansbury's devoted East End supporters were not alone in feeling sad over his defeat. The *Daily Chronicle* said: 'The House of Commons is deprived of a politician whose courage and transparent honesty were always admired even by those who differed from his judgement.'

On November 28, a five-day, nation-wide pillar-box attack began.

Various types of harmful fluid were posted, and although some letters were only stained, others had the addresses completely obliterated. In answer to the public outcry, Pethick Lawrence wrote:

> The women have not gathered themselves together and encamped in battle array upon Primrose Hill, because to take such a course, in view of modern conditions, would have been to court instant defeat; but they have adopted a far more effectual modern equivalent. They have struck a blow at civilisation from within.

Amendments to the Manhood Suffrage Bill were to come up for debate in the new session of Parliament, although it was rumoured that Asquith, Churchill and Harcourt had threatened resignation if such a measure were adopted. Lloyd George and Sir Edward Grey, however, had spoken in favour of the amendments and before the new session opened the two ministers agreed to receive a deputation of working women. The idea was Sylvia's. While campaigning with Lansbury in Bow, she had come directly in touch with the East End poor, and she felt that the women would make a moving impression if they spoke for themselves.

The scheme developed, and finally a group representing working women from all over the country met in London on January 23. Shepherded by Mrs Drummond and Annie Kenney, they went to the Treasury to state their case before the two Cabinet Ministers. Beatrice Harraden accompanied the deputation:

> There was great dignity in the way in which the women stood up, one by one, and stated their cases and the need of the vote. The effect they produced on Lloyd George and some of his colleagues present was cumulative. These gentlemen were having the privilege of listening to a continuous human record, given with dignity and fearlessness, in simple direct language.

Teachers, nurses, shop assistants, domestic servants and factory women were among the professions and trades represented. Mrs Leonora Cohen of Leeds told of the tailoresses who worked for three-pence halfpenny an hour while men were paid sixpence halfpenny an hour for the same job: 'In slack time the girls go day after day to the factory and get no work given them. A hunted look comes over their faces as they realise they are being driven on to the streets. Raise their status, Mr Lloyd George, help them to get rid of that hunted look.'

Mrs Bigwood spoke on behalf of the sweated workers of the East End. 'I earn six shillings a week making pinafores and buy my own cotton and fire and gaslight.' Mrs Ward Brown, a little laundress from Poplar, told of the drudgery of wielding a seven-pound iron and standing over a hot stove all day. 'Men can't do it. They've tried them. We ought to have the vote now. It's a shame we've not got it already, Mr Lloyd George.'

Dressed in her fisherwoman costume, Mrs King from Scotland gave a dignified and imposing speech. 'Give me my vote, Mr Lloyd George,' she said, after telling of her strenuous work. 'I've come four hundred miles to get it and I want it before I go back.'

A pitbrow lass, Miss Morgan, had come in her working dress and clogs to speak for her comrades. Unknown to the assembled statesmen, she was a local heroine—the Florence Nightingale of Hulton Mine. When three hundred and forty-four miners were killed in the Hulton pit disaster, she had worked unceasingly for nearly three days, taking charge of the casualties and dead.

The twenty speakers were selected from a group of three hundred, and cleverly arranged so that each personality should stand out. Beatrice Harraden says that Mrs Drummond was the General at the General's very best. Her witty and good-natured temperament gave her a free pass into any camp, but she managed this deputation with an added finesse that brought sincere compliment from Lloyd George himself. In spite of the moving speeches, and one stormy interlude when Annie Kenney cross-questioned the Chancellor, the ministers would not commit themselves. The three hundred members of the deputation therefore remained in London prepared for any action that might follow, and meanwhile they spent the evening at the Drury Lane pantomime.

On the very same day, the Speaker ruled in Parliament that the women's suffrage amendments would so alter the new Franchise Bill that their inclusion would necessitate an entirely new Bill being drawn up. By the beginning of the next week the Franchise Bill itself was withdrawn and a new pledge to women was substituted, but clearly it was worthless.

All the suffrage societies protested. On the evening of January 27 Mrs Despard was arrested for holding a demonstration in Trafalgar Square, and at the same time, Mrs Pankhurst announced in the London Pavilion that only a Government measure or the resignation of Lloyd George and Sir Edward Grey could now prevent guerrilla warfare.

Meanwhile Annie Kenney and Mrs Drummond had been trying to negotiate with Lloyd George but their letters and personal interviews met with no success. The working women were still in London and on Tuesday, January 28, they met in the Horticultural Hall. After a short council of war led by Mrs Pankhurst, Mrs Drummond set out for the House of Commons with her deputation of twenty.

H. W. Nevinson describes the scene in *Votes for Women*:

A day of wet fog had been followed by an evening of drizzle that later turned to heavy rain. The police were drawn up in lines across all approaches from the hall to the Houses of Parliament and large crowds of little shop-boys, corner-boys, drunkards, brothel-bullies and others to whom the Government had proposed giving the vote, stood waiting in the slush.

A crowd of police instantly pounced upon the little party of women and attempted to break it up. Pushing straight on, Mrs Drummond, with about half a dozen supporters, turned into Rochester Row. When she came exactly opposite the doors of St Stephen's Church, the three policemen who were closely following her suddenly sprang upon her. The largest and most brutal seized her by the waist as one 'collars' a man in Rugby football, lifted her off her feet and dashed her violently upon the stone pavement.

There she lay, moaning, stunned and almost unconscious. She was raised to her feet, and covered in mud, without her hat, and hardly able to walk for pain, she went on. The women who were holding Mrs Drummond up still moved as rapidly as they could. The small procession was allowed to pass through the solid cordon of police and at last came up against the St Stephen's door.

As Mrs Drummond advanced towards Inspector Rogers to demand entrance, he produced a letter from Lloyd George refusing to receive the deputation, and offering only a private inter-view next day. In her fine Scottish accent, and with that voice which always seems to have a smile in it, even at moments of the most violent crisis, Mrs Drummond replied: 'Now, Mr Rogers, we are only a deputation of twenty or less, and we want to go quietly into the House. If you don't let us there'll be trouble. Enough of this tomfoolery.'

Police fell on the women and tried to drive them off. Orders were given that arrests should be made without further violence, but it was too late to prevent rough handling and in vain Mrs Drummond protested that she would walk quietly. Two policemen seized her and dragged her like a drunken criminal past the gates of Palace Yard and towards Cannon Row Police Station. At the road across Westminster Bridge the crowd of men yelled and booed.

As soon as the failure of the deputation was announced, many windows were broken and some thirty women were immediately arrested. During the rest of the week, there were further militant attacks on larger shops and Government property. 'I didn't fancy window smashing,' said Mrs

Cohen, who had spoken for the tailoresses, 'but I had come to London, and I didn't intend to return to Leeds without making my protest.'

It was already Saturday, and she had been in London more than a week:

> I pondered the matter very carefully, went out and bought a guide of the area giving the places of interest—museums, art galleries, etc. I then decided I would go to the Tower of London, remembering Colonel Blood, who once tried to steal the Crown Jewels. My hostess was much against the idea, but I was determined. Having no missile, I took out a bar from a grate, filed it down, packed it in a small parcel and started out for the Tower.
>
> I was very nervous and journeyed round and round on the tube train before summoning up courage to alight at Mark Lane Station. On arrival at the Tower, I found a party of school children in front of me, which gave me a little time to pull myself together. Then I went to the Literature Department, and I bought a guide to the Tower and some post cards before making my way to the Jewel House. There I found a crowd of schoolboys, but being tall, I could see over their heads. Swiftly, I decided my plan of action. Two Beefeaters were guarding the cases and patrolling round the room. At the moment when these two were separated by the greatest distance, with all my might I threw my missile on to the glass case which held the Regalia of the Orders of Merit. I remember one was the Order of the Garter and another, I think, was the Order of St George. There was an awful crash of breaking glass.
>
> The two Beefeaters rushed at me, and grabbed me by the shoulders, demanding why I had done this thing. I told them it was because of the Government's treachery to the working women of Great Britain in withholding an Enfranchisement Bill to give votes to women. The room was cleared. The Governor of the Tower came rushing in. He also demanded my reason for smashing the case, to which I gave him the reply I had already given to the Beefeaters.
>
> I was then arrested and taken by policemen to a place downstairs which I thought was a dungeon. There I was detained until arrangements had been made to take me to a police court. Later, I was escorted by the Beefeaters to Leman Street Court, and, as it was a Saturday morning, by the time we arrived there we were being followed by a procession of school children and spectators.
>
> The police cell into which I was put had been inhabited the night before by someone, and was in a filthy state. I felt I couldn't bear to remain in it and started to kick at the door until I was let out. After

my complaint about the filthy cell, I was conducted to the matron's room. In due course the superintendent of the division arrived. He started to ask questions, saying first: 'I think I've seen you before.' I replied: 'You ought to know—it isn't for me to tell you!' However, he was kind. Being Saturday morning it looked as if I should have to stay in the lock-up all the week-end. But the superintendent made telephone enquiries, and discovered that Thames Police Court had not yet finished its session. He thereupon made arrangements for that court to take my case as the next item on their register. Soon I was taken along and my case was heard.

It was necessary to get in touch with the Lord Chamberlain in whose charge the Crown Jewels are placed. He gave evidence that the cost of damage to the glass was seven pounds. I was committed for trial and I was bailed out by my hostess, Mrs Morrison, a sister of Professor Gilbert Murray. My case was to come up at the next quarter sessions in that division.

As we drove along the Strand in a taxi, news vendors were selling papers and showing posters which announced: 'Suffragette's Raid on the Tower of London', and Mrs Morrison commented: 'What a wonderful protest you've made. This is going to do more good for the cause than any of the protests made hitherto.'

When committed for trial, the policy was that we had to defend ourselves and plead our own cause. When my case was heard before a judge and jury, I pleaded that the court had no jurisdiction over it, that an error of judgement had been made in committing me for trial, as the court below could have dealt with it. I told the court that my husband had secured an estimate from an expert for four pounds, seventeen shillings and sixpence, to replace the damaged glass case by an exact replica, and that this sum, being under five pounds, gave me the right to appear before the lower court. The judge addressed the jury. My witness swore to do the replacement for four pounds nineteen and six, but the jury couldn't decide, so the judge said I must have the benefit of the doubt and the case was therefore dismissed.

Now full-scale militant warfare broke out. Telegraph wires were cut, golf greens were attacked with trowels and messages were burnt in the turf: 'Votes or War'—'Justice before Sport'—'No Votes, no Golf'—'No Surrender'. Golf was a favourite sport of many Cabinet Ministers, and it was reported that the links at Walton Heath where Lloyd George played were guarded by fifty caddies, day and night. Several of the royal houses —Kensington Palace, Kew Palace, Hampton Court and Holyrood—

were temporarily closed to the public and there was also talk of shutting museums and art galleries.

On February 8 plants were wrecked in the greenhouses at Kew and four days later a refreshment kiosk in Regent's Park was burned down. Mrs Pankhurst had tried to hold a truce before the withdrawal of the Franchise Bill but now she openly pursued a policy of incitement and after each of her meetings militancy took a new turn.

The house being built for Lloyd George at Walton Heath was damaged by a bomb on February 19. 'We have tried blowing him up to wake his conscience!' said Mrs Pankhurst in public. 'I have advised, I have incited, I have conspired. The authorities need not look for the women who have done what they did last night. I accept the responsibility for it.' She went on to say that, if arrested, she would prove by hunger striking that punishment unjustly inflicted on women who have no voice in making the law cannot be carried out.

On the afternoon of Monday, February 24, Mrs Pankhurst was arrested at her flat in Knightsbridge and taken to Scotland Yard. Her case came up at Epsom the following day, and she was finally committed for trial at the Old Bailey on April 1. Until that time she was allowed conditional bail. It seemed inevitable that Mrs Pankhurst would be given a long sentence, and there was much public speculation as to how McKenna would now deal with hunger strikers.

The latest cases of forcible feeding had caused much general concern. Useless attempts had been made to feed May Billinghurst, a cripple, and Lilian Lenton was released by alarmed authorities immediately after the first operation:

> I was determined to stop them if I could and all the time they were trying to push the tube down I kept coughing—coughing incessantly. Somehow food must have reached the lung for intense pains came round my chest and I found it impossible to breathe... They were obviously very frightened and upset... When I got out, I sent a post card to my parents: 'Out, double pneumonia and pleurisy, but quite all right!'

Perhaps Sylvia Pankhurst thought that, by exposing the horrors of forcible feeding, she could put a stop to the practice before her mother's inevitable reimprisonment. Twice she courted arrest, and when eventually imprisoned and forcibly fed she smuggled a letter out of prison giving gruelling details of her struggles to overcome the authorities.

'If you take a woman and torture her, you torture me,' said Bernard Shaw, speaking on forcible feeding:

These denials of fundamental rights are really a violation of the soul. They are an attack on that sacred part of life that is common to all of us, that part which has no individuality, that part which is real, the thing of which you speak when you talk of the 'life everlasting'. I say—with an absolute sense not of saying anything mystical to you, but of saying to you something that is most ordinary common sense. I say that the denial of these fundamental rights to ourselves in the persons of women is practically a denial of the life everlasting.

Many people were saying: 'Let the women starve. Provide them with food and send details of the meals to the Press. If they refuse to eat, and die, the public will know it is not the fault of the authorities.' Deportation to St Helena was proposed, and fines without option of imprisonment, but the most practical suggestion was a ticket-of-leave system. The hunger striker would be released when her life was endangered, but she would have to return to prison again as soon as she recovered. On these lines, McKenna drew up a Prisoners' Temporary Discharge for Ill-Health Bill, and it was immediately hurried through Parliament before Mrs Pankhurst was tried.

At the Old Bailey on April 3 Mrs Pankhurst was sentenced to three years' penal servitude 'Shame!' cried all the women, as the judge finished making his pronouncement. 'Shame! Shame!' they called rising to their feet, and as Mrs Pankhurst was led away they burst into deafening cheers. The judge ordered the court to be cleared and the Suffragettes then filed out, defiantly singing the Marseillaise. Still cheering, they joined other supporters outside, and they followed Mrs Pankhurst's carriage to Holloway.

As soon as she arrived in prison Mrs Pankhurst began a hunger strike, and four days later the Press reported that she was lying in her cell in an exhausted condition and that her release was expected at any moment. 'Whatever may be her fate,' said the Press, 'the W.S.P.U. is unrepentant.' At the London Pavilion meeting on Monday, April 7, Annie Kenney said that the W.S.P.U. policy was unchanged. 'Its attack is still upon property, and property alone. The policy of attack on human life is left to the militant opponents of the Home Rule Bill.' Here Annie was referring to Sir Edward Carson and Andrew Bonar Law who were stirring up militancy in Ulster.

Mrs Pankhurst's imprisonment marked the beginning of a long and continuous series of arsons and attempts to wreck empty buildings—stations, boatyards, sports pavilions and churches. Children played the 'Suffragette Game', placing home-made bombs on neighbours' doorsteps, and parading with handwritten sandwich boards threatening 'Votes or Boms'.

On April 8, the day after Annie's Pavilion speech, she was arrested, and she appeared at Bow Street Magistrates' Court on the following afternoon. Although remanded until the hearing of her case in the High Court, she was now prevented from taking any further part in the organisation of the movement. In the late summer Christabel decided that in such an event Grace Roe should succeed Annie, and since the autumn Grace had been working in London as Annie's understudy. She had been a strong support at headquarters during the critical first months of 1913, and she was now ready to take over Annie's part.

Grace had accompanied Annie to the trial with Arthur Marshall, the W.S.P.U. solicitor, and H. D. Harben, a firm friend of the union who had stood bail. As they were returning to the W.S.P.U. headquarters after the trial, Marshall told Grace that he had overheard a comment in court which indicated that the authorities had noticed her, and he warned her to be careful.

Danger was more imminent than she had realised. The Government wished to wind up the movement, and was only at a loss in view of proofs of overwhelming support for the women. At a Suffragette meeting at the Albert Hall on April 10 fifteen thousand pounds was raised, and Mrs Pankhurst's release on April 12, after a ten-day hunger strike, encouraged further sympathy. Mrs Pankhurst came out of prison in a dying condition, and under the terms of McKenna's new Bill—named by Pethick Lawrence the 'Cat and Mouse Act'—she was to return to prison in fifteen days' time. Summoning her last strength she had torn her licence to shreds in front of the prison authorities in defiance of the new measure.

Mrs Drummond and Lansbury had been speaking for the union since Mrs Pankhurst's arrest in February. They had organised a series of Sunday meetings in Hyde Park and both had addressed the Albert Hall meeting on April 10. On April 15 all W.S.P.U. meetings in the metropolitan area were prohibited and summonses were served on Lansbury and Mrs Drummond. A preliminary hearing of their case was taken on April 18, and they too were then remanded conditionally pending their trial in the High Court.

On the same day two members of the Women's Freedom League captured the Monument. Equipped with two heavy iron bars, a flag of their league, a W.S.P.U. flag and a large banner inscribed, 'Death or Victory', they climbed to the top of the tower. After diverting the attention of the two guards, they managed to take over the gallery and when they had barricaded the doors and hoisted their flags, they showered down leaflets on the huge crowd of working men who had gathered below.

In spite of the prohibition, Suffragette meetings took place in Hyde Park and on Wimbledon Common the following Sunday, and later in the week Mrs Despard protested from the plinth in Trafalgar Square. Meanwhile a week of nationwide arson and bombing of empty buildings preceded Mrs Pankhurst's expected return to prison. On Monday, April 28, her licence expired, but she had no intention of complying with its terms and she remained at Hertha Ayrton's closely guarded house in Norfolk Street where she had been staying to recuperate. On Tuesday the Home Office sent a message to say that officials would come to fetch Mrs Pankhurst at noon, and by the time they arrived a crowd had gathered outside the house. As the detectives and prison doctor were admitted, the crowd booed and waited anxiously. Only a few moments later the officials came out again. Mrs Pankhurst was too ill to be moved.

On the morning of April 30 Grace Roe left her father's home in Norwood feeling weighed down by responsibilities:

> I was on the verge of sending a telegram to say that I would not be at the office when I realised that this was no way to carry on the work that had fallen on my shoulders.
>
> I went to London and when I stepped off the 28 bus at Kingsway, I was mildly surprised to see small groups of police standing about. It was ten o'clock when I arrived at Lincoln's Inn House, and I immediately started work on the plans for the forthcoming summer fête—'All in a Garden Fair'. The map was spread out before me and I was dictating memos and interviewing organisers when there was a sudden stir and a stamping of feet.
>
> Some of the staff rushed into the room. 'We are raided!' they said. 'They have arrested Miss Kerr and Mrs Sanders and they are now in the editorial department.' At that moment the C.I.D. burst in and ordered me downstairs. I casually picked up the map and my papers from the desk, put them in my despatch case and made my way to the ground floor. I was wearing an inconspicuous navy suit and a close-fitting hat and was able to mingle unnoticed with the chatting office girls.
>
> The entrance hall was packed with speakers and workers and as soon as I came down, Marjorie, one of the typists, darted up to me, blue eyes sparkling and cheeks flushed. 'Miss Roe,' she whispered, 'I've got the leader,' and she patted her chest. Marjorie had happened to be in the editorial department just as Rachel Barrett was

being arrested and seeing the manuscript in Christabel's handwriting on the desk, she had seized it.

I managed unobtrusively to get word to many of the friends and workers to meet me at the 'bun house' at the corner of Kingsway and Holborn as soon as they were free. I moved forward with the office girls, passed the police who looked into my despatch case, and walked out of the building. I went quietly to the 'bun house', where there was already a small gathering, and they told me that the police had also been at the printers and seized all the copy for *The Suffragette* which was to go to press that day.

We made plans over tea. Mrs Dacre Fox and Joan Wickham left directly to find a printer. Cecily Hale, Emma Wylie and some others went to Maud Joachim's house in Victoria to write up the story of the raid for the forthcoming paper, and another group went along to the W.S.P.U. rooms in Westminster.

We needed money to carry on the immediate affairs of the movement, and all who had the authority to sign cheques on the official account had been arrested. I hurried out and took a taxi to my personal bank. I dashed through the main office into the back room and said, without as much as by your leave: 'I want five hundred pounds now. If I haven't got it in my account I've got bonds here to meet it,' I added. 'And I want to write a letter to my father.' I sat down at the desk and wrote: 'Don't worry about me, but do not try to get in touch with me. I am all right.' I handed the note to the manager and said: 'Will you please hold this letter for my father and ask if he will call at the bank tomorrow.' I came out with my money and dashed back to the Westminster rooms.

During this time Dorothy Bowker arrived at my home in Norwood to find plain-clothes men were already there watching the house. She managed to collect the papers for which she had come and succeeded in getting away without any trouble.

As I arrived at the Westminster rooms, Mrs Dacre Fox and Joan Wickham drew up in a taxi with a printer. I got into the taxi with them and went on to Maud Joachim's flat. The group there had by this time composed enough material for an eight-paged paper which could appear the following day the printer said. I asked Gerald Gould who was there if he would go with the printer to see the paper through the press, as I expected to have to leave for Paris that same evening. I then dictated a letter to be sent to all organisers and secretaries, telling them that they should get out on to the streets, sell the paper, and carry on.

Gerald Gould and the printer left with the material, and I made my way to Mrs Hertha Ayrton's house where Mrs Pankhurst was lying very ill. She looked transparent and terribly frail. 'Well, Grace, we won't be able to get the paper out for a few days.' 'We have already gone to press, Mrs Pankhurst.' Her face lit up. She was delighted. It was important to get news to Christabel, and it suddenly occurred to me that Barbara Ayrton could go to Paris at once, tell Christabel about the raid and explain that I would come as soon as I could. It was agreed, and Barbara left on the afternoon boat for France.

I went back to the Westminster offices where members and friends were all waiting to know what they could do to help. After I had answered continuous questions for nearly two hours there was a sudden lull. I was conscious that someone was sitting in a chair beside me, and a voice said: 'Shall we win?' 'Yes,' I answered, hardly recognising my own voice. 'Thank God!' said the friend at my side. It was Emily Wilding Davison.

Louie Hatfield came up to me and whispered: 'Do you realise you are being closely watched? If you're not careful you will be arrested.' I felt exhausted and I must have had a temperature. 'Where shall I go?' I asked. 'What do you suggest I should do?' I decided we should go to the Marshalls, and Louie came with me to their house in Geyfere Street. There I changed into some of Mrs Marshall's clothes—a black check suit and a toque with an osprey feather covered with a black spotted veil which made me look a much older woman, and different from anything I had ever looked before. Later in the evening Mr Marshall accompanied me as his wife to Victoria, and I left for Paris, via Havre.

Immediately I set foot on French soil I sent a telegram to Christabel—alias Amy Richards—and when I finally arrived at the Avenue de la Grande Armée, Christabel and Mrs Tuke greeted me with open arms. I had only been there a few minutes when we saw in the paper that there had been further Suffragette arrests. We realised that probably warrants were out for all the leading organisers. Should I be redisguised? Mrs Tuke wanted me to dye my eyebrows gold saying that it was quite impossible to disguise my eyes. However, I declined to have my eyebrows dyed, and eventually returned as I was, dressed in Kitty Marshall's clothes. Christabel thought that, as I was impersonating Mrs Marshall, it would be a good idea to return to her home.

After a rapid two hours' conversation, I had to return at once to London and as I was about to leave Christabel, a friend called. She was Phyl Keller, a charming young girl who lived in Paris with her mother. We left together and hailed a taxi en route for the Gare du Nord. It occurred to me, just as Phyl Keller was about to leave the taxi, that it would probably be unsafe to correspond direct with Christabel in future, and I asked Phyl to give me her address. I seemed to know that we might have to use it immediately.

On arrival at Southampton I sensed danger, and was soon aware that many detectives were watching the boat. I stepped into a first-class carriage and lay back in a corner seat feeling ill and exhausted, but my brain was working rapidly. There were only two other people in the carriage besides myself—a man and his wife, an elderly lady dressed in black. Apparently I looked ill, for the lady immediately sent her husband to get a cup of tea. While he was gone, detectives came along the train searching into every carriage. When they reached mine, the little elderly lady was standing at the window. 'Go away! Go away! There's a young lady in this carriage who is very ill indeed.' The detectives passed on, and soon the train steamed out of the station.

During the journey to London I did not outwardly recover, but my thought was concentrated on my arrival at Victoria Station. I knew that I could well be recognised by the Westminster bobby who with a friendly greeting would stop my taxi to take my ticket as I left the station. I had been arrested three times on deputations to the House of Commons. Now I had to avoid recognition at any cost. On arrival, I decided to cross over to the suburban line. I hailed a taxi and drove to Gayfere Street, but not without the old taxi driver having to stop once to ask a London policeman the way.

We neared the Marshalls' home and I saw, on the other side of the street, secret-service men standing on guard outside the house of one of the ministers. The upstairs lights were on in the Marshalls' house and I realised that they had retired. I jumped out of the taxi, ran up to the front door and gave the danger knock. Immediately Mr Marshall was there. 'Oh! Come in—I'll pay the taxi,' he said in a very English drawl. I entered, and he closed the door saying: 'Grace Roe, there is a warrant out for your arrest!'

Next day I sent for Louie Hatfield and gave her all the messages for the staff. The same day, a new home was found for me just off Piccadilly—a spacious flat owned by an elderly lady.

That evening, dressed for the theatre in Mrs Marshall's evening clothes, I left in a taxi with Mr Marshall and we were driven to Piccadilly. In the heart of the theatre world we left the taxi, Mr Marshall escorted me to a waiting car and we parted. Louie was in the car. We drove on, and quickly reached the new destination where we were met by a charming old lady. She gave us a warm greeting and I gave my alias, Miss Courtney. 'But, that is not my real name,' I said. 'My dear, it is much better that I should not know your name.' Then, opening the doors of a beautiful living-room, dining-room and bedroom all on one floor, she said: 'Make yourself at home.' A lovely fire, comfortable arm-chairs, books, desk, and every comfort met my gaze.

It was evening. I was feverish and felt really ill—so ill that Louie was up with me all that night. When morning came I still had a temperature, and felt I must be alone to make a big decision. So I sent Louie out and gave her enough work to last at least four hours. I told her to go and spend some time with Annie—to stay with her as long as she wished.

Once by myself, I sat down at the desk in the bay window and took a sheet of paper. I made two columns—the one side headed *For*, the other *Against*. The *Against* was completely filled. There was one word on the other side—'Loyalty'. I got up and paced up and down the room. Then I sank into a very comfortable arm-chair in front of the fire, and suddenly I relaxed and felt myself almost in another world. When I came to myself once more, it seemed that my mind was made up. Nothing could stop me going on, whatever happened.

When Louie returned, she explained how she had told Annie that I would not be able to take over—that I was much too ill. Where-upon I started giving Louie instructions about the many things to be done. 'Annie said . . .' she broke in, 'Annie said, "Nonsense! There is nobody else to take on the job but Grace." '

Next day, two members of the Actresses' Franchise League came to give me a new disguise. This time I was dressed as an elderly lady and I had to remember that all my movements must be slow.

I moved to Hampstead but felt in danger all the time. Just as things were at a pitch, Mrs Mansel turned up. She was recovering from a serious operation and the moment she read the papers came straight to London to help me. When she saw me she went into peals of laughter—I looked so odd in my disguise! We had a good talk and she was in no doubt that, if I was to be able to carry on the work, then I must have a settled place in which to do it.

She had no sooner left than I fled to a flat that Christabel had used at one time, but the feeling of danger followed me. I went next to visit Annie and Rachel and tried to talk to them about the work, but they seemed very vague about everything. I told them that some-thing made me feel I should not go back to the flat. Annie said: 'Act on your own intuition—don't go back,' and at that moment Louie Hatfield came in and told us that, within half an hour of my leaving, the flat had been raided. 'Why don't you go to one of the hotels near the British Museum,' said Annie, 'and take Louie with you?' This we did, but I was miserable. The walls were very thin and I realised it was quite unsafe to talk in the room we were in.

Meanwhile Mrs Mansel had seen Christabel in Paris and she came back with instructions to find a flat for me. It seemed an interminable time but it must have been only a few days before I found myself in a quiet upstairs flat in an old house in Earls Court. Mrs Mansel said she had taken the flat for a young lady who had come from Australia for the London Season. 'The young lady' arrived with no clothes, not even a toothbrush, only the names and addresses of the valued members and organisers of the W.S.P.U.

Before I went into this flat, the Actresses' Franchise League came to the rescue and I was redisguised as a chorus girl. Charlie Marsh, who did much secret work for me, had a similar disguise. My transformation was golden and her wig was black. We certainly made a striking pair, but it was a very good disguise indeed. Our costumes were so cleverly designed that only the wrong type of man looked at us! We called ourselves 'The Sisters Blackamore'.

By this time an underground set-up was being formed. Joan Wickham came to stay with me and messengers travelling by circuitous routes went between Christabel and myself taking letters and important news. At least a channel was now in the making, and soon secretaries came regularly.

At this time, I had a man caller, always immaculately dressed. He was Mr Herbert Goulden, Mrs Pankhurst's brother, whom many of us called 'Uncle Herbert'. He was a frequent visitor and often came in the evenings, bringing important news. He seemed always to be by my side when I had a problem to solve. The flat was now the heart of the W.S.P.U. in London and Lincoln's Inn House made a wonderful front. The head of the information department, Cecily Hale, called often, bringing last-minute news. Mrs Mansel, as cousin of the Liberal Chief Whip, was virtually immune from arrest and she was now a constant visitor to the flat. She presided at the weekly At Homes, and was the vital link between the commander in exile and the chief organiser in London.

Chapter Ten: Death for the Cause 1913

CIVIL LIBERTIES AT STAKE—'LET MRS PANKHURST DIE'—
EMILY WILDING DAVISON KILLED AT THE DERBY—THE W.S.P.U.
STAFF TRIED FOR CONSPIRACY—MOCKERY OF THE CAT AND
MOUSE ACT.

The Suffragette of May 9 showed a picture of Lincoln's Inn House with the flag again flying, only twenty-four hours after the raid. 'Every attack which the Government have ever made upon us has left us stronger than before,' said Mrs Pankhurst. Now A. H. Bodkin, speaking on behalf of the Public Prosecutor, said that inflammatory speeches must be stopped, *The Suffragette* must be stopped and that all subscribers to Suffragette funds were in an 'awkward position'. 'Can a newspaper be suppressed?' asked the *Manchester Guardian*, and the article continued: 'If the W.S.P.U. is an illegal combination for committing offences against the law, and nothing else, by all means let it be suppressed. But if the union is not illegal and cannot be suppressed, neither can its members or subscribers be punished.' 'Who the devil is Bodkin anyway?' asked the public.

Sidney Drew, the printer of the emergency copy of *The Suffragette*, had clearly no other connection with the W.S.P.U. but he was tried at Bow Street with Mrs Drummond, Annie Kenney and the rest of union personnel charged with conspiracy. Although acquitted, his release was conditional, and when four days later another printer, Edgar Whitely, was arrested for producing the next number of the paper, a storm of protest broke out. In order to uphold the freedom of the Press, Keir Hardie and Ramsay MacDonald suggested that they should take over the publication of *The Suffragette*, MacDonald assuming right of censorship. Whether the offer was genuine, or merely a political move, it was obviously not acceptable and finally the Athenaeum Press agreed to print the paper. At the same time the Home Office made a statement that there never had been an intention to suppress *The Suffragette*.

On the Sunday after the raid thirty thousand people gathered in Trafalgar Square for a mass rally in defence of free speech, and on the same afternoon Suffragettes in Hyde Park made a sport of holding meetings and dodging the police. Each speaker came equipped with a flag and a camp stool, and at a suitable moment she quickly mounted her stand and unfurled the colours. Immediately the crowd came stampeding towards her: 'Free speech! Free speech!' they yelled and hemmed her in on every side. Frantically, the police tried to force their way through the mass of people who did everything to obstruct them. 'Shame!' roared the mob as police whistles blew for reinforcements. When the police eventually managed to break through, they often found the woman gone and they would hear her voice coming from the centre of another crowd a little way off. Although some speakers were arrested, the excited crowds rallied to defend the women, and meetings continued all over the park until sundown.

In the weeks following the raid on Lincoln's Inn House the papers were filled with stories of burning mansions, damaged churches and gutted railway stations. 'Bombs have been found in St Paul's Cathedral and elsewhere,' said the Press. 'London is "locked up", and very great nervousness prevails.' Public sympathy was therefore not altogether with Mrs Pankhurst when she was rearrested on May 26.

Still weak and exhausted from the hunger strike, she had moved from London to Dr Ethel Smyth's house in Woking hoping to be able to recover in the country and in the company of her one great friend. Detectives had followed her to the cottage and were posted all round the garden amongst the bushes, 'I never went to the window, I never took the air in the garden without being conscious of watching eyes,' says Mrs Pankhurst and in spite of all Dr Ethel's efforts, she found the situation unbearable. 'I determined to end it and to resume my position as an ordinary human being in this country.'

The W.S.P.U. car was summoned to fetch Mrs Pankhurst back to London and as it drove up to Coign, bringing Dr Flora Murray, a detective placed himself strategically at the gate. A few moments later Mrs Pankhurst—frail and drawn—came slowly out of the house supported by Dr Ethel and Nurse Pine. When she reached the car, the detective stood in front of the door to prevent her entering, and asked her where she was going. 'I was in a weak state,' says Mrs Pankhurst, 'much weaker than I had imagined, and in refusing the right of a man to question my movements, I exhausted the last remnant of my strength and sank fainting into the arms of my friends.'

Later she was driven to London by the police and at Bow Street Court she was formally committed again to prison. Scarcely able to speak, she protested against the inhuman conditions of the Cat and Mouse Act, and defied the Government to let her die. Dr Ethel watched her being taken off to Holloway: 'The last we saw of her was the bright brave smile which is all we have to live on till we see her again.'

'Let her die,' said some people and the *Daily Sketch* 'Man in the Street' prophesied:

If Mrs Pankhurst dies, as she will die of course because she is a woman weakly, advanced in years and suffering from a defective digestive system, if she dies, the public conscience will be shocked. The man in the street who has light-heartedly consigned Mrs Pankhurst and all her works to the devil, will say solemnly: 'This must not occur again.'

At the beginning of June, while arson and destruction of property were rampant, the Suffragettes held their summer festival at the Empress Rooms. Of all the W.S.P.U. fêtes this was the most feminine with its profusion of flowers and seventeenth-century garden. Children dressed as brownies, elves and butterflies flitted about selling the paper. Live hens roosted in the beams of an old-world barn—the produce stall—and Suffragette waitresses in white offered strawberries and cream. The only sign of militancy in the decor was the large statue of Joan of Arc dominating one end of the hall.

Emily Wilding Davison went to the fair with Mary Leigh on June 3—the opening day. Together they stood before the statue and read out the words on the pedestal: 'Fight on and God will give the Victory.' They stayed on at the fair until late in the evening. Emily was happy. 'I shall be at the fair every day except tomorrow. I'm going to the Derby tomorrow.' 'What are you going to do?' 'Ah!' she said, smiling mysteriously. 'Look in the paper and you will see.'

Early the next morning Emily rushed into headquarters. 'I want two flags,' she said. 'What for?' 'Ah!' 'Perhaps I'd better not ask.' 'No, don't ask me.' Dressed unobtrusively, and with a flag wound round her hidden beneath her coat, Emily bought a third-class return ticket to Epsom and travelled in a packed train to join the fashionable racegoers and the riff-raff assembled on the Downs.

As the time for the great race approached, she stood beside the course at Tattenham Corner in the front line of the dense crowds. At last the horses came round the bend in a great sweep thundering closer and closer. The King's horse came near. Emily slipped under the railings and in a second she was on the course with flag unfurled, grasping the horse's bridle. The animal swerved, the jockey was thrown, and Emily, caught up with the horse as it fell, rolled over and over, headlong across the turf. Stewards and spectators rushed on to the course to attend to the casualties. The jockey was not seriously hurt and the horse was unharmed, but Emily was unconscious. She never recovered, and four days later she died.

In spite of her determination to sacrifice herself, Emily loved life. She had a great sense of fun and her former headmistress describes the 'peculiar brightness of her look—a brightness that no photograph could reproduce'. Besides being a keen sportswoman, Emily delighted in literature, music and the theatre and she was interested in many subjects and questions that had no direct bearing on the movement. A verdict of death by misadventure was recorded at her inquest, but nevertheless it was difficult to find a clergyman prepared to conduct the funeral. Eventually the Rev. C. Baumgarten, the Vicar of St George's Church, Bloomsbury, agreed to take the service. All the arrangements for the ceremony and a great procession were organised by Grace Roe from hiding. Any public demonstration at this time involved great risk, for in making an appearance many of the leading Suffragettes were exposed to arrest.

Dr Ethel Smyth helped Mrs Pankhurst to dress for the funeral: 'She looked pecularly ill and the long wait told on her.' After a five-day hunger strike Mrs Pankhurst had been released from prison again at the end of May, but she was far too weak and emaciated to leave her bed on the expiry of her seven-day licence and it was only her determination to attend the funeral that now gave her strength enough to get up. When the carriage arrived at Westminster Mansions where she was staying, crowds watched Mrs Pankhurst come out of the house in deep mourning. Immediately four detectives approached, a conversation took place on the steps, and within a few moments she was being helped into a taxi bound for Holloway. Crowds pressed round the car before it could get away. 'God bless you, dear: keep up your spirits!' called the working women to the frail figure at the window.

The funeral on Saturday, June 14 was the last and most moving of all the Suffragette demonstrations. It had the simplicity and intimacy of the prison release processions of earlier days, but a solemn sadness replaced the joyful exuberance. In spite of Mrs Pankhurst's absence, her carriage dramatically took its place in the procession and was driven empty behind the coffin. Emily's friends, the familiar figures that had once been so outstanding—the Joan of Arc, the Bandleader and the Horsewomen—now walked beside the coffin as one, and Charlotte Marsh, the Standard Bearer, led the procession carrying a huge wooden cross. Long lines of women in white held madonna lilies; Suffragettes in purple and black followed bearing irises and peonies and between the bier and Mrs Pankhurst's empty carriage walked the 'conspirators'—Annie Kenney, Rachel Barrett and the office staff awaiting trial. Dressed in their familiar everyday clothes, they stood out from the uniformed ranks as marked women.

While the bands played solemn music of Chopin, Handel and

Beethoven, the procession accompanied Emily's body from Victoria Station to King's Cross where she was to leave London for burial at Morpeth, her Northumberland home. Midway the procession halted for the short impressive funeral service at St George's. Triumphantly, almost gladly, the Suffragettes sang out the last hymn, 'Fight the good fight with all thy might'.

Crowds lined the route of the procession, awed and silent. Women wept, and there were tears on the faces of many men. Although strong forces of police were on duty, they did not actively come to the women's help when a band of hooligans made a rush at the procession as it was nearing the station. 'If it hadn't been for the cross,' said Charlotte Marsh, 'we wouldn't have got through, but everybody just fell back when they saw it.'

The trial of the conspirators opened in the High Court after the weekend of the funeral. Mrs Drummond was ill and could not appear, but the other Suffragettes together with Edwy Clayton came up before Mr Justice Phillimore on Monday morning. Clayton was a scientist and author—a keen suffragist with a wife and daughter both active W.S.P.U. and Church League members. Now he was implicated because of correspondence discovered at Annie's flat which suggested he was carrying out experiments with certain chemicals for the use of the W.S.P.U. Annie, speaking in her own defence, denied any knowledge of the incriminating letters, which she said belonged to her sister Jessie.

On June 17, the final day of the trial, Mrs Winston Churchill and Miss Violet Asquith were among the spectators in court. Annie Kenney made an inspired speech explaining the reasons for the Suffragette agitation, but in spite of the jury's recommendation to mercy, the judge gave heavy sentences:

Edwy Clayton	Analytical Chemist	21 months
Annie Kenney		18 months
Miss Kerr	General Offices Manager	15 months
Mrs Sanders	Financial Secretary	12 months
Rachel Barrett	Assistant Editor of *The Suffragette*	9 months
Geraldine Lennox	Sub-editor	6 months
Agnes Lake	Business Manager of *The Suffragette*	6 months

Nothing specific could be proved against the office staff and they were clearly of good character as Judge Phillimore implied before giving sentence: 'You have of course departed from your natural good sense and refinement of feeling. Now I am afraid I must treat you all as people who have done very serious injury to the public peace and who must be kept away from doing mischief, and you must be made to some extent an example to others.' 'I never desired nor intended to go to prison,' says Miss Kerr, 'and I always felt somewhat like St Paul "not meet to be called" a Suffragette. To my huge astonishment I was now transformed into the villain of the piece.'

All the conspirators were placed in the third division and the judge stated that none should be released in any circumstances. They were hurried by night to distant and separate gaols—Wormwood Scrubs, Maidstone, Holloway, Lewes, Canterbury, Bristol and Warwick. Within ten days, in spite of the judge's decree, all had been released after hunger striking, and they were back in London, weak, emaciated and seriously strained by the ordeal. Some were rearrested, but they had to be let out of prison again almost at once. Mrs Pankhurst, too, was on release after a forty-eight-hour hunger and thirst strike which had left her in a half dying condition.

Shaw commented on the Government's lack of decent feeling: 'Suppose Mrs Pankhurst dies! Will the Government merely because it has contrived that she shall die out of Holloway still cry, "don't care," as it did by arresting Mrs Pankhurst before Miss Davison's funeral instead of after it?'

Shaw then goes on to say how Asquith, in a recent debate, for the first time opposed the franchise for women explicitly on the ground that woman is not the female of the human species but a distinct and inferior species naturally disqualified from voting as a rabbit is disqualified from voting.

A man may object to the proposed extension of the franchise for many reasons. He may hold that the whole business of popular election is a delusion, and that votes for women is only its reduction to absurdity. He may object to it as upsetting a convenient division of labour between the sexes. He may object to it because he dislikes change, or is interested in business or practices which women would use political power to suppress. But it is one thing to follow a Prime Minister who advances all, or some, or any of these reasons for standing in the way of votes for women. It is quite another to follow a Prime Minister who places one's mother on the footing of a rabbit. Many men would vote for anything rather than be suspected of the rabbit theory. It makes it difficult to vote for the Liberal party and then look the women of one's household in the face.

If Mrs Pankhurst dies, public opinion will consider that the

Government will have executed her. Mr Asquith will not be moved by that; in his opinion it will matter just as much as killing a rabbit.

After the release of the conspirators, Shaw said: 'The women who want the vote say in effect that we must either kill them or give it to them. In spite of lawyers' logic, our conscience will not let us kill them. In the name of common sense let us give them the vote and have done with it.'

The Cat and Mouse Act was proving a failure and the Home Secretary was ridiculed:

> That great Tom-fool whose name is McKenna
> Becomes a Tom Cat when in a dilemma.

Long letters condemning the Act appeared in the Press and numerous protest meetings and demonstrations were held. On July 11, during a debate on the franchise in the House of Commons, a toy pistol was fired from the Strangers' Gallery, and a man threw a shower of mousetraps down on to the floor of the House. Although some 'mice' were missing, and others on release were committing new outrages, McKenna still firmly persisted in upholding the Act.

When Sir Edward Busk, Chairman of the Conference for the Repeal of the Cat and Mouse Act, called at the Home Office, McKenna smilingly told him that he could hold out no hope for the repeal of the measure. Mrs Mansell-Moullin, the wife of the eminent surgeon, wrote a report of the interview:

> The lawyer met the great Tom Cat
> And shook him by the hand
> He said: 'I've called to try my best
> To make you understand
> That British people won't endure
> The "Act" you think so grand.'
>
> 'It grieves me sore to hurt the mice,
> And give them needless pain,'
> Said sly Tom Cat; then licked his paws
> And purred and purred again.
> 'But if you think I'll own I'm wrong
> Why, then you ask in vain!'
>
> 'If twenty mice in twenty traps
> Should die in half a year
> Do you suppose,' the lawyer said,
> 'That that would make it clear?'

'I doubt it,' said the great Tom Cat
And smiled from ear to ear.

'You've had your chance,' the lawyer said,
'And if that senseless grin
Is all the answer you can raise
To try to hide your sin
The trap you've made will catch yourself
And shut you firmly in!'

Just before the W.S.P.U. offices were raided, Christabel had adopted a
new line of policy. In a series of articles in *The Suffragette*, she set out to
prove with many facts and statistics that prostitution was unnecessary,
harmful and degrading. Two months later on July 10 a somewhat
sensational procuration case came up in the High Court, but very little
information was given in the Press:

> Mme Queenie Gerald (26), an actress, was sentenced to three
> months' imprisonment in the second division at the London
> Sessions for offences under the White Slave Traffic Act. Wearing a
> black silk costume with a white collar and lace tie, she made a
> striking picture in the dock and she pleaded guilty in a whisper.

This was the first prosecution to come under a new statute, and the
Chairman of the London Sessions was lenient in his sentencing. As
Queenie Gerald had pleaded guilty, the girls involved in the case were
not required to give evidence.

Because the case had received so little publicity, the Suffragettes felt
that the facts should be exposed, and they quickly found out details of
the case and the names of the prominent people who were involved. The
Daily Sketch very soon took up their cry for more information:

> The woman was sentenced, that was all the public heard of the
> affair. Letters have been found, signed by men of high position,
> revealing an organisation for procuring young girls and little
> children. The evidence was not produced in the case because the
> men concerned were persons of importance. The law of libel makes
> it impossible to give names but the *Daily Sketch* knows the names of
> people mentioned in this article.
>
> Other persons also know the names. Some would speak if the law
> of England would protect them for telling the truth. Others are
> silent because they are guilty.

The matter finally reached a stage where questions were asked in the
House, and the Home Secretary was obliged to answer for the Govern-

ment. 'I was unaware of any of the names until after the trial was over,' said McKenna and he firmly denied that any Members of the House of Commons were involved in the case.

Although every W.S.P.U. speaker took up the cause of white slavery, and destruction of property continued, the main business of the union was now to prove its indestructibility by defying Government coercion. Under the Cat and Mouse Act, women's health deteriorated to such an extent that they could no longer be imprisoned for more than three or four days. The newly adopted thirst strike had a rapid and dangerous effect on the body and the periods of release for recovery extended far beyond the terms of the licence. Although ill and weak, Mrs Pankhurst and Annie Kenney now proposed to address the W.S.P.U. Monday At Homes at the Pavilion, and as 'mice', they escaped from the heavily guarded houses where they were staying, and by an elaborate series of ruses appeared together on the Pavilion platform for four successive weeks.

Mrs Pankhurst's escape from a flat in Little Smith Street was arranged to take place on the night of Saturday, July 19, and Olive Bartels— Grace Roe's future understudy—was to call for her at eleven o'clock.

Dressed in a blue evening cloak, and carrying flowers, Bartels drove in a taxi from Chelsea. As she came up to Big Ben, it was five minutes to eleven:

I thought Gosh! I'm still five minutes too early. So I said to the cabman: 'My goodness, I've forgotten to send a telegram. Drive me up to Charing Cross Post Office.' I ran into the post office, wrote something on a bit of paper, came out again and said: 'Now, drive me to Victoria Mansions—number twelve.'

Two detectives were sitting in a doorway on the opposite side of the road watching the house and muttering.

I drew up in the taxi, my flowers in my hand—a great bouquet—not a word said—jumped out—ran upstairs—they thought just visiting (it was a block of flats)—leaving flowers. As I rang the bell of the flat (of course they were all just inside waiting), the door opened immediately and Big Ben struck out eleven. 'What organisation!' said Mrs Pankhurst.

Meanwhile a party of pretty girls in evening dress came down the road and several young men came towards them. They were apparently friends for they stopped to have a chat in front of Mrs Pankhurst's flat. A taxi drove up to the entrance and down the stairs came a frail-looking lady heavily veiled and supported by her nurse. The young men and girls were quite interested at the proceedings and Mrs Pankhurst's name was mentioned as she was recognised by the group. The taxi door was flung open, and the lady bundled in with the police following with orders to the driver to go straight to Holloway.

The lady meanwhile appeared to be in a collapsed condition with her head well down, and it was only after having gone a good distance that she threw off her veil and the police discovered that they had not got Mrs Pankhurst as their prisoner but a stranger. Back at the flat, another car had driven up, and into it the real Mrs Pankhurst got and was driven off to the Marshalls' house in the country.

On Monday, Mrs Pankhurst and Mrs Marshall drove to the Pavilion meeting by car. 'Mrs Pankhurst had a useful veil. They were the fashion in those days and helped to disguise people quite a lot,' says Mrs Marshall.

Annie Kenney arrived at the Pavilion as an old lady, with a plum in each cheek to fill out her face. She tells how she drove up in an ancient cab and intended to go into the meeting with the audience.

When we arrived at the front entrance I saw in a flash my own special detective. His eyes were piercing each individual. I couldn't speak—the plums were going to be my downfall. In a second they were out. 'For God's sake drive on; don't you see Detective Renshaw? Get to the stage door entrance as quickly as possible.'

'We got safely inside the hall,' says Mrs Marshall, 'but then the game was up.'

A number of detectives were there and one of them seized Mrs Pankhurst. 'Women, they are arresting me!' she cried and there was a regular scrimmage—friends trying to save her and foes to arrest her. I held on to the detective's tie with one hand and in the other I had a small suitcase, but I was had up for smacking the detective on his face, which of course I should not think of doing. In the struggle, Mrs Pankhurst and all of us got pushed into a small room, and the lights were turned off and the table overturned. It had all sorts of literature and *Votes for Women* buttons and badges on it.

Another witness said that a man struck out wildly with a thick stick:

Several people were hit over the head and blood splashed down all over the floor and on to the literature table. When the lights went on again, I saw Mrs Pankhurst for the first time standing in the far corner looking very shaken as if she had been badly knocked about.

'Mrs Pankhurst gave me instructions to tell the audience of her regret at not being able to speak,' says Mrs Marshall, 'but I never got near the platform as everyone in the room was arrested. Off to Vine Street we were taken, and a huge crowd in Piccadilly saw us go.'

Meanwhile Annie Kenney had managed to enter the Pavilion unnoticed:

> Once safely inside, I flew like the wind. The old lady suddenly turned into a brisk flapper. The meeting started. It was known that I was to attempt to run the blockade, and the one thing discussed among the audience was—should I get in or shouldn't I. The air was electric. Everyone had taken their seats on the platform when in I strolled waving my licences. The enthusiasm was unbounded.

Having been arrested at the previous Monday meeting, Annie was imprisoned and released after a drastic hunger and thirst strike and now, still on licence, she could speak temporarily without rearrest. A reporter says she was pale and wan and scarcely able to walk, but she nevertheless insisted on standing to address the audience as it was 'more defiant'. Greatly excited, she spoke about her licences as 'a proof of the misguided Liberals', and then she put them up for auction.

At the Pavilion on the following Monday Annie, wearing a long coat and thick veil, walked on to the platform and gaily throwing off her disguise she asked the audience: 'I wonder if you recognise me?' In the middle of the meeting, Mrs Mansell Moullin, the chairman, quietly remarked: 'I have another speaker, ladies and gentlemen, I call upon Mrs Pankhurst.'

The curtain at the back of the stage was drawn aside, and Mrs Pankhurst was wheeled up to the chairman's table. The cheering that greeted her subsided and changed to an awed silence when the audience realised how very ill she was. Then slowly and deliberately, Mrs Pankhurst delivered her speech. 'We shall fight on,' she ended, 'and I know we are going to win very soon.' Her licence was sold for one hundred pounds. Annie impulsively ran forward and embraced her again and again before the invalid chair was slowly pulled to the back of the platform, and disappeared behind the curtain. After the meeting, men and women fought with police outside the Pavilion to protect Annie from rearrest, but they were eventually overcome and Annie was taken back to Holloway.

Towards the end of her four-day imprisonment, Annie became delirious, and her heart was seriously affected by the hunger and thirst strike. Other Cat and Mouse prisoners were being released in a state of collapse and there was growing protest at all levels of society.

On August 5 and 11 both Mrs Pankhurst and Annie Kenney were allowed to speak freely at the Kingsway Hall, possibly because the International Medical Congress was being held in London. Throughout their stay, the delegates were made aware of the Cat and Mouse question by daily poster parades outside the Albert Hall where the congress met. Sandwich boards proclaimed in several languages: THE ENGLISH GOVERNMENT IS MURDERING WOMEN.

Chapter Eleven: Armed Women 1913–14

It was the holiday season and in the middle of August Mrs Pankhurst and Annie Kenney left England quite openly to spend some time with Christabel in France. For a while they stayed at Deauville as the guests of the wealthy American Suffragette, Mrs O. H. P. Belmont, and from here Mrs Pankhurst planned to make yet another lecture tour in the United States before returning to England.

While the leaders were away, the Suffragettes kept themselves in the public eye through an extensive paper selling programme. At resorts all over the country the W.S.P.U. established pitches, in some places speakers would address the crowds, and each week *The Suffragette* contained a double-page spread of holiday campaign snapshots, showing the success of the project. The paper also gave detailed accounts of the members' activities:

> On Thursday, eight of us dressed as gypsies climbed into an old decorated cart and made seats for ourselves on our bundles of luggage and provisions. The crowd collected outside Lincoln's Inn House and we flicked the old horse up as we drove off from Kingsway to carry our message to the women of Kent. The mare certainly required a good amount of 'wigging' and no one knew her name. It was suggested we should call her 'Christabel' or 'Pankhurst', but as she stopped all the progress and activity in the Strand she was at last named 'Asquith'.
>
> The first night we reached Halstead and we approached the farmer to know if he would lend us a field. After dispelling the farmer's idea that we had come to burn his haystacks, and the boy's idea that we had come to smash the windows, the whole family set to work to make us comfortable.

The Suffragette, sold so light-heartedly, contained articles which probed deeper into the implications of the movement than ever before. In a

211

series of articles on sexual excesses, Christabel finally and unashamedly embarked on a criticism of male behaviour as the only means by which women could secure respect. 'What after all is there to lose?' she said. 'Any man who is alienated from the suffrage cause by the W.S.P.U. policy on the sex question is a man who gives himself away.'

Many of the clergy were now behind the movement and they saw Christabel's point of view that there is a violence that is righteous as well as a violence which is unrighteous. 'Many times over in the history of the Church violence has been used in the name of religion,' she said. 'All the forces of progress are working in favour of the movement,' wrote the Bishop of Lincoln in *The Times*. 'It cannot be set aside.' In a sermon, the Rev. E. H. Taylor said: 'In my opinion the new force has won already and the sufferings inflicted on the standard bearers are due to the fury of the defeated foe.'

On August 7 a deputation of one hundred and sixty clergymen arrived at Downing Street to present a memorial to the Prime Minister, but, although Asquith received the petition, he declined to give an audience. By no means all the clergy were sympathetic, and in churches where the priest was not prepared to intercede for the Cat and Mouse prisoners, organised Suffragette choirs would break into the service chanting prayers for their comrades.

Shaw's *Androcles and the Lion* was running currently in London and the Suffragettes realised that it would be a very apt play at which to make an interruption. The Brackenbury sisters, great Shavians, were horrified at the suggestion, but Christabel felt that all was fair at this stage. On the night of Saturday, September 13, a group of Suffragettes attended the performance and when in the play the Christian martyrs are rebuked, a woman rose from her seat: 'That is just what McKenna says to the Suffragettes.' 'McKenna, McKenna, McKenna,' echoed women from all round the theatre.

In preparation for the leaders' return a bodyguard was formed, and the recruits came from every walk of life. A housemaid, unknown to her Suffragette mistress, belonged to the group, and whenever there was an important militant event she would mysteriously disappear.

Gertrude Harding was to become their leader.

It was a proud moment for me when Grace Roe told me that I was to be the one to select and organise this band of women. She gave me unstinted help and advice from the start of this strange assignment or I should never have known where or how to start. All volunteers had to be carefully selected. They must be completely trustworthy, in good physical shape and be ready at a moment's notice to do battle with the police in defence of Mrs Pankhurst.

Scotland Yard did their best to introduce spies into our ranks so that they could learn what the women were armed with. After some thirty recruits had been accepted, they were notified to come to Lincoln's Inn House for our first evening meeting when weapons would be distributed. They all turned up full of curiosity as to what the weapons would be and it was somewhat of an anti-climax when each member of the Bodyguard was handed a neat little Indian club with instructions to tie this around her waist under her skirt.

During the next few weeks we met in different places for practice, and we took instruction in jiu-jitsu from Mrs Garrud. Sometimes the meetings would be in a basement lent by a sympathiser, or in some studio with skylights. We had to keep changing our meeting places because it was found that police were intercepting the notices sent out to tell the Bodyguard where to meet. One night, when the meeting had just started in a large studio, we discovered two faces peering down from the skylight. All proceedings were stopped at once and the women were told to go home. As each one stepped outside a flash-light picture was snapped by a group of waiting detectives, and a man followed behind every member of the Bodyguard as she left. I was the last to leave and the same thing happened—first the flash-bulb, then the lone man waiting fell in behind me. Of course the idea was to find out the names and addresses of every member of the Bodyguard.

A ridiculous game of hide-and-seek began; I stopped at a sweet shop, only to find my shadower waiting when I emerged. After a few more such incidents, I decided to carry the war into enemy country —and did so. 'What do you mean by following me?' I fiercely demanded. 'I'm sorry miss, but it's my orders,' a rather apologetic voice replied. I tried to keep up an aggressive front and told him that he should be ashamed of himself. Then, in an amiable way, we agreed that it was all a game of wits. If I managed to fool him, I won, if I didn't, he was the winner.

Off we started again with a greatly speeded up effort on my part. When a tram came along, I would board it—and so would he. Then off I would jump with the detective not far behind. This seemed to go on for ages, and then I made a great effort. There was a bus just moving away and I hopped on board and sat down on the only vacant seat near the door. My pursuer foolishly, but decently, went upstairs. Quickly I jumped off the still moving bus, and ran like a hare down a dark side street. I flattened myself against a shadowy doorway. Running footsteps came and passed on down the street. Soon I was in a taxi, heading for home, feeling just a little bit elated with success.

The following morning I heard how other members of the Bodyguard had fared. Some had managed to get home safely, but poor Mrs Barry and her daughter were not so fortunate. They walked all night long without being able to throw off their pursuers. Exhaustion was setting in, and when the two men began to sing: 'Art Thou Weary, Art Thou Languid', that finished it. They headed straight for home with one thought—bed.

On October 1 Miss Kerr and Mrs Sanders returned to Lincoln's Inn House to resume work after their holidays. No attempt was made to arrest them during the morning, but as they left the building for lunch, there were violent scenes outside the headquarters as police struggled with crowds of supporters before taking the two women in charge once more.

Later that week, Annie, in a buoyant mood, was smuggled back from Brittany so that she could appear at the Monday At Home on October 6. This time she reached the theatre in an actress's hamper labelled: 'Marie Lloyd—Pavilion'.

At the start of the meeting, Annie emerged from a dressing-room and took her place on the stage. The building was surrounded by uniformed and plain-clothes policemen, and wild cheers greeted her appearance. All was peaceful until Annie rose to speak. 'There are detectives all round,' she said gaily, 'so I had better start.' As the sound of the cheering died away, a low rumbling sound could be heard in the wings, and a tramping of heavy feet almost drowned the sound of Annie's voice. Detectives stormed on to the platform, the Bodyguard rose and Annie made a dash to escape. The police lashed out with sticks, beating her rescuers over the head, and Annie was dragged out with her dress almost torn off.

In the street, she was marched to a taxi waiting to take her back to Holloway. 'Woman after woman flung herself on to the vehicle in an endeavour to help Miss Kenney,' said a reporter. 'The cab was in the centre of swirling humanity, which surged backwards and forwards, heedless of the traffic. Finally a passage was cleared and the vehicle drove off with a woman clinging to the driver's seat.'

After the fight, the Pavilion meeting continued with an auction of trophies. Two detectives' hats sold for five pounds each, and the stick with which Annie Kenney was beaten fetched twenty-five dollars from an American. Next morning it was announced that no more militant

Suffragette meetings would be held at the Pavilion—the management had cancelled the contract.

It was expected that Annie would be released within two or three days, and when she was kept in prison longer there was grave concern for her health. People of influence pleaded for her release and Grace Roe, disguised as a chorus girl, called on the Duchess of Marlborough and begged her to put pressure on the Government. During the interview the Duchess walked up and down the room, wringing her hands in great distress. After a nine-day hunger and thirst strike, Annie was finally released—scarcely able to speak and only fit to lie on a stretcher. In this condition, she continued to attend meetings and whisper defiant words to the awe-struck audience.

The situation was intolerable. While Annie was in prison, McKenna reintroduced forcible feeding in the case of Mary Richardson and Rachel Peace, on remand for arson. Shortly afterwards the prison doctor was waylaid outside Holloway by a woman he had once fed by force, and she thrashed him with a sjambok while the public inertly looked on. Pieces of hard chalk wrapped in paper labelled 'Death or Release' were thrown at the windows of doctors' houses in Harley Street. A chorus of women offered up prayers in Westminster Abbey as soon as McKenna's announcement became known, and at the West London Synagogue on October 11, women chanted: 'May God forgive Sir Herbert Samuel and Sir Rufus Isaacs for consenting to the torture of women.'

On October 17 the Bishop of Winchester begged the militants to call a truce, suggesting positive methods of compromise by which they might further the cause. To his letter in *The Times* of October 25 Annie replied: 'We want no truce and no amnesty. What we want is peace after the vote is won. Does a soldier lay down his arms simply because he is under fire?'

It was quite obvious that the Cat and Mouse Act was no deterrent in the case of arson. 'Mice', such as Lilian Lenton, who had been released, had disappeared, and it was suspected that they were partly responsible for the numerous fires ravaging empty buildings all over the country. In October a typical week's record of Militancy was outlined in *The Suffragette*: 'GIGANTIC FIRE AT YARMOUTH—Timber Yards a Sea of Flames, Damage estimated at over £40,000. CONFLAGRATION AT SURREY MANSION—Two Rooms completely gutted. FOOTBALL STAND BURNT TO THE GROUND. HAYRICKS ABLAZE. GOLF GREENS CUT UP'.

Very few women were prepared to undertake this type of militancy and it was not, as some of the public believed, carried out in a spirit of random destruction. In every instance of arson, the manoeuvre was carefully considered and planned before volunteers took any steps.

Human life was sacred, the W.S.P.U. ruled that 'not a cat, dog or canary should be harmed', and this rule was miraculously upheld without any known exception.

Mary Richardson had several times been arrested for taking part in protests against the Cat and Mouse Act in the summer of 1913. She describes how she felt when, as a 'mouse', in hiding, she was called on to undertake a burning:

> Arson! the word had haunted me for so long, I had known I should not escape in the end. I must pay the full price demanded of a Suffragette. What brought me some relief personally was the knowledge I belonged nowhere. I had no home and so there was no one who would worry over me and over whom I would worry. I must do more than my fair share to make up for the women who stood back from militancy because of the sorrow their action would have caused to some loved one. It would have been the same with me had I been in their position.

Before embarking on the project Mary Richardson felt rebellious and unhappy, but she nevertheless carried out her task in the face of overwhelming obstacles—a dense fog and a terrified companion, who failed to make the difficult entrance into the grounds of the mansion they were to burn. Mary Richardson lit the fire alone and then rejoined her partner for the escape:

> We went as fast as we could but we were both groggy from fatigue and the mental strain of the whole ugly business. After a while we heard the clanging of the bells of the fire engines. We staggered on and made renewed efforts to get as far away as we could. For a long time we seemed to be walking along outside a high wall . . . The fog was becoming dense, and we were still outside the wall. I began to feel we were condemned to walk beside it for ever in punishment for our sins.

As they stumbled along two tall figures loomed out of the fog. 'Aren't you two out a bit late?' one of the policemen asked. 'Just step across the road. We've been looking for you for the past hour.'

Meanwhile Mrs Pankhurst arrived in America on October 18 only to hear that she was to be deported. Although there had been speculation as to whether she would be allowed to land, it was a great shock to her to find herself detained among the illegal immigrants on Ellis Island. She remained there for two days while Mrs Belmont and lawyers made elaborate negotiations on her behalf.

Her case was taken up by the American Press:

The immigration authorities at Ellis Island and in Washington have decided—for the moment at least—that this brave little old lady, whose name now blazes in electric light o'nights on the tower of Madison Square Gardens, is not moral enough to set foot on the streets of New York. The American people are dead tired of this sort of official foolishness. America is being made the laughing stock of Europe by the priggishness and pedantic literalism of the immigration authorities. It is doubly and trebly absurd that people like Mrs Pankhurst, who represent the rising democratic spirit of Europe, and who come here just to make a call, should be insulted and sent back!

At last, on October 20, Mrs Pankhurst was admitted to the country by order of the President. The English papers reported that the Suffragette leader had many troubles when she tried to land in New York, but not the least of them was the importunate reporters who being Americans, made her say all sorts of things she'd never thought of.

'Mrs Pankhurst, some people in this country say that the shadow gown and the slit skirt and all that sort of thing come from the influence of the Suffragettes on feminine morals. And the feminine point of view— and the tango and the rag songs too, they say they came in with the Suffragettes.' Mrs Pankhurst smiled mischievously. 'The tango? I thought that was of African origin. Do they have "Votes for Women" clubs on Upper Nyanza?' Mrs Pankhurst's smile deepened, so did the enigmatic expression in her blue eyes. 'Eve, in the Garden of Eden, rather an odd idea of dress she seemed to have, didn't she? I wonder if she was a Suffragette too.'

Soon after Mrs Pankhurst's arrival the American authorities made an ineffective attempt to suppress *The Suffragette* because of Christabel's increasingly frank articles on the white slave traffic. 'Everyone is talking about this,' said Nurse Pine who had accompanied the leader. 'It has raised about as much comment as Mrs Pankhurst herself.' However, threats to circulators of *The Suffragette* were not taken seriously, the ban was soon lifted, and there was an increased demand for the paper. These incidents had great advertising value, and Mrs Pankhurst was welcomed everywhere. The Americans appreciated her quick un-hesitating answers to their questions and her tour was an unqualified success.

A great demonstration was to be held at the Empress Theatre, Earls Court, on December 7 to welcome Mrs Pankhurst on her return. The W.S.P.U. were intent on doing everything in their power to prevent her being arrested. All likely ports were guarded, but at Plymouth, where she was expected to arrive, the Suffragettes organised a full-scale campaign to get the townspeople to assist them in defending Mrs Pankhurst. On December 4 crowds of people anxious to help waited on the quay in cold rough weather.

Mrs Pankhurst had heard from W.S.P.U. headquarters on the night before arrival that she was to be arrested but no one knew exactly how it would be managed. In fact she was arrested at sea. As the *Majestic* anchored outside port, the bay was cleared of all small boats. A police tender was sent out to fetch Mrs Pankhurst and the Press tender that should have met the liner was held back by two huge grey warships. Mrs Pankhurst describes how the passengers crowded to the deck rails to see what would happen next:

> Suddenly a fisherman's dory, power-driven, dashed across the harbour directly under the noses of the grim war vessels. Two women, spray-drenched, stood up in the boat, and as it ploughed swiftly past our steamer, the women called out to me, 'The cats are here, Mrs Pankhurst! They're close on you.' Their voices trailed away in a mist and we heard no more.

Soon the police were on board, Mrs Pankhurst was arrested and as she refused to go willingly to the tender they had to carry her. The police boat then steamed away down the coast to land at Bull Point—a port closed to the public. From there Mrs Pankhurst was driven across Dartmoor and taken to prison in Exeter. Four days later, on December 8, weakened by hunger strike, she was released and she returned to London—just too late to attend the welcome demonstration that had been arranged for her. When her train arrived at Paddington, double rows of women lined the platform to greet her as she was carried on a stretcher into an ambulance bound for Lincoln's Inn House.

Next day she left to see Christabel in Paris, but now she was continually shadowed, and although she travelled back to England on October 13 before her licence had expired she was arrested on the Dover Express. Instead of Suffragettes, a double row of policemen and detectives lined the platform at Victoria. *The Suffragette* described the scene under the headline, GOVERNMENT IN A PANIC—DARE NOT FACE THE BODYGUARD. The detectives pushed Mrs Pankhurst from the train, dragged her along the platform to a car, and took her back to prison.

This time Mrs Pankhurst lay on a concrete floor for two days and refused to be examined by the prison doctor. On the third day she announced the intention of walking the floor of her cell until she was released or died from exhaustion. 'All day I kept to this resolution, pacing up and down the narrow cell, many times stumbling and falling, until the doctor came in at evening to tell me that I was ordered to be released on the following morning.'

Every day since Mrs Pankhurst's return Suffragettes had spoken out in churches, restaurants and theatres for the abolition of the Cat and Mouse Act, but on December 13 a most dramatic appeal was made before the King and Queen. 'Amazing Scenes at the Opera', read the news placards next day. The occasion was a production of Raymond Roze's newly composed *Joan of Arc*. The royal party had just arrived after the first act, when three women stood up in a box opposite them and unfurled a banner: KING GEORGE, WOMEN ARE BEING TORTURED IN YOUR MAJESTY'S PRISONS.

Joan Wickham then began to speak, and after making a dignified appeal for an end to the Cat and Mouse Act she said:

> We wish to draw an analogy between the opera Your Majesties are witnessing and the things that are happening around you today. The same policy of persecution is adopted towards women fighting for principle and ideals today as was adopted towards Joan of Arc in the Middle Ages!

On December 18, just after Mrs Pankhurst's release, a bomb exploded inside the prison wall at Holloway, and at the same time a pathetic letter was sent out by Rachel Peace who was being forcibly fed. She said that she could no longer continue to hunger strike without losing her mind as she was suffering from such terrible hallucinations. For a short period she took food normally, but as soon as she resumed the hunger strike at the beginning of January, and was fed by force again, the terrifying visions returned. On January 22, when Gertrude Ansell was released from Holloway, she told of hearing screams which she believed came from Rachel Peace, now suspected to have been transferred to a padded cell.

The clergy had already held a great demonstration on December 5 to protest against forcible feeding, and now the militants, led by Mrs Dacre Fox, turned to the bishops and asked them to investigate. A deputation met the Bishop of London on January 26, and on January 28 he visited Holloway and interviewed Rachel Peace. Apparently she looked healthy and answered his questions calmly with little complaint about her treatment.

The bishop's subsequent report did not satisfy the W.S.P.U. and in a letter which was published in the Press, Mrs Dacre Fox wrote: 'A whitewash brush, my Lord Bishop, has been placed in your hand. You were urged to insist upon seeing for yourself the operation of forcible feeding. Your investigation of the horrors of forcible feeding was no investigation at all.'

The W.S.P.U. demanded a further inquiry, and the bishop interviewed two more women who responded in the same placid way as Rachel Peace. It was only when one of these, Phyllis Brady, was released on February 11, that it was confirmed that drugging, which had been suspected, was in fact taking place. Tests proved that Phyllis Brady had been given bromide and she said: 'During the interview with the Bishop of London I felt dazed and stupid. He asked me various questions with regard to prison and forcible feeding. I told him the matter was very painful but felt too limp and feeble to speak with emphasis and give him any real impression of the sensation and effect.'

After this discovery bishops throughout the country were asked to intervene with the Government. Some were embarrassed, others showed sympathy, but none would take any open action. In the House all drugging allegations were denied, and it was stressed that the Suffragette prisoners could secure immediate release by undertaking to renounce militancy.

Since the split with the Pethick Lawrences, Sylvia Pankhurst had separated herself from the main body of the W.S.P.U. She had established headquarters in Bow and gathered round her a loyal group of East End working men and women who were prepared to stand by her and fight if the need arose. Twice during July Sylvia had spoken in Trafalgar Square, and the crowd, led on by her East End supporters, had set out on a mass march to Downing Street with the spontaneity that the Suffragettes had tried so hard to win five years before.

Sylvia could now with confidence jump from a platform into a crowd knowing that they would do their utmost to save her from arrest, and it became a regular sport for the East Enders to 'fight for the safety of Miss Sylvia Pankhurst'. She outwitted the police by endless disguises and her escapes often involved extreme discomfort. Once Lansbury's two sons removed her to safe hiding, tied up in a sack among a cartload of firewood. Inevitably some of her numerous meetings ended in arrest, but as soon as she had recovered from imprisonment—hunger, thirst and sleep strike—she relentlessly appeared in public again.

After a summer holiday and lecture tour in Scandinavia, she returned to speak at a welcome meeting in Bow Baths on October 13. She had been talking for some ten minutes when suddenly the audience called out: 'Jump, Sylvia! Jump!' They rose and as she leapt into their outstretched arms, detectives with drawn truncheons stormed on to the platform. Chairs were slung down on to the police from above and men climbed down from the galleries to do battle on the platform. The chairs were hurled back into the audience, police brandished their truncheons freely, Suffragettes and East End women were caught up in the fight and several were severely injured.

Sylvia, surrounded, left the Baths and escaped to safety escorted by a prize fighter. Later Willie Lansbury guided her out of the area and saw her into a taxi bound for Hampstead. Next day, Sylvia, disguised and with a dummy baby, set out to speak at Poplar Town Hall, but she was recognised and rearrested at the entrance. After her subsequent imprisonment, she, too, appeared at meetings on a stretcher.

A Peoples' Army, equivalent to the Bodyguard, was inaugurated on November 5. Drilled by Army officers, it was to be more military in character than Mrs Pankhurst's force of women, and Sir Francis Vane, the appointed leader, obviously visualised it as a battalion of troops. He soon realised, however, that the task of assembling a mixed corps was no straightforward one, and he resigned his position. Nora Smyth, Dr Ethel's niece, was eventually responsible for drilling the Army.

Sylvia was always open to accepting offers of help from men, and she had continually worked in close co-operation with members of the Labour Movement. Her appearance at the *Daily Herald* Albert Hall meeting on November 1 caused the Press to remark: 'Every day the industrial and the suffrage rebels march closer together.' 'Independence of all men's parties is the basis of the W.S.P.U.,' said Christabel, refuting this statement:

In the French Revolution, the world saw women guillotined on equal terms with men, and afterwards denied political enfranchisement. Some day, when differences of right and status between men and women are abolished, then the need for a distinct and separate women's movement may disappear. But at the present time the need of it is very urgent.

A split between the sisters was inevitable, but before it became official, there was an interesting correspondence between Christabel and Henry Harben. It was he who had suggested that Sylvia should appear on the Herald League platform for he believed that the move would benefit both parties. Christabel had strongly disagreed, and after the event Harben wrote:

Two points arise out of the meeting. The first bears out my point of view—the second bears out yours.
(i) The meeting was undoubtedly the most remarkable of modern

times; that such a meeting should have been possible at all, shows the enormous strides made by the *Daily Herald* Movement in its short eighteen months of existence—and that the greatest ovation of the evening should have been given to your sister (who, by the way, made a very fine speech), the whole audience standing up and wildly waving handkerchiefs, will I think, make the Home Secretary pause and think before he touches her again; had it been Annie Kenney, as I had hoped, it would have been exactly the same. (ii) But there is another side to the question, and curiously enough that meeting has made me come round more to your view than I was inclined to do before. All the men speakers except Lansbury, Lawrence and myself were obviously giving the women lip-service and dragging them in as an afterthought. There was no real feeling on the woman question. The ovation to Sylvia was to the rebel and not to the woman. I came away strengthened in my suspicion that sooner or later, if our movement gets very strong, it may kick away the women's support which has helped it so much in the early days, even as the Labour Party itself has done. The meeting owed almost everything to the women. The idea of an Albert Hall demonstration, the promise cards, the stewarding by scores of attractive girls in red caps of liberty and red sashes. Prisoners free as a result of the hunger strike—all this struck me as very successful mimicry which has now become part of the stock-in-trade of agitation. Yet, in a few years' time, if you have not by that time got the vote, some of the people in that hall, and many of those who have grown up round our movement, will be just as prepared to sell you as the Liberals or Labour people have done.

Finally, at Christabel's request, Sylvia travelled to Paris with her uncle Herbert Goulden, and the situation was resolved at an upsetting meeting between the sisters. On February 7 Christabel officially announced that Sylvia's East End Federation was an entirely separate organisation from the W.S.P.U. The Press, eager for a truce, took every opportunity to suggest that the split would involve a change in W.S.P.U. policy. The *Daily Sketch* said:

Not all of us approve of violence for the simple reason that it offends the public, whose sympathy we must gain before we can succeed in our object.

Christabel was formerly the apostle of violence, Sylvia followed her. But whereas Christabel has a sense of humour, her sister has none. You will note that her organisation does not guarantee to protect human life, which shows a lack of sense of proportion.

Perhaps wit, ingenuity and a sense of proportion can do more for the movement than a whole arsenal of bombs. You will see if the W.S.P.U. does not make you laugh soon. We cannot persuade Sylvia that her earnestness is too deadly, but we can at least be merry and bright ourselves.

Militancy continued, but a further round of brilliant escapes enhanced the reputation of the W.S.P.U. On two occasions Mrs Pankhurst spoke from the balcony of a guarded house and then announced that she would defy arrest and descend into the crowd. On February 10, while a force of police and detectives waited below to recapture her, she left the house between lines of the Bodyguard rhythmically swinging Indian clubs at Mrs Garrud's instruction, and made her getaway in a taxi.

Gertrude Harding tells how a real fight took place in Scotland on March 9, when Mrs Pankhurst arrived to speak at St Andrew's Hall, Glasgow:

> Her whereabouts was now a mystery except to a chosen few. The Bodyguard were alerted for duty, and in a spirit of great adventure we met at Euston Station ready to take the night express north. In order not to excite suspicion, we posed as a travelling theatrical group on our way to an engagement in Scotland. The women spent an uncomfortable night in a third-class carriage sleeping on their clubs, but were in good form when the train pulled in to Glasgow Station. We took rooms in Sauchiehall Street, again letting it be known that we were a theatrical group. The meeting was to be that night, and while the Bodyguard rested, I went off to find out what was happening at St Andrew's Hall.
>
> Olive Bartels was in charge of all arrangements and had already put in many days' hard work getting everything in readiness for the big event. Public interest had been greatly aroused by handbills and newspaper notices advertising that Mrs Pankhurst would speak at the meeting. There was considerable doubt that she would ever manage to get inside the building without being arrested, and all this served to keep the interest at fever pitch. Bartels, looking anxious and keyed-up, took me around to see what kind of reception had been dreamed up for the police should they crash the party. Standing before the platform, one admired the three garlands of flowers and leaves stretching across the front, which upon closer look turned out to be strands of barbed wire camouflaged. On the platform itself, chairs for the Bodyguard had been carefully arranged behind the speaker's table. There were also seats for the chairman

and other ladies who might be present. Leading from the platform were two entrances, one of which led to the basement, and the other to the balcony. After getting the set-up firmly fixed in my mind I went back to the hotel.

The Bodyguard, now awake and refreshed, were anxiously waiting for news. It was by now getting on towards five o'clock and we decided to have something to eat and go on to the hall early. It was a little after six when we arrived there, and the first thing we heard was that fifty policemen had marched into the building at six o'clock and occupied the basement. The meeting was scheduled for 8 p.m., but already the crowds were beginning to collect and a cordon of police had surrounded the entire building. When the time came for the doors to be opened to admit ticket holders, each person was closely scrutinised by plain-clothes detectives and police. It seemed impossible that anyone could escape detection, and there was a growing feeling of tension inside the great hall as it began to fill up.

The Bodyguard had been briefed and were all in their places, quietly easing their clubs around to the most convenient position for a quick draw. Before I left London, Grace Roe had cautioned me against doing anything that could cause arrest. This was in keeping with the rule that once a volunteer became a paid organiser she must refrain from militant acts or behaviour that might lead to her arrest. So there I was, sitting in the midst of the Bodyguard with no weapon and feeling an awful heel.

By half-past seven, every seat had been taken, and even the boxes were full. Some of these, close to the platform, were occupied by old ladies who had come out of curiosity and not because they approved of the Suffragettes.

Eight o'clock came and passed, but still no Mrs Pankhurst. Tense whispers went through the audience. Some were openly predicting that she would never make it. Then suddenly—as if she had floated from the skies—a little figure in grey appeared on the platform. Mrs Pankhurst *had* made it. There was a sort of stunned silence and then a wild clapping and shouts of welcome. This quickly died down as she began to speak.

At the moment those of us on the platform heard the sounds of heavy boots approaching and an instant later the head of a huge policeman appeared in the doorway with others close behind. Then, to my amazement, Janie Allen, tall and handsome in a black velvet evening gown, arose from her seat and pointed a pistol straight at the man in the door! There was a loud explosion, and the policeman tried frantically to push back those behind him, thinking, no doubt, that he had been mortally wounded. But the pressure behind him was too great and soon the platform was filled with the policemen using their truncheons without mercy. Miss Allen's blank pistol shot had both startled and angered them. The Bodyguard met them head-on wielding their clubs. It was a fantastic scene of violence with Mrs Pankhurst in the middle of milling police and Bodyguard.

To add to all this turmoil, the audience now began to join in with shouts of disapproval against the police. The elderly ladies who had no use for Suffragettes, rose up in their boxes and using umbrellas as weapons, they began hammering on the heads of two policemen trying to climb on to the platform with the help of the 'garlands'. They let go in a hurry when the barbed wire came to light!

The speaker's table was overturned and chairs flew about in all directions. I found myself looking up at a very large policeman with truncheon lifted ready to descend on my head. For some unknown reason, he lowered it, and tossed me instead into a pile of overturned chairs. Many of the Bodyguard had been struck on the head and some were found later to have suffered slight concussion.

The police were in an indescribable state of excitement, shouting, pulling and dragging at Mrs Pankhurst as though they all wanted to seize her at once. They broke into several pieces the chain that she was wearing round her neck, tore off her fountain pen, tore off a velvet bag which was securely attached to her waist and tore the velvet ribbon around her neck.

When at last they got Mrs Pankhurst into the street, a crowd was being held back by uniformed police and a cab was standing waiting. Some of the police got in and then they pushed and they pulled Mrs Pankhurst into the vehicle. There was a police matron already inside. She was standing up and looking horror-stricken at what was going on.

Every seat in the cab was occupied. The matron stood, and Mrs Pankhurst was compelled to crouch on the floor at the detectives' feet. She was very much shaken, her ankles and legs were badly kicked and the skin was broken. She appealed to the police to let her sit down with the matron. 'No, you are only a prisoner,' they said. 'You are a bad woman,' shouted one of the detectives striking her on the back. 'There will be murder soon,' said another, and the man who had seized Mrs Pankhurst on the platform exclaimed exultantly: 'It was I who got her— I got her—It was I.'

The citizens of Glasgow were shocked. In London next day Mary Richardson slashed the Rokeby Venus. In justification of her action, she wrote: 'I have tried to destroy the picture of the most beautiful woman in mythological history as a protest against the Government for destroying Mrs Pankhurst who is the most beautiful character in modern history.' The London galleries were closed as a result of the incident, and the slashing of the picture soon became world news.

Mrs Drummond had been at the Glasgow meeting and she spoke in Edinburgh on the following day.

It was my duty when I saw it was the attempt of the Government to stop that great meeting to step into the breach, but what was I met with? When I stated in the passage that I would continue the meeting, the authorities said: 'You won't.' I said: 'I will,' and I did. I was myself hunted from room to room and, I am sorry to say, to the back of the platform where the Government's hirelings always like to carry out their dirty work. But I am glad to say that I was rescued by working men, and in a group of these men I was taken, or rather I was carried, on to the platform. Immediately it was seen that I was there, a policeman rushed forward to push me off the platform. It was evident that they had got their orders that I should not speak. But I spoke.

Mrs Drummond continued to hold boisterous meetings up and down the country and she was eventually arrested on Saturday, April 4, after driving a dogcart through Hyde Park. The occasion was Ulster Day and Carson and the Unionist militants had freely set up platforms, while the Suffragettes were forbidden to speak. As the police tried to drag the cart away, Mrs Drummond jumped off and was carried by the crowd to another part of the park. Here she was lifted shoulder high to address her cheering supporters. Two attempts to arrest her were prevented, but at last the police seized her and she was taken off to Marlborough Street Police Station.

'You might just as well listen, because *I* am going to talk for a change,' she said in court on the Monday morning. The magistrate had already ordered her out once because she refused to remain quietly in the dock. Her second and third appearances were equally disruptive. 'This is tomfoolery, and I do not intend to listen to you,' she shouted before her case was put off until Wednesday.

When the trial was resumed, a policeman was hastily put in the witness box to give evidence and although little could be heard above Mrs Drummond's voice, it was soon clear that the magistrate was about to pass sentence. To prevent him proceeding, Mrs Drummond tore herself free from her police guard, ran out of the dock and dashed round the court. She crashed into the door of counsels' enclosure, knocking the prosecutor's chair. 'Do go back,' he pleaded, rising from his seat. 'You sit down, you Jack-in-a-box,' she said to him, and addressing the magistrate she remarked: 'I suppose you have been seeing Bluebeard at the Home Office—the man who tortures women.' 'Forty shillings or one month,' said the magistrate, and Mrs Drummond was quickly taken out. 'You have not done with me,' she shouted as she left the court.

Her fine was paid, and Mrs Drummond, undeterred, continued to address the public. She spoke at a great W.S.P.U. meeting in Lowestoft on April 15, which coincided with the conference of women teachers in the town. Everyone expected that Mrs Pankhurst would speak, but she was still unwell after her treatment in Glasgow and instead Annie made a dramatic reappearance. It was the first time she had been seen since she spoke at the W.S.P.U. autumn meetings from a stretcher. Meanwhile, she had been staying as a 'mouse' at 2 Campden Hill Square —the Brackenburys' home—now closely guarded and used for convalescing Suffragette prisoners. Before the Lowestoft meeting Annie escaped from 'Mouse Castle' on a moonlit night, dressed as the black cat of the pantomime.

On the evening of April 15 police and detectives surrounded the Lowestoft Hippodrome and arc lamps flashed on to the people as they arrived. Disguised as an 'auntie' with a schoolgirl niece, Annie came in with the public and managed to get through to the dressing-rooms unrecognised.

Wild enthusiasm greeted Annie's unexpected appearance halfway through the meeting. She came forward to speak:

The only way you can stop militant methods is by giving women the vote and the sooner you learn the lesson the better. We shall go on, and on, and on, and go to prison and come out of prison and be as bad as ever. In fact we shall go from bad to worse. Take me for instance, I was only a mild little Suffragette at the beginning, when I merely went to heckle Cabinet Ministers at political meetings—it makes your blood hot to see the way you are treated by Cabinet Ministers. Afterwards I did one thing and then I did another and it subsequently meant imprisonment. They thought they would crush us if they put us in prison. When you are on hunger strike and thirst strike, your suffering is very great; your tongue is swollen, your lips are swollen and your mouth is swollen. The whole body twitches and you have unendurable sensations. But you have no fear at all, though you know perfectly well you may never leave prison alive.

There is something in this movement that no power of opposition whether of the Government or the people can stop.

After Annie had finished speaking Mrs Drummond said: 'I wonder how many of you to-night have realised the determination that is behind the action of Miss Kenney in coming here. If I were to pick one of you to do as she has done, you would shrink behind your chair.' By this time Annie had already left the stage to prepare for yet another escape.

Mrs Drummond continued to appear on W.S.P.U. platforms, and she was finally summonsed at Harringay on May 1 for alleged incitement to disorder. 'I have no time for such nonsense,' she said, flinging the paper back at the waiting detectives. Mrs Dacre Fox received a similar summons and on May 14, the day appointed for their trial, they called at the houses of Sir Edward Carson and Lord Lansdowne, demanding the Irish Unionist leaders as 'fellow militants' to give them protection. Their efforts were unsuccessful.

Early in the afternoon, as Sir Edward was leaving his house, Mrs Drummond made several desperate attempts to get near him in order to present 'a little work' she had compiled. Each time she approached, three men guarding Carson—detectives according to Mrs Drummond—pushed her away, and she could do no better than drop her book into Sir Edward's car after he had climbed in. She then subsided on the doorstep and showed a reporter a duplicate of the work. It contained one hundred and fifty pages of typewritten matter comparing speeches by Lord Lansdowne and Sir Edward Carson on behalf of Ulster, with others by members of the W.S.P.U.

I only wanted him to be a sportsman and accept my book. We are both in the same boat, and he should extend the hand of fellowship. I believe I am supposed to be appearing at some police court today, but I have not the slightest idea at what time, and I do not propose to be there.

Mrs Drummond and Mrs Dacre Fox were arrested and on May 15 they appeared in court. Both skilled speakers, they made a mockery of the proceedings, talking continuously so that no one else could say a word. Mrs Drummond read out every one of her pet passages in the speeches of 'those gamesters', interspersing the performance with witty and pointed comments which met with irrepressible laughter while the legal farce went on in dumb show. She was sentenced to one month and as she was carried out of court she shouted: 'I shall not serve it, and I shall be coming to your doorstep next. No Cat and Mouse Act for me!'

Chapter Twelve: No Surrender 1914

THE MARCH ON BUCKINGHAM PALACE—GRACE ROE ARRESTED—
APPEALS TO THE KING—THE W.S.P.U. OFFICES RANSACKED—
RAMPANT TERRORISM—VOTES A POSSIBILITY—MRS PANK-
HURST'S NINTH HUNGER STRIKE—WAR—THE STRUGGLE IN
HOLLOWAY.

A deputation to the King was to be the final national militant event. The manoeuvre took months of planning and representatives from all over the country volunteered to take part, and go with Mrs Pankhurst to Buckingham Palace.

Mrs Higginson was a Lancashire member from Preston.

They told us months beforehand so we had time to make our preparations. We left our houses in very good condition and good baking behind us, and people who wouldn't go to prison would look after my children while I was away. One took a girl and one took a boy, and one came to look after my husband, and he arranged to have his holidays at that time.

An empty house in Grosvenor Place which overlooked Buckingham Palace gardens was lent to the W.S.P.U. Mrs Marshall tells how, three days before the appointed time, women started to gather at the house. 'Some were dressed as maidservants and some as visitors and they kept arriving in ones and twos, quite unostentatiously, but not going away again; Mrs Pankhurst was also there. It was a very big house with endless stairs and large rooms and our numbers gradually increased.'

'Two hundred of us arrived from north, south, east and west,' says Mrs Higginson, 'and we didn't know each other. The Londoners know each other, but we don't, we've come from foreign parts!' She then goes on to tell how they had to form into groups of ten and appoint a captain and vice-captain.

While we were sat on the floor they passed a slip of paper to each person. We'd to read, mark and inwardly digest it very thoroughly, because if you didn't get arrested then you had to go to the address on that paper. All those papers were burnt while we were there—that was the end of that lot—and we set out.

We came out of the house, ten abreast; the police were taken by surprise. The placards had: 'Bayonets to meet the Women', but we went on. If your captain falls then your vice-captain takes over, and it's ten little nigger boys we had to play; and you'd keep pushing on and you'd become captain in your turn. Well, it didn't work out like that because those Whitehall police maimed us, they mauled us about the shoulders and we were all of us black and blue the next day.

The *Sphere* reported:

It was a warm sunlit afternoon and as the little band headed by Mrs Pankhurst, pale and determined, swung along past the back wall of the King's garden a large crowd gazed with interest on their movements. It soon became evident that ahead of Constitution Hill would be the centre of disturbance. The women were there met by others who had been waiting with the ordinary spectators. The police closed the main gates and much trouble occurred at the side entrances into Constitution Hill. Some women pulled at the mounted constables, trying to get them off their horses and tugged at the horses' reins while others climbed on the railings.

Mrs Marshall, knowing how horrid it was to have police horses backed on to her, had brought up from her country house a pair of secateurs, which she intended to use for cutting one side of the horses' bridles:

The police would not then be able to guide their horses and ride us down. They were naturally furious with me for I managed to cut three different bridles. They were trying to hit me with their batons and they had to get off their horses of course to try and repair the damage I had done. I was having a very nasty time with the roughs who always seem to gather when there is trouble with the police, when four gentlemen, one a parson, clasped their hands together and formed a ring round me. They made their way to a taxi-cab and got me safely inside and stood there until the taxi got away.

One contingent of women threw eggs filled with coloured powder while another group made a systematic attempt to cut policemen's braces. Members of the Bodyguard wielded Indian clubs and the police retaliated—wringing their assailants' arms—beating the women with batons about the shoulders and throwing them to the ground. There were many arrests and a temporary police station was set up within the wall of the Wellington Arch. Here, as soon as they were brought in, the captured Suffragettes smashed everything in sight.

Mrs Pankhurst and her bodyguard had miraculously managed to slip through the Wellington Gates just as they were closing. They passed the police cordon at the bottom of Constitution Hill and nearly reached the front of the palace before Mrs Pankhurst was seized. A huge inspector rushed forward to claim his prize, and as he carried Mrs Pankhurst bodily past the group of waiting reporters, she called out: 'Arrested at the gates of the Palace—tell the King!'

Mrs Higginson was not arrested and she tells how they finally petered off, one or two or three at a time, to the address they had been given.

When we got there, it was a very large house and a table was set with cakes the size of a halfpenny. Well, Lancashire people have a good appetite, they're not expecting little halfpenny buns! You could have cups of tea, but I wanted something to eat. Anyway, I didn't get anything.

And do you know, we were there till half past nine at night and then they asked us to come into a small room in twos and threes. On the floor there were two suitcases full of stones and they said: 'Sorry we've kept you waiting so long but there are no loose stones in London and so we had to go to Southend for our ammunition!'

Armed with her stones, Mrs Higginson went out into Whitehall with a companion to protest by window smashing. Mrs Marshall was also on the raid and broke a Cabinet Minister's window with a cricket ball—'an expensive missile, but you cannot find stones easily in London.'

There were sixty women arrested and two men after the scenes on 'King's Thursday'. As soon as they reached the police station, many of the women exchanged clothes and all refused to give their names. Although they were allotted numbers, the trials were a farce.

Number One was brought in on her knees, Number Three was dragged in and refused to be tried. When she was finally forced into the dock, she threw folded paper at the magistrate. The next woman turned her back on him—another was only prevented by four policemen from climbing over the dock rails and then more paper and a bag of flour were thrown by some of the spectators in court.

Sir John Dickinson ordered the court to be cleared and there was a new start. Number Eleven threw her boot at the magistrate; Number Fourteen shouted, 'Hip, hip, hurrah!' continuously. The next two women were placed in the dock together and as one called Sir John 'a rusty tool of a corrupt Government', the other referred to him as a 'wicked old man'. A succession of women made similar protests and most of them, after refusing to be bound over, were discharged.

On the afternoon of the Buckingham Palace attack, police raided a flat in Maida Vale and Nellie Hall, her mother and sister and two other women were arrested. In the flat the police discovered a small arsenal; a haul of beach pebbles was found amongst window-smashing equipment and during the search a woman entered with a basketful of stones covered with lettuce. Doubtless this discovery occasioned the long wait for ammunition on Thursday night.

The Hall family were pioneer members of the W.S.P.U. Leonard Hall had been a leader of political agitation in Manchester in the time of Dr Pankhurst, and the two families were close friends. Nellie and her sister—younger than the Pankhurst girls—were still at school during the years of peaceful militancy. Now Nellie, in her early twenties, was one of the most active and energetic of the W.S.P.U. underground workers. At this critical stage in militancy, her family, including her father, had come down from Manchester to be at her side.

In connection with the discoveries at the Maida Vale flat, a warrant was issued for the arrest of Grace Roe, and on Saturday, May 23, Lincoln's Inn House was raided. Grace had come out of hiding and since the autumn of 1913 she had been openly working at headquarters. Now detectives stormed into her private office. 'Where is Grace Roe?' they demanded, unsure of her identity. 'Why don't you find her?' she calmly replied. She walked downstairs to the main office, asked to see the warrant, and then gave herself up for arrest to the chief inspector.

Since she had become Chief Organiser, Grace had held the W.S.P.U. together for a year without a break. One of the organisers who worked closely with her said that 'she went about her duties with a light heart, always with her eyes fixed on one thing, inspiring us who were fortunate enough to work under her.'

No conclusive evidence could be found against Grace and, when brought into court on Saturday afternoon, she refused to submit to trial. She had to be lifted into the dock and her loud protest drowned all the proceedings: 'I glory in the fight women are making. You think you can imprison us, but we shall hunger strike and thirst strike and you can do nothing with us at all.'

On remand, Grace was taken to Holloway—and four days later she was already being fed by force. Christabel had sensed that Grace was going to be arrested after the Buckingham Palace deputation and when Grace visited her in Paris on the previous Sunday they had spoken about it.

Now Christabel could only advocate that women should be given the vote 'at once'. She seemed to realise that the fight as such was ending and she concluded in her *Suffragette* leader of May 29: 'The Militants will rejoice when victory comes in the shape of the vote, and yet, mixed with their joy will be regret that the most glorious chapter in women's history is closed and the militant fight over—over, while so many have not yet known the exultation, the rapture of battle.'

Individuals still struggled on to try and reach a turning point. On May 22 Annie Kenney as a 'mouse' went openly to Lambeth Palace to take sanctuary and to persuade the Church to take action. She was given an interview by the Archbishop of Canterbury and then announced her intention of staying at the palace. Instead the police were called and Annie was taken back to Holloway. Six days later, released and desperately ill, she returned to the archbishop's palace on a stretcher and lay on the cobbles outside the barred gates until she was removed to the workhouse infirmary. Next day, Annie tried to approach the Bishop of London at Fulham Palace. The bishop was out, and on his return, late in the afternoon, he invited Annie in for tea, but she left the palace in the evening and there the *entente* ended.

On Sunday, May 24, Sylvia Pankhurst headed the East London Federation May Day Procession to Victoria Park, Bow. She was chained by the wrists to a bodyguard of twenty-five women armed with purple, white and green staves. At the park gates the procession was stopped and the chained demonstrators defended themselves fiercely as police tried to separate them from their followers. Eventually they were driven into the park, the gates were closed against the rest of the procession, their chains were smashed with truncheons and Sylvia, hatless and dishevelled, was recaptured and taken off in a taxi.

At about this time Mrs Pankhurst wrote in a letter to Dr Ethel Smyth, 'Grace Roe is being *drugged* and forcibly fed. How can one stay in a country so horrible? Yet life is sweet and one loves one's fellows.' Grace and Nellie Hall appeared together at Marylebone Police Court on May 29 to face a conspiracy charge. Both women were obviously under the effects of sedation and they had to be carried in.

Nellie Hall, with cut mouth, swollen hands and torn clothes, protested in a whisper—'I won't be tried. You cannot try us until you nearly kill us. How would you like to have tubes put down your throat?' Still protesting, she struggled to get out of the dock and fainted, falling heavily on the floor. 'Remove that woman,' said the magistrate.

Grace then began: 'I say we absolutely refuse to be tried in the court today . . . People are supposed to be innocent until they are proved guilty. I tell you, if instead of these farces in court you would have a measure giving votes for women, the whole thing would end . . .'

Drowsiness seemed to overpower her, but Grace rallied again to describe the horrors of forcible feeding: 'It is not only the torture one goes through, it is the terrible memory all day and all night . . . Nobody who has not been forcibly fed knows what it is. All day long you see the prison door open. You see the doctors and wardresses coming in to feed you. They seize hold of you and they fling you down . . .' Her voice trailed away and she lay back exhausted.

Again and again she gathered up strength to disrupt the proceedings as witnesses tried to give evidence. 'I have been drugged. They are drugging women in prison because they know that however much we are tortured we shall never give in.' Finally, as no witnesses could be heard, the magistrate had to call an adjournment.

The militants now centred their activities on gaining the personal attention of the King. On the day after the Buckingham Palace deputation, a royal party attended a charity performance at His Majesty's Theatre. In spite of all security precautions a number of Suffragettes were present and the play was ruined by constant interruptions. From all sides of the theatre came a call: 'Release Mrs Pankhurst! Release Mrs Pankhurst!' Someone cried out at the King: 'You Russian tsar,' and while carpenters were busy trying to dislodge a woman who had chained herself to the stalls, another Suffragette climbed up on to the stage and with arms outstretched towards the royal box, she pleaded for an end to prison torture. Stage hands rushed 'on to remove her.

During the Sunday morning service at Westminster Abbey, a large group of women chanted from Poets' Corner—'Enlighten the heart of George V, and open the eyes of his ministers that they may cease to persecute our women.'

A few days later on June 4 a most sensational and dignified protest was made before the King in the Palace. Mary Blomfield, on being presented with her sister at Court, dropped on her knee when she came into the royal presence and begged the King, in a loud clear voice: 'For God's sake stop forcible feeding.' The Queen turned pale. The orchestra began playing a tune. There was a slight scuffle and the two women were escorted away.

The Blomfield family regarded the affair with 'the utmost disgust'. 'It may be a strong term to use,' said Lady Blomfield, 'but the occasion requires it.' She made a personal call at the Palace to beg forgiveness for the incident, and shortly afterwards she left the country with her daughters for a prolonged stay abroad.

It was then announced that there would be no garden parties at Buckingham Palace or Windsor that season. In spite of a press statement that it would be impossible for any unauthorised person to gain admission to the royal grounds, on June 6 the news placards proclaimed: 'A man in the Palace.' As an act of bravado, an engineer, Pike, climbed into the grounds by night, entered by a window and before he was caught he explored several rooms, in one removing his own clothes and donning a suit which he found there.

This Suffragette-inspired midsummer madness was intolerable, and now a determined effort was made to smash the organisation and hound down the ringleaders. Olive Bartels took over from Grace Roe. She had for some time been disguised as a widow—'Dead black—black everything, except for a tiny white ruff around the neck—the gloom—I almost began to think I was a widow.' Her task was practically impossible. 'There is no peace for the Suffragettes,' said the *Daily Sketch*, after Lincoln's Inn House had been ransacked and the Westminster offices were raided. The homes of influential members were also raided and searched in the hope of discovering a secret base, while the office staff went from private house to private house skilfully evading the police and keeping the routine campaign going.

Although drawing-room meetings, poster parades and self-denial week went on as usual, uncontrolled militancy was rampant. To the Suffragettes there was no longer any standard of values; fighting was breaking out in Ulster where gun-running had gone uncensured and in England unconvicted prisoners were being tortured. The militants slashed more valuable pictures and with bombs and fires created nationwide destruction of property.

In an attempt to curb these activities, prominent persons were sent to Holloway to try and force the Suffragette prisoners to renounce militancy and secure their freedom. Experts came to the prison to try to establish that the women were lunatic. Grace Roe tells how one day a visiting magistrate looked in at the door of her cell but was told by the officials that she never talked to anybody. 'I beckoned to him. He entered and we held a conversation until I lay back exhausted. This little man with greying hair paced back and forth in my cell and then, as if speaking his thoughts out loud, he said in a low tone, "Very sane, very sane indeed," and walked out.'

During a debate in the House on militancy, McKenna said that they had to deal with a phenomenon absolutely without precedent in our history. The sympathy of the respectable classes was so great that the work of the police was heavily handicapped. Lord Robert Cecil said: 'The public will soon take these things into their own hands—that means lynch law.'

All proposed solutions proved impracticable. In reply to the popular statement, 'Let them die', McKenna said that the women would be prepared to, and one martyrdom would bring on a host more. 'Coupled with their hysterical fanaticism they have a courage that stands at nothing.' Deportation was rejected and McKenna said that it was impossible for the Government to go against medical opinions with regard to lunacy. McKenna refused to discuss the franchise question and his only practical solution was to threaten subscribers to the W.S.P.U. funds. He appealed to the Press not to give headlines to militant acts, and if possible not to report at all.

The *Daily Graphic* was quick to answer a non-militant complaint that suffragists received no publicity, and this paper devoted a page each day to articles by members of all non-militant suffrage groups, setting forth points of view on the prevalent unrest. The extremists had at last succeeded in forcing the general public to consider the whole problem and people were now only too glad to hear the women's cause advanced by professed anti-militants.

Clearly, Government attitude was also changing. On carrying out a threat to hunger and thirst strike on the steps of the House of Commons, Sylvia Pankhurst finally prevailed on Asquith to receive a deputation of her East End women. On June 20 the Prime Minister met a small group and admitted that votes for women was now a possibility, but he offered no proposals.

The less militant suffrage societies felt that the interview was a great move in the right direction, but Christabel was sceptical. 'Once upon a time, Mr Asquith stood at the point of "Never", now he has reached the stage of "if".' Such advanced thinkers as Annie Besant suggested the opportunity of a truce, but the W.S.P.U. would accept no compromise. Mrs Pankhurst summoned all her remaining strength and came out of hiding on July 8 having announced in the Press that she was going to resume official work. She arrived on foot at Lincoln's Inn House quite openly, and was greeted by an overjoyed office staff. It was only when she left the building a few hours later that a detective stepped forward to arrest her and take her back to prison.

Orders were given on this occasion that Mrs Pankhurst must be searched. Her persuasive speeches to the matron and wardresses met with no response; they had their instructions and meant to carry them out. Standing against the wall, Mrs Pankhurst declared that she would resist searching:

Then they all set on me, I think six, I am not quite sure as to the number—and I hit out and resisted as long as I could. I was finally overcome. Some held my legs, some my arms and they stripped me and took everything from me, searched all over my body, and then finally put some clothes on me again and took me to my cell. I was feeling very ill and exhausted.

The following morning Mrs Pankhurst was informed that she would be tried by the visiting magistrates for using insulting language and assaulting a wardress. Due punishment followed—solitary confinement and the forfeit of privileges. However, within three days Mrs Pankhurst was released severely shocked, and after her ninth hunger strike, quite unfit to remain in prison.

Four days later on July 16 she intended to speak at a great protest meeting at the Holland Park Hall. An ambulance was sent to fetch her from the house where she was recovering and Mrs Pankhurst was brought out on a stretcher, 'her face dead white against her black evening dress, her eyes bright and feverish, and her hands shaking. Through all her self-control and determination there was clearly shown the strain of the past torture.' Police and detectives were waiting in force and Mrs Pankhurst was lifted into the ambulance and driven once more to Holloway.

The Holland Park meeting proved that there was overwhelming support for the movement. In spite of all McKenna's threats, fifteen thousand pounds was raised and Annie Kenney and Mrs Dacre Fox, both 'mice', appeared on the platform, evading arrest. Mrs Mansel, now much to the fore as an organiser, presided at the meeting and read a message from Mrs Pankhurst: 'The Government, having released me on four-days licence, are now taking me back to prison to prevent me speaking to you here tonight. At the risk of killing me, they have silenced my voice but there are silences more eloquent than words.' Mrs Pankhurst was in fact released again as soon as the meeting was over.

Events in Ireland shortly turned attention from the Suffragettes; shooting broke out in the streets of Dublin. The situation was grave and Carson was received by the King. Mrs Pankhurst, in a final attempt, sent a letter to the Palace maintaining the women's right to be received on the same terms as the Irish rebels, but her messengers, Lady Barclay and the Hon. Edith Fitzgerald, were refused admission. A week later even Ireland faded to insignificance when war in Europe suddenly became imminent.

The situation in Holloway had never been worse. Grace Roe and Nellie Hall were dragged into court again, each time looking more ill and emaciated. Grace's brother was at the final hearing of her

case at the Old Bailey on July 8. He wrote to his fiancée afterwards:

> All the women in the back of the court protested that the trial was
> unfair and were all ordered out of court till there were no women
> left. Grace and Nellie Hall were given three months and they have
> already done six weeks. Grace has never done anything militant in
> her life. Their pluck is tremendous and it makes one ill to think of
> everyone going their own selfish way without enquiring the rights or
> wrongs of the question.

Terrible reports of forcible feeding had been given by the released
prisoners and the medical profession publicly denounced the operation.
The Bishop of London wrote in *The Times*: 'We are not justified in
treating delicate women in this way. The process seems to leave them
physical and mental wrecks which is incompatible with a Christian
civilisation to allow.'

On July 30 Mary Richardson was released for an appendix operation
after weeks of forcible feeding. She had been in the cell next to Grace
Roe. 'While rejoicing that Mary Richardson was out,' says Grace, 'now
came the worst ordeal—the empty cell and the feeling of being utterly
alone.'

> One day in early August, there came over me a terrible foreboding of
> approaching tragedy. On that morning a big German wardress
> grabbed my head as I was about to be forcibly fed. She shouted
> 'Long live the Kaiser!' and I knew that the war had come. Soon
> news filtered into the prison through the prisoners' organiser the
> Hon. Edith Fitzgerald that several countries were at war.
>   The prisoners were now calling, 'G.R., G.R.!' and, lying very
> weak in my cell, I heard them telling how officials and prominent
> persons were trying to persuade each one to give an undertaking.
> With a strength not my own I climbed up to the window of my
> cell and answering the calls said: 'Give no undertakings, all will be
> done from outside.' This was picked up by a nearby prisoner and
> echoed and re-echoed around the prison court yard.

In this last desperate struggle to resist, the women won.

On August 10 an unconditional release was ordered and immediately
Mrs Pankhurst declared a suspension of militant activities: 'What is the
use of fighting for a vote if we have not got a country to vote in? With
that patriotism which has nerved women to endure torture in prison for
the national good, we ardently desire that our country shall be victorious.'

On August 11, the following comment appeared in the *Daily Herald*:

The remission of sentences on the suffrage prisoners was a natural step; for people have not been slow, at the very outset of this war, to turn to the women for aid. Let us note above all that it has not been aid in the task of destruction.

To ask the aid of women at a period of national crisis involves two things. It means in the first place that we recognise them as a part of the nation. It means in the second place that their help is a thing worth having. The first point is the recognition of their citizenship and of that the vote is the one adequate symbol. The second point is the recognition of our stupidity in so long delaying what we now acclaim as a thing of value.

Postscript

SIX MILLION WOMEN WIN THE RIGHT TO VOTE. On January 11, 1918 the Press announced the women's triumph. 'Is it not wonderful that the war has brought us victory?' wrote Mrs Pankhurst.

Her own understanding and command of the war issue had been phenomenal. After nine years of strenuous suffrage work she still had the energy to play a monumental part in saving the country from invasion. Her followers were at first bewildered by her immediate declaration of loyalty to Government and country:

> Her eloquence did much to persuade us that she was right, but what mostly persuaded us was the fact that she herself bore no bitterness, no ill-will to those who, but a year earlier, had decreed her to be a criminal. Those who had brought her to death's door were now accounted as allies in the nation's hour of peril.

In the foreword to her book Mrs Pankhurst gives some impression of her true feelings as she temporarily called a halt to the suffrage struggle in 1914.

> The militancy of men, through all the centuries, has drenched the world with blood, and for these deeds of horror and destruction men have been rewarded with monuments, with great songs and epics. The militancy of women has harmed no human life save the lives of those who fought the battle of righteousness. Time alone will reveal what reward will be allotted to women.

The influence of the Suffragettes undoubtedly prepared women for the part they were to play in the crisis. The movement had trained thousands to work in co-operation with one another and to take on new responsibilities. Mrs Pankhurst was confident that women could be employed in industry, transport and agriculture in order to liberate men for fighting, but at first no opportunity was given for them to prove themselves.

Christabel advocated several vital measures for dealing with the national crisis, and during the first months of the war Mrs Pankhurst addressed vast audiences all over the country, recommending food rationing and universal national service—ideas that were adopted only later.

By the summer of 1915, the war had reached disastrous proportions. Trade unionists were refusing to allow women to work in the munitions factories and supplies were running dangerously low. 'Women are prepared to sacrifice, serve and suffer,' said Mrs Pankhurst in June 1915. 'We are only waiting to be told what to do.' The crisis became so serious at the beginning of July that the Minister of Munitions, Lloyd George, approached Mrs Pankhurst and begged her to organise a demonstration to prove women's willingness to help in war work. Mrs Pankhurst's 'Call to Women' met with such an overwhelming response that sacks of mail arrived at the W.S.P.U. Kingsway headquarters by every post.

A huge procession marched through the streets of London on July 17. WE DEMAND THE RIGHT TO SERVE proclaimed the float heading the procession. Tables were placed at points along the route, and the signatures of over eleven thousand women were collected during the forty-five minutes' march. Mrs Pankhurst and the deputation leading the women were welcomed by Lloyd George at the Ministry of Munitions and it was then agreed that the registration and national organisation of women should be undertaken at once.

When Lloyd George became Prime Minister, the W.S.P.U. continued to give him unqualified support and Mrs Pankhurst's help was invaluable in the promotion of industrial peace. She went down the mines to speak to the men threatening strike action and convinced them that national unity came before partisan interests.

In 1918 the new franchise law admitted women over thirty only, and Mrs Pankhurst's reaction was to emphasise the need to educate women to make a wise and constructive use of the vote. On June 14, 1928 she died, just as the Bill giving equal voting rights to all men and women over twenty-one received the royal assent. Mrs Pankhurst was only sixty-nine and had she lived longer she might have helped the younger generation through her wisdom and experience to understand the meaning of political equality. A re-separation of the sexes seemed to defeat the purpose of all that suffragists had been fighting for.

Bernard Shaw wrote after the suffrage struggle: 'People who are shown by their inner light the possibility of a better world based on the demand of the spirit for a nobler and more abundant life, not for themselves at the expense of others, but for everybody, are naturally dreaded and therefore hated by the Have-and-Holders.'

The Suffragettes were cruelly persecuted and misrepresented for their efforts to achieve basic equality but since that era of restriction, the structure of society in this country has essentially changed and the barriers between the sexes are also dissolving. This is an age of transition and of many sensational upheavals. The differences between men and women really are less, and future achievement will certainly come through their working together as complementary equals.

Appendix: Outstanding Events in the Suffragette Campaign 1903–14

1903
October 10 Inaugural meeting of the Women's Social and Political Union.

1904
May 12 Mrs Pankhurst holds a protest meeting outside the Houses of Parliament following the talking out of a Women's Suffrage Bill.

1905
October 13 Christabel Pankhurst and Annie Kenney are thrown out of the Manchester Free Trade Hall and subsequently imprisoned.

1906
January General election and return to power of a Liberal Government. Suffragettes campaign against Churchill as Liberal candidate for N.W. Manchester.

February 19 First London meeting of the Suffragettes at the Caxton Hall. A deputation of women arrives at the House of Commons to find the doors of the Strangers' Entrance closed to them.

February Mrs Pethick Lawrence joins the movement.

April 25 Keir Hardie introduces a women's suffrage resolution in Parliament. Suffragettes in the Ladies' Gallery protest as Members ridicule the measure.

May 19 First great women's suffrage demonstration. The Prime Minister, Sir Henry Campbell Bannerman, receives a deputation of three hundred and speaks of opposition to women's suffrage within the Cabinet.

June 21 Annie Kenney and two working women are sentenced to six weeks' imprisonment for attempting to call on Asquith after his refusal to receive a deputation.

August At Cockermouth, Christabel establishes the W.S.P.U. by-election policy.

September The W.S.P.U. open official headquarters at Clement's Inn.

October 23 Opening of Parliament. Rebuffed members of a women's suffrage deputation protest in the Lobby of the House of Commons. The arrested include Mrs Pethick Lawrence and Mrs Cobden Sanderson. All are sentenced as common criminals. Several are shortly released from prison having broken down, and under public pressure the Home Secretary transfers the others from the second to the first division, thereby recognising them as political prisoners.

1907

February 13 First Women's Parliament at the Caxton Hall. A Suffragette deputation to the House of Commons persists against a force of mounted police to try to reach the House. The confrontation results in over fifty arrests.

March 8 W. H. Dickinson's Women's Suffrage Bill is rejected.

September Mrs Despard, Teresa Billington Greig and Edith How Martyn break away from the W.S.P.U. to form the Women's Freedom League.

October The Pethick Lawrences bring out the first number of *Votes for Women.*

1908

January 17 While Suffragettes chained to railings cause a diversion, Mrs Drummond attempts to get into a Cabinet Council meeting at 10 Downing Street. The authorities in sentencing the women to imprisonment revert to placing them in the second division.

February 11, 12, 13 Three-day session of a Women's Parliament. Suffragettes try to reach the House by a Trojan Horse method. The first arrest of Mrs Pankhurst (February 13).

February 28 A Women's Suffrage Bill put forward by H. Y. Stanger is carried by a majority of one hundred and seventy-nine votes.

June 21 Great Hyde Park meeting. Purple, white and green become the Suffragette colours.

June 30 The public is asked to support a Suffragette deputation to Parliament. Huge crowds watch Suffragettes being turned away from the House. Two women break windows of 10 Downing Street in protest.

October 11 In Trafalgar Square the public are invited to help the Suffragettes to 'rush the House of Commons'.

October 13 Mrs Pankhurst, Christabel and Mrs Drummond are arrested and eventually imprisoned with some thirty other Suffragettes who had tried to 'rush the House'.

October 28 Two Women's Freedom League members chain themselves to the grille of the Ladies' Gallery in the House of Commons. Officials, unable to detach the women, have to wrench the pieces of grille out of the surrounding stonework. The House is temporarily closed to strangers.

October Start of an organised campaign of heckling cabinet ministers.

December 22 Triumphal procession round the West End to celebrate the release of the leaders.

1909

February 18, 24 Deputations to Parliament from the Women's Freedom League and the W.S.P.U. Mrs Despard, Mrs Pethick

Lawrence and Lady Constance Lytton are among the arrested. Their preferential prison treatment causes public comment.

March 19 Second reading of Geoffrey Howard's Electoral Reform Bill proposing votes for women. Despite the vote in favour, Asquith states that such a Bill would only be acceptable as a Government measure.

March 22 Lancashire Suffragettes lead an unsuccessful deputation to the House.

May 13/26 The Woman's Exhibition at the Prince's Skating Rink in Knightsbridge.

June 29 The 'Bill of Rights' deputation. Mrs Pankhurst and eight well-known women attempt to take a petition to Parliament, claiming that: 'It is the right of the subject to petition the King.' The deputation is rejected and a highly organised manoeuvre follows. Windows of Government offices are broken and one hundred and eight arrests are made. In the police court the women claim that their action is justified by the Bill of Rights. While all but the stone throwers are remanded, the case is referred to the High Court. The test case of Mrs Pankhurst and the Hon. Mrs Haverfield is heard in December. They are found guilty and fined and the cases of the other ninety-two women are dismissed.

July 5 Marion Wallace Dunlop, in prison for rubber-stamping a passage from the Bill of Rights in St Stephen's Hall, begins a hunger strike in protest against second-division treatment.

July 13/14 Stone throwers in Holloway mutiny and adopt the hunger strike. The majority are released within a week.

August 13 M.P.s and the Home Secretary visit Holloway accompanied by one of the hunger strikers. Prison conditions about which the Suffragettes complained are soon afterwards improved.

August/September Cabinet ministers, waylaid and pestered by Suffragettes, are closely guarded in public, and Suffragettes are banned from Liberal meetings.

September 17 Barricades are erected in Birmingham in anticipation of Suffragette disturbances during Asquith's visit. In defiance the Suffragettes shower down stones from the roof of the hall where the Prime Minister is to speak.

September 24 The start of forcible feeding in Birmingham causes a public outcry. Within a few days H. N. Brailsford and H. W. Nevinson resign their positions on the *Daily News* in protest.

October 9 Militant demonstration on the occasion of Lloyd George's visit to Newcastle. Among the twelve women imprisoned, Lady Constance Lytton and Jane Brailsford receive preferential treatment.

1910

January General election. A Liberal Government is returned with a reduced majority.

January 14 Lady Constance Lytton, disguised as Jane Warton, leads a protest demonstration in Liverpool and is imprisoned and forcibly fed without a thorough medical test. She is released, seriously strained, on January 23 when her identity is discovered.

February 14 The Suffragettes declare a truce in view of the proposed Conciliation Bill drawn up by Lord Lytton and H. N. Brailsford.

March 15 Churchill rules that political prisoner treatment shall be given to all offenders whose crimes do not involve moral turpitude.

June 14 The Conciliation Bill is introduced in Parliament by D. J. Shackleton.

June 18 Ten thousand Suffragettes march in a two-mile-long procession from the Embankment to the Albert Hall. The public is sympathetic.

June 21 Asquith receives deputations from constitutional suffragists and from anti-suffragists.

July 11/12 A debate on the Conciliation Bill results in a majority of one hundred and thirty-nine votes in favour of the proposals. No time is allowed for a further reading during the session.

November Differences between the Lords and the Commons necessitate the dissolving of Parliament.

November 18 Black Friday. Suffragettes try to gain assurance from the Prime Minister of a future for the Conciliation Bill. He refuses to meet their deputations, and in subsequent attempts to reach the House of Commons the Suffragettes meet with violence and brutality from police and plain-clothes men. Several women are seriously injured and two later die as an immediate result of their treatment. Altogether one hundred and nineteen arrests are made, but charges against the offenders are withdrawn next day at the direct instruction of Churchill.

1911

Coronation Year. The Suffragettes resume their truce.

January 21 Dr Ethel Smyth gives the first performance of her newly composed 'March of the Women' and presents the piece to Mrs Pankhurst.

April 2 Suffragettes boycott the national census. All-night activities are organised by groups who are absent from home at the time of enumeration.

May 5 The Conciliation Bill is again debated and the vote shows a majority of members in favour.

June 17 All suffrage societies unite in a procession of forty thousand supporters from every class and profession. The demonstration includes historical and empire pageants. There is general anticipation of victory.

November 7 By announcing a Manhood Suffrage Bill, Asquith 'torpedoes' the conciliation proposals.

November 17 Asquith receives a deputation of Suffragettes and suffragists after announcing that women would only be included in an amended Manhood Suffrage Bill. He refuses to make any concessions.

November 21 Mrs Pethick Lawrence attempts to lead a deputation to the House of Commons from the Caxton Hall but all ways are blocked by police. An organised stone-throwing raid on the windows of shops and Government offices follows involving two hundred and twenty-three arrests.

1912

March 1 Mass window smashing in the West End. After persistent warnings which gain no response from the Government, the Suffragettes announce that they intend to use the 'argument of the stone', and give notice of a demonstration on March 4. Unannounced, a manoeuvre led by Mrs Pankhurst is carried out on March 1. Mrs Pankhurst is arrested.

March 4 A further outbreak of window smashing takes place.

March 5 Police raid the W.S.P.U. headquarters at Clement's Inn. The Pethick Lawrences are arrested, Christabel escapes to France and Annie Kenney secretly becomes the chief organiser in London.

May 15/22 Mrs Pankhurst and the Pethick Lawrences are tried at the Old Bailey and sentenced to nine months' imprisonment.

June 19 A Suffragette hunger strike begins in Holloway as a protest against the preferential treatment of the leaders.

June 22 Large numbers of Suffragettes in Holloway are fed by force. Mrs Pankhurst defiantly prevents the authorities from feeding her, while other Suffragettes barricade their cells and Emily Wilding Davison throws herself over the prison staircase.

June 24 Mrs Pankhurst and Mrs Pethick Lawrence are released.

June 27 Pethick Lawrence is released from Brixton.

July 18 A hatchet is thrown into Asquith's carriage on the occasion of his official visit to Dublin. Suffragettes attempt to fire the Theatre Royal where Asquith is speaking. For their part in the protest Mary Leigh and Gladys Evans are sentenced on August 7 to five years' penal servitude. Both women hunger strike and are released within nine weeks.

July 19 Helen Craggs is arrested for attempted arson.

August 21 Pethick Lawrence has been made responsible for damages involved in the Suffragette window-smashing outbreaks. Bailiffs enter the Mascot, the Pethick Lawrences' country home.

September 12 Christabel's whereabouts become public.

October 17 At an Albert Hall meeting Mrs Pankhurst outlines a new militant policy and W.S.P.U. members hear of the split between the Pankhursts and Pethick Lawrences.

October 18 The first number of *The Suffragette* appears.

November 9 Letter-box damage begins.

November 11 George Lansbury resigns from Parliament on the women's suffrage issue. After a strongly supported election campaign he loses the seat on November 26.

November/December Widespread letter-box attacks.

1913

January 23 A deputation of working women led by Mrs Drummond put their case before Lloyd George and Sir Edward Grey and demand proof of the ministers' professed support for women's suffrage. In the House of Commons the Speaker rules against a woman's suffrage amendment to the proposed Electoral Reform Bill.

January 28 Militant demonstration by the working women's deputation.

January/February Golf greens are ruined and telegraph wires are cut.

February At a series of Suffragette meetings Mrs Pankhurst openly encourages a policy of stronger militancy.

February 12 The burning of the Regent's Park refreshment kiosk is the first incident in a continuous programme of Suffragette damage to empty buildings.

February 19 Lloyd George's newly built house at Walton Heath is damaged by a bomb and Mrs Pankhurst is arrested on February 24 in connection with the outrage. She accepts full responsibility.

March 18 After a public outcry against the latest forcible feeding of Suffragettes, a majority of Members are against the practice and many think that the women should be left to die. On this point McKenna firmly disagrees, foreseeing mass Suffragette martyrdom.

March 25 The Prisoners' Temporary Discharge Act (the Cat and Mouse Act) is introduced to prevent Suffragette hunger strikers from securing unconditional release.

April 3 Mrs Pankhurst is sentenced at the Old Bailey to three years' penal servitude.

A record of a typical week of attacks on property which follow Mrs Pankhurst's imprisonment.

April 3 Four houses are fired at Hampstead Garden Suburb. Three women damage the glass of thirteen pictures in the Manchester Art Gallery. An empty railway carriage is wrecked by a bomb explosion at Stockport.

April 4 A mansion near Chorley Wood is completely destroyed by fire. A bomb explodes at Oxted station.

April 5 The burning of Ayr racecourse stand causes an estimated three thousand pounds' damage. An attempt to destroy Kelso racecourse grandstand is discovered.

April 6 A house at Potters Bar is fired. A mansion is destroyed at Norwich.

April 7 An attempt to fire stands on Cardiff racecourse is discovered. Fire breaks out in another house in Hampstead Garden Suburb. In the ruins of Dudley Castle the Suffragettes charge one of the ancient cannons and cause a shattering explosion.

April 8 'Release Mrs Pankhurst', cut in the turf at Duthie Park, Aberdeen. The word 'release' is twelve feet long.

April 9 A haystack worth a hundred pounds is destroyed near Nottingham.

April 9 Annie Kenney is arrested. Grace Roe secretly takes her place.
April 12 Mrs Pankhurst is released under the Cat and Mouse Act.

A record of Mrs Pankhurst's imprisonment under the Cat and Mouse Act.

1913	April 3	Imprisonment.
	April 12	Release.
	May 26	Rearrest at Woking.
	May 30	Release.
	June 14	Rearrest before Emily Wilding Davison's funeral.
	June 16	Release.
	June 21	Rearrest at the London Pavilion.
	June 24	Release.
	December 4	Rearrest at Exeter.
	December 7	Release.
	December 13	Rearrest on Dover Express.
	December 17	Release.
1914	March 9	Rearrest at Glasgow.
	March 14	Release.
	May 21	Rearrest outside Buckingham Palace.
	May 26	Release.
	July 8	Rearrest at Lincoln's Inn House.
	July 11	Release.
	July 16	Rearrest at 2 Campden Hill Place while setting out on a stretcher to attend a W.S.P.U. meeting.

1913
April 15 The Home Office prohibits Suffragette open-air meetings. Suffragettes defy the order and police make little attempt to enforce the rule.
April 16 Mrs Drummond and Lansbury are arrested for disturbing the peace.
April 30 The W.S.P.U. Headquarters are raided, heads of department are arrested and police confiscate copy for the forthcoming *Suffragette*. Grace Roe eludes the police and organises the printing of an edition of *The Suffragette* which appears on sale next morning. Grace Roe, disguised and in hiding, continues to operate as Mrs Pankhurst's chief organiser in London.

May/June Continual demonstrations are held in defence of free speech and the freedom of the Press.

June 4 Derby Day. Emily Wilding Davison stops the King's horse and is seriously injured. She dies on June 8.

June 14 Emily Wilding Davison's funeral.

June 9/17 Annie Kenney and the arrested Lincoln's Inn staff are tried for conspiracy and sentenced to long terms of imprisonment. They are sent to distant and separate gaols but shortly return to London on release after hunger striking.

July/August Mrs Pankhurst and Annie Kenney defy the Cat and Mouse Act and between periods of imprisonment they escape from closely guarded recuperating quarters and address W.S.P.U. meetings at the London Pavilion. During the July meetings either one or the other is rearrested.

July 10 The Piccadilly Flat case. The lenient sentencing of a procuress under the new White Slave Traffic Act causes the W.S.P.U. to investigate undisclosed facts in the case and to embark on an anti-prostitution campaign.

July/August Many sections of the public protest against the Cat and Mouse Act.

August 3 Protest chanting begins in churches. Suffragettes interrupt the Litany at St Paul's with prayers for Mrs Pankhurst.

August Mrs Pankhurst, Sylvia Pankhurst and Annie Kenney go abroad.

September 13 During a performance of *Androcles and the Lion* the Suffragettes make analogies between their position and that of the Christian martyrs. Interruptions are later made at other plays.

October 11 Mrs Pankhurst leaves France for her third visit to the United States. She is held up as an undesirable at Ellis Island. On October 20, she is admitted to the country by order of the President.

October/November Annie Kenney and Sylvia Pankhurst return to England. They appear in public between imprisonments and accompanied respectively by the Bodyguard and the People's Army, they defy arrest. Finally, weakened by prison experiences, they each speak at meetings from a stretcher.

December 4 Mrs Pankhurst returns from America and is arrested at sea.

December 5 The clergy protest against renewed forcible feeding.

1914

January 26 After serious reports about the condition of Suffragettes in Holloway, Mrs Dacre Fox organises deputations to bishops asking them to take action.

January 28 The Bishop of London investigates conditions in Holloway and interviews Suffragette prisoners. He finds nothing to justify reports of ill treatment.

February Further deputations to bishops are organised.

February 7 Christabel announces that Sylvia's East End Federation, which has worked persistently in conjunction with the Labour Party, is no longer connected with the W.S.P.U.

February 10, 21 With the help of the Bodyguard Mrs Pankhurst escapes from guarded houses having first publicly announced from a balcony her intention of doing so.

February 20 A statement in *The Suffragette* alleges that tests on released prisoners show evidence of bromide drugging.

March 10 Mary Richardson slashes the Rokeby Venus in protest against the brutal rearrest of Mrs Pankhurst at Glasgow on the previous day. Public galleries are temporarily closed.

May 21 A mass Suffragette deputation goes to Buckingham Palace. After a fierce confrontation with the police, an organised window-smashing campaign takes place. Police discover a Suffragette arsenal at a Maida Vale flat.

May 23 Police raid Lincoln's Inn House and Grace Roe is arrested. Olive Bartels, disguised as a widow, takes her place, running the organisation from a series of changing bases.

June 11 At a debate in the House McKenna refers to militancy as 'a phenomenon absolutely without precedent in our history'.

June 16 At a meeting at the Holland Park Skating Rink, fifteen thousand pounds is raised. Annie Kenney is smuggled into the hall, and after speaking she leaves in disguise undetected.

June 20 Asquith receives a deputation from the East End Federation.

August 10 Six days after world war is declared all Suffragette prisoners are unconditionally released. Mrs Pankhurst suspends militancy and calls on her followers to help defend the country.

Bibliography

Letters of Constance Lytton, ed. Betty Balfour (Heinemann, 1925).

Towards Woman's Liberty, Teresa Billington Greig (Garden City Press, Letchworth, 1907).

The Treatment of the Women's Deputation by the Metropolitan Police, Brailsford and Murray (The Woman's Press, 1911).

So Rich a Life, Clara Codd (The Institute for Theosophical Publicity, Pretoria, 1952).

The Life of Emily Davison, Gertrude Colmore (The Woman's Press, 1913).

Memoirs of a Militant, Annie Kenney (Edwin Arnold, 1924).

Prisons and Prisoners, Constance Lytton (Heinemann, 1914).

My Idealed John Bullesses, Yoshio Markino (Constable, 1912).

Unshackled, Dame Christabel Pankhurst (Hutchinson, 1959).

My Own Story, Emmeline Pankhurst (Eveleigh Nash, 1914).

The Suffragette, E. Sylvia Pankhurst (Gay and Hancock, 1911).

The Suffragette Movement, E. Sylvia Pankhurst (Longmans, Green, 1931).

My Part in a Changing World, Emmeline Pethick Lawrence (Gollanz, 1938).

Fate has been Kind, Lord Pethick Lawrence (Hutchinson, 1942).

Suffrage Annual and *Women's Who's Who*, ed. A.J.R. (Stanley Paul, 1913).

Laugh a Defiance, Mary Richardson (Weidenfeld and Nicolson, 1953).

The Unexpurgated Case against Woman Suffrage, Sir Almroth E. Wright, M.D., F.R.C.S. (Constable, 1913).

Index